THE ANATOMY OF THE MUSIC INDUSTRY

HOW THE GAME WAS & HOW THE GAME HAS CHANGED

Dr. Logan H. Westbrooks

Ascent Publishing
Los Angeles, CA

Project Manager LaRita Shelby: SB Music, Media & Marketing
Edited by Dee Robinson the RightWriter
Cover Design by Jessica Godbee, Concept by Prophet X

Printed in the United States of America
First Edition: 2015

PCN 2015913038

SAN 990-0306

ISBN 978-0-6925022-2-8

"I'm glad to see that Logan Westbrooks has expanded on his groundbreaking book on the music industry. Logan is a well-respected veteran of the music business and knows of what he writes. I highly recommend it."

Attorney Larkin Arnold
Former Senior Vice-President
CBS/Sony & Arista Records

"The historical past provides the framework for innovation that has and continues to redefine the business of music. 'The Anatomy of the Music Industry' traces this history through the voices of those who contributed to it, including African American pioneers."

Portia K. Maultsby, Ph.D.
Laura Boulton Professor Emerita of Ethnomusicology
Indiana University-Bloomington

"Logan Westbrooks is a trailblazing music industry executive. He has a vast wealth of knowledge and insights acquired from decades of experience and rigorous study. His book is required reading for those seeking insight into the anatomy or constituent structures that make up the complex institution known as The Music Industry. 'The Anatomy of the Music Industry' provides a much-needed view from the bridge to help navigate an industry shaped by changing technologies and global networks of distribution and consumption."

Dr. Scot Brown
Historian
UCLA Departments of African American Studies and History

"Music, like everything, constantly evolves. But we must know where we come from to know where we are heading. This book can help illuminate the possibilities."

Tony White
Director
Music and Entertainment Education
Los Angeles Unified School District-Beyond the Bell Branch

IMPORTANT MESSAGE

For my wife Geri
and
For our love of music…

CONTENTS

ACKNOWLEDGEMENTS

I'd like to thank Dr. Johnnie B. Watson, President of LeMoyne-Owen College and the Board of Trustees of LeMoyne-Owen College for bestowing upon me an Honorary Doctoral Degree of Humane Letters in 2014. I also thank Dr. Portia Maultsby and Indiana State University for hosting me as a lecturer on Black Music, and I thank the University for recognizing the importance of enshrining historical documents from my personal collection as well as other artifacts housed in Indiana State University's Archives of African American Music & Culture.

Ms. Dee Robinson also deserves special thanks for her writing help and assistance, and for excelling beyond any expectations as well as her caring insight and knowledge that she so graciously shares. Thank you to the many writers, transcribers, interviewees and those who demonstrated untiring efforts to meet all of the deadlines. To my project manager, interviewer and supervising editor LaRita Shelby, and to our artistic web designer Prophet X of ProphecyWebDesigns.com, thank you. To our transcribers Brian Allen, Bria Allen and Ricki Jae Morris, I humbly thank you. To Miss Veronica Ahktar, thank you for being a champion, enduring long hours and helping us to bring the project to completion, you are sincerely appreciated. Thank you to Gil Robertson for your special assistance in securing some key interviews.

To all of the industry professionals who granted us your time and so generously shared of your expertise, this book could not have been possible without you.

I would also like to thank those who had an early impact in my career: Ronnie Mosley, Wendel Bates, George Gerkin, Irwin Steinberg, Lou Simon, John Sippel, Clive Davis, Bruce Lundval, John Hammond, Goddard Lieberman, Jim Tyrell, Walter Yetnikoff, Clarence Avant, and especially Marnie Tattersall for structuring The Harvard Report. Where would I be without my circle of friends and family? Thank you also to the students, journalists, artists, producers and music enthusiasts who constantly inquire about the music industry. I am humbled that you cherish the part of music history that I was blessed to participate in, and I am inspired by those of you who are eager to mold the present and future of the music industry.

To my wife Geri, thank you for your constant love and support. You have been my partner throughout this journey.

INTRODUCTION
LaRita Shelby

To say that the music industry is an ever-evolving entity is an understatement, especially given the fact that nowadays technology advances at lightning speed. With that being a given, there are fundamental dynamics that are relevant for any era of music in the past, present or future—a great song, a great team to help market and promote the song, and fans who are excited enough to respond to it with the end result being some type of purchase that leads to a profit.

The industry used to present one primary business model, which was the record company. Within it lay an infrastructure that financed the administrative staff and fueled the creative dreams of a plethora of musical acts, whose songs have become a part of our daily lives. Through this book Logan H. Westbrooks has provided a venue for many behind the scenes stories of the strategies, the work ethic and the passion exuded by the industry professionals who took the time to share with us.

You will learn what industry executive saved Janet Jackson's musical career when the label was ready to drop her. You will find out who defied their music label to do a grassroots street promotion for Prince when he was just getting started. When Black music divisions were phased out at major labels, another executive found a home helping a start-up Gospel label launch the career of Kirk Franklin & The Family, and many more. This book also reveals the educational preparation that many executives in the music industry have earned, amassing degrees in marketing, economics, business and accounting. There are also some who took non-traditional self-taught avenues and were quite successful.

Now that the digital age is here to stay, we were fortunate in garnering interviews with experts in the digital music medium such as David Wasserman from Latin Cool Now and our youngest contributor Greg Savage from DIYMusicbiz.com. It was also exciting to speak with multi-faceted producers and musicians who have managed to keep their businesses intact and up to speed with today's climate in the industry. Kashif, Jay King and Larry Blackmon from Cameo are just a few who offer an abundance of insight in this regard.

Each and every entry is an inspiration from the former days of music, and an education about the new Anatomy of The Music Industry. As a former international radio broadcaster and current contributor to Lee Bailey's Electronic Urban Report, it was a delight to facilitate these conversations. I learned something new with each and every one. As an artist who attempted to single handedly promote my own jazz product years ago, I now understand the great value of infrastructure and the budget that accompanies a solid marketing campaign.

I'd also like to thank every investor and angel donor who has sacrificed their resources for the sake of artistic expression, especially music. Yes, currently technology provides access to do many things in an instant, but to quote an African proverb: "Strategy is better than strength."

The great news is that this book is like a one-on-one consultation with some of the brightest minds in the business. Their knowledge pool has helped to make millions of dollars in the music industry worldwide. Hopefully, the generous offering of their expertise will help you, whether you are an artist, producer, promoter, marketer, manager, conductor, arranger, educator, a music fan or historian.

ABOUT LOGAN H. WESTBROOKS, HON. D.H.L.

Dr. Logan H. Westbrooks is one of the first African Americans to work as a major label Music Executive. Westbrooks' impact in the music industry is undeniable. He is recognized as a pioneer who paved the way for African American Music Executives of today.

He has worked in most of the music capitals of the world, including Europe and Africa. He partnered with Don Cornelius and Dick Griffey in the formation of Soul Train Records, while teaching a course called *The Anatomy of a Record Company* at California State University. He also conducted the "Quincy Jones Workshop" there on campus. He has held top management positions at Capitol, Mercury, CBS and CBS International. Westbrooks is also credited as the co-architect of "The Harvard Report."

A Memphis native, he grew up across the street from LeMoyne-Owen College in the LeMoyne Gardens housing project. He graduated from Booker T. Washington High School and attended LeMoyne-Owen College for a time before moving on to Lincoln University in Jefferson City, Missouri, where he earned a Bachelor's Degree in Business Administration in 1961.

Westbrooks began his musical journey as a management trainee at RCA Victor and moved to its record division within two years where he promoted such legendary artists as Sam Cooke and Elvis Presley. He later joined Capitol Records as its first Black territory salesman for the South and West sides of Chicago where he promoted Black, Country and Pop artists, including Lou Rawls, Nancy Wilson, Nat King Cole, the Beatles and more.

Westbrooks' star was on the rise. Capitol Records promoted him to Regional Promotional Manager to secure airplay for all of the label's Black music releases through the major urban centers in the Midwest. His success led to another promotion in 1970 to Administrative Assistant to the Vice President of Marketing. Not long after that, Mercury Records in Chicago recruited him to serve as their National R&B Promotions Director where he handled the releases for such artists as Jerry Butler, Gene Chandler, Melba Moore, Errol Gardner, Buddy Miles, and Rod Stewart.

His success then captured the attention of one of the industry's most iconic executives, Clive Davis. Mr. Davis hired Westbrooks at music giant CBS Records as the company's first Director of Special

Markets in its newly created Black Music Division. Within the first year, he and his staff hit the ground running, marketing "Backstabbers" by the O'Jays, "If You Don't Know Me By Now" by Harold Melvin & the Blue Notes, and "Me and Mrs. Jones" by Billy Paul. His phenomenal success in the United States naturally led to an international career. CBS named him the Director of Special Markets for its Columbia Records label, as well as Managing Executive of CBS Africa and CBS in Paris, France. These opportunities led to him assisting The Jackson Five's first tour of Africa in 1974.

Westbrooks climbed aboard Soul Train Records two years later as partner with Don Cornelius, and as the label's Vice President of Marketing. He later formed his own label Source Records, which was home to music legends Chuck Brown & the Soul Searchers, Sharon Paige, Harold Melvin & the Blue Notes and Smash (which was composed of the DeBarge brothers). The label's string of hits included the chart topper "Bustin' Loose," which later was sampled by rapper Nelly on his Grammy Award-winning song "Hot in Herre."

Westbrooks is a consummate industry professional who helped to shape and redefine music during a stellar career that spanned more than 50 years. He now leverages his business and marketing prowess at his real estate investment firm—Westbrooks Management. In May of 2014 he was bestowed the highest honor from LeMoyne-Owen College in Memphis, Tennessee, when he received an Honorary Doctorate of Humane Letters for his outstanding lifetime achievement in business, the arts and community service. His personal papers, Source Records memorabilia and personal artifacts are archived at Indiana University in Bloomington, Indiana, and can be accessed online at: http://www.indiana.edu/~aaamc/general.html.

A short video highlighting his career can be viewed online at: http://www.youtube.com/watch?v=WnWKjBxfbWU.

An interview with *Open Vault* discussing the music industry can be viewed online at: http://openvault.wgbh.org/catalog/35beed-interview-with-logan-westbrooks-part-1-of-2 (Part 1) http://openvault.wgbh.org/catalog/511c5c-interview-with-logan-westbrooks-part-2-of-2 (Part 2)

Additional information is available at loganwestbrooks.com.

PREFACE

What's old is new. The old music industry is dead, long live the music!

The music industry is not actually dead or dying, but a large-scale change has come. When discussing changes in the music industry, I'll use the terms 'old model' and 'new model' because the differences are very stark. With that being said, the discussion about the old model being in transformation is over. It is not transforming; it has already transformed. The major change has already taken place—namely, from the physical format to the digital format. This transformation is not totally complete, however, but the model I worked under is taking its last breaths. The new model is exciting, open, fluid, and operating under a continual flow of updates.

Artists are now taking control. There was a time when this concept was unheard of and would not have been tolerated. At that time, record labels were in the unique position of having complete control of what artists produced and what listeners heard. Major labels were the only way in for artists to create, promote, and monetize their music from production to radio to the stores. Technology has changed all that to the detriment of the majors and to the benefit of artists and listeners. The gatekeepers have been removed and the gates have not only been opened, but eliminated. By its resistance to change and its unwillingness to share the wealth, the old model has helped to diminish its own power.

Music lovers are no longer just consumers. Being a consumer connotes a business relationship. Music lovers can now be considered listeners who do not necessarily have to purchase the music to consume it. It's no longer about owning a physical disc of a song. Today, it's all about access, and there are bold new ways to get what you want, how you want it, and when you want it. When you want it is now done at astronomical speed, like immediately. You no longer have to wait for music to get to the store or for the store to open. If you hear a song you like that you never heard before at two o'clock in the morning, there's an app called Shazam that allows you to hold your Smartphone in the air and grab the song's digital fingerprint. You can then download it.

The changes have been truly amazing and once the technological floodgates were opened, it happened with lightning speed. That puts the onus on artists—no longer dependent on labels—to be innovative and find creative ways to capitalize on their product. That's not as difficult as it once was because the Internet has become the great equalizer, connecting people and villages across the globe with just one click.

But, it is the listeners who are truly the ones in charge of the current model. The law of supply and demand is totally up to them. In order for it to be win-win, artists only need to create beautiful music that listeners find irresistible. One part of both models that will never change is the quality of the music itself. Some of it will be good and some not so good, and the good and the bad of it will come out in the wash. But, good music is good music and you can't change that.

During my career as a record executive, I was directly involved in the careers of many artists who became superstars—the Beatles, Paul McCartney, Johnny Mathis, Johnny Nash, Sly Stone, Santana, Billy Paul, the O'Jays, Harold Melvin & the Blue Notes, and many other acts. They created classic songs with compelling lyrics and magnificent music with live orchestration that will live on in its timelessness.

The old model might not have been ideal, but, My God, look at what magic it produced. It was what it was, and it got us where we are today. In a couple decades, another generation will look back at what is today's new model and be glad that era is over. It's called progress.

Let the music play.

CHAPTER ONE

THE NEW ANATOMY

Introduction of Streaming

Having been a fully-active participant as a record executive in the old model and now an eye witness with a deep interest in the new model, I continue to be transfixed and impressed with the transformation of the music industry. Some technological fixtures of the new model are inarguably better than the old model, and some are arguably controversial. Streaming music is a component of the new model that I think is controversial because it directly impacts artists' revenue. It is the main aspect of the new model that I still grapple with because it seems that the music creators are getting a raw deal.

Streaming: Friend or Foe

Streaming music is delivering audio without downloading, which is more like borrowing the music rather than buying it. Great for the listener, but how does the artist fare? Streaming has increased exponentially with more than 50 billion songs being delivered in just six months in 2013 through companies like YouTube, Pandora, and Spotify. There's also Rhapsody, Xbox Music, iTunes Radio, Slacker, Nokia Music, Songza, Google Music, Rdio, iHeartRadio, Deezer, and a host of others. Spotify, however, has taken streaming a step further by allowing users to download songs, not just stream them.

Two new streaming services are subscription only—Tidal, owned by rapper/entrepreneur Jay Z, and Apple Music—which will probably be Spotify's biggest competitor. Apple Music has the potential to become a behemoth. It combines its subscription streaming service with global radio-like programming where artists and fans can connect. It will be pre-installed on all iOS and OS X devices allowing for streaming and eliminating the need for downloading.

There are successful established artists such as Will.i.am, who complain that these things give artists and content creators a raw deal and questions the fairness of YouTube and Vevo for branding association through ads while not considering the artists. Initially, Apple Music was not going to pay content creators during their three-month free trial period. Superstar Taylor Swift single-handedly persuaded them to pay artists by withholding her latest album *1989* from Apple Music's catalog.

David Lowery, who leads the rock band Cracker and is the most outspoken advocate for artists' rights, wrote an open letter to Emily White of NPR "All Songs Considered" when she said she paid very little for her music library. He was responding to a letter she wrote in which she said that she does not pay for music, yet grapples with the moral implications of not paying for it. Lowery explained to her how the actions of her generation impact artists' revenue. Link to the full article: http://thetrichordist.com/2012/06/18/letter-to-emily-white-at-npr-all-songs-considered/.

Also, in January 2014, David Lowery testified on copyright law before the U.S. House of Representatives subcommittee. He addressed the committee on Courts, Intellectual Property and the Internet.

Other artists have also organized to fight against being left out of the revenue pie due to streaming services like Spotify. Meanwhile, the major labels received huge advances for their catalogs and the listeners who get free music are also benefitting.

Do Artists Benefit?

Artists earn a minuscule amount—fractions of a penny per stream. The premise behind streaming is that those fractions of a penny will add up. But, having more listeners hasn't necessarily translated to more money for artists. "Low" by David Lowery & Cracker was played a million times on Pandora and he received $16.89. He and the other songwriters also shared $42.23 for the million plays. In comparison, 1,900 plays of the same song on commercial radio earned $1,400. That's a significant difference in payout.

In 2013, the rock group DafPunk had "Get Lucky", the most successful song in the world with 104,760,000 streams. They got about $26,000 (that amount does not include downloads and commercial radio). With over one hundred millions plays, $26,000 is a pittance and is a sad exchange for such a popular song.

Cellist and successful Indie artist Zoë Keating shared her 2013 payouts from downloads and streaming through services like iTunes, Spotify, and YouTube by posting the information in a public document through Google Drive. Keating said that she posted her information to help other Indie artists gain a better perspective of streaming revenue, and to understand who pays what among the different services. Her post generated a lot of discussion about the subject. Streaming has become a contentious issue for many content creators, and there are a number of superstar artists who have begun to complain about the low payout artists receive from streaming.

Collectively, artists have earned over a billion dollars through streaming services. Worldwide the music industry earned more than 28 billion dollars, including all sales. Though the technology of streaming is here to stay, the artists will continue to lose because free streaming completely removes any incentive to pay for music. With a download app at your disposal, it can become addictive to stream and download at no personal cost to you. The ease of streaming from a legal site removes the moral paradigm of receiving it for free.

The old music industry model was transformed by the digital impact, and now streaming has transformed song delivery. Legal down-loading permits the listener to get any song they want to buy, but now streaming permits music lovers to listen to any song they want for free.

Under the old model, the Baby Boomer Generation as well as Generation X heard music through the radio, waited for it to reach record stores (could take weeks), visited the record stores, paid for the record or CD, took it home, and then played it on a record player or CD player. But, it's vastly different for Millennials—Generation Y (those born between 1980-2000) and Generation Z (those born after 2000). Many of the new generation of music listeners expect music to be free.

Generations Y grew up with the new technology, and Generation Z was born into it, so it's in their DNA. Generation Z is connected online through their gadgets (phones, laptops, tablets) 365 days a year, 24 hours a day. That means total music access when and where they want it. It's the way the music experience was introduced to them, so it's understand-able that they cannot readily see the harm it does to artists or content creators. Also, from their perspective digital music exists in infinity, meaning even if they take a digital copy, it's still out there, so they don't see it as stealing.

In addition, commercial radio is guilty of repetitive playlists that focus on major-label artists, many who follow the cookie-cutter template for songs and offer very little in terms of ingenuity. Terrestrial radio ownership is now concentrated in the hands of a very few, so the process gets replicated all over the country—a handful of artists and a handful of songs. College radio, non-commercial radio, satellite radio, and Internet radio are viable alternatives that offer refreshing options in music. Even though commercial radio and major labels are still dominant, streaming is also contributing to their diminishing power.

There is music played on streaming services that you will never hear on commercial radio. If commercial radio was not so entrenched with keeping Indies out, people would gravitate back there rather than turning away from it now that there are other options. The fact is, however, that commercial radio is very limited, extremely predictable, and, dare I say, quite boring to the new generation of listeners.

In my estimation, there is a need for accountability on both sides of the equation in order to bring more equity and opportunity for different artists to be heard—Indie artists in particular. Technology has nothing to do with artists not getting airplay on commercial radio. That issue is driven by something else that is as old as radio itself and pre-dates digital music, downloading, streaming, and the Internet. It's called payola and greed, which have nothing to do with technology, and it is questionable if that will ever change.

ARTISTS & PRODUCERS

INFORMED SOURCES

Larry Blackmon
Jonathan Butler
Marquis Hill
Kashif
Jay King
Joanne McDuffie-Funderburg "Jo Jo"
Dorie Pride
Stephanie Spruill

CHAPTER TWO

LARRY BLACKMON

Artist, Writer, Producer, Founding Member of Cameo

"I thank God for giving me what I wanted, and this is the closest thing to immortality that you're going to get."

Larry Blackmon is the founder of the group Cameo. His résumé extends 40 years in the music industry, and his hits include legendary jams such as "Candy," "Single Life," "Shake Your Pants," "Word Up," and "She's Strange." Co-founders of the group also include Tomi Jenkins and Nathan Leftenant. Larry, who prefers to be called LB, spoke to us about his career and the origins of the group.

Larry Blackmon:
It started out as the New York City Players, and at that time we had…Goodness, I can't remember how many people we had at that particular time. I'd say about maybe eight altogether. We had a female with us and a couple of other people, and it evolved into Cameo through changes and evolution. It became Cameo, I would say, in 1976. I believe that's when it was, I may not be exact. I believe that's when we did our first deal with Casablanca Records. It was a disco song called "Find My Way." After that song didn't do as well as they expected, I asked them if they would come in and listen to our original material because we didn't write that song. I produced it and arranged it, but we didn't write it. Cecil Holmes came in and listened to our original material. He thought we should go ahead, and that's what we did. Our first deal was a single deal.

Then we did an album deal with Casablanca Records. Chocolate City was the name of the logo label, and Cesar Holmes ran that division. Neal Bogart was the president of the company. I think he thought we were a White group, not that it mattered at all. He didn't treat us any differently. So we recorded that. At the time I was working at a clothing store on Wall Street. One day I was fitting a customer for a suit when I heard this slot on the radio called the World Premier. That particular slot would play 12 times a day, and whenever I heard that slot, that particular song would become a hit. As I'm fitting this customer, I heard the introduction to the World Premier segment, and then our song "Rigor Mortis" came on. I asked one of our associates to finish with that customer. I went to my locker, I got my things, and never turned back.

Cameo amassed a string of hits in the 1980s. The guys looked good and sounded good. They were smoking hot and exciting to watch. It was the era of full bands with musicians who were equally versed on instruments, on vocals and with choreography. We asked LB for a few highlights of being a part of a group versus being a solo performer.

Larry Blackmon:

It was exciting for us because that's all I ever wanted in life since I was 14 years old. I started playing drums in a drum and bugle corps. Then my first year of Junior High School I played in orchestra, and the second year I played baritone bass clef horn, then the last year I played drums again. I grew up, not far from the Apollo Theater. When I was five, my aunt used to take me to see all of the late great Black artists, from Jackie Wilson to Sam Cooke. You can't name one that I had not seen.

Then I started going to the Apollo myself. I would play hooky from church and take my sister to my cousin's house after putting in the offering, and then make it to the matinees on Sunday. I would see everyone from Otis Redding to Bill Cosby, and needless to say James Brown. I saw anyone that you could mention. And that's why I guess I went to college for the entertainment business, because carrying all of that with me is what I integrated into the groups that I was a part of since I was a drummer.

After high school I went to Julliard on an extension program because my parents couldn't afford the tuition. This all happened around the same time. I didn't care for Julliard because I didn't study any of the music that I learned about. Everybody that I did learn about was dead, from Beethoven to Tchaikovsky. But, I did that for my résumé, because if things didn't work out for the group, then I would become a pit musician (as in orchestra pit) on Broadway. So, having that on your résumé wouldn't hurt. Not many people finished, but I went the same year that Robin Williams was there. I went at night, of course. From there we recorded "Rigor Mortis," which was a hit.

For our second album, *We All Know Who We Are*. It had "I Just Want to Be" on it. Our first went Gold, and our second went Gold. Then there was *Ugly Ego*, the third album. They shipped too many copies, so it took longer to catch action. I think they shipped 300,000, and they regretted that because it took a while for it to show itself as a hit. Then they did several others.

After playing clubs most of my life, the requirement I had for the act was that you had to play and sing. Gwen Guthrie was a part of what turned into the New York City Players. It was a band called East Coast, and we did one album on ABC Records.

Gwen Guthrie was quite talented. While they were with us, she and another musician in the group wrote, "Supernatural" performed by Ben E. King. They enjoyed some success as writers. Gwen, of course, went solo and was with the same label—Polygram. Polygram bought 51 percent of Casablanca, which became The Polygram Group.

The joke that I used to tell a lot was that we were with the label longer than the presidents or any of the employees. Although there was always an A&R person, and a vice president and so forth, they left us alone because we did our own material, and we didn't need their help. And for us, we wanted to make our music radio friendly. Being a part of society, we felt we knew what people wanted to hear. They would say, radio is playing ballads now, and I would come up with an up-tempo. We knew our audience and we played to our audience.

After the time ended with that company, we explored a couple of relationships. The music industry as a whole is not fair as a business; it never has been. It's totally backwards, and we decided never to do anymore deals with any other record companies.

2014 saw the release of a double CD set of past hits and a few live hits such as "Candy." There are a couple of others that we have never recorded live before. So, that's what we're in the process of doing, and that brings us current.

What are the things that newcomers should look out for, especially if they're a part of a group when approaching any type of a music deal?

Larry Blackmon:

Well, let's say the standards have changed a great deal in the industry. What to look out for is to make sure you own your copyrights and that you maintain them. Record companies were notorious for setting you up to take your copyrights, as they attempted to do with us and were successful to a lesser degree. Have someone that you can trust such as an attorney.

Even in the music business there were attorneys you couldn't trust because there were always promises coming from the record companies that they would give them (the attorneys) something under the table, or split some of the income from the acts with the attorneys that brought the acts to the record company. There were all kinds of notorious, nefarious, scandalous, bullcrap, and I want it to be seen that way.

What hurts me most emotionally, is that we, as humans, can conduct business in such a predatory way when people such as myself come from modest means and we are creative. They want to take our property and also be predatory because of the racial divides. Pretty much, that's what it is, and I walk by faith and not by sight.

I continue to walk that way, and I have no apologies or explanations or excuses for anything. I thank God for giving me what I wanted, and this is the closest thing to immortality you're going to get. Because people will know twenty and thirty years and a hundred years from now…people will know who we are and what we did, and we did it well. We are continuing to do it also, walking by faith, you're all in. You're all in!

Groups can change their course over the years, both personally and professionally. We asked LB to expound on the evolution of Cameo.

Larry Blackmon:

Well, we've decided over the past three years to tour continually. Whereas before, we put out an album and then we toured. We started out that way and we wanted to go back to that because this is what we do for a living, and this is what we enjoy. So as long as people want to see Cameo, we'll be there to be seen. Most of our members have been here for over ten years, so they're called 'a lifer.' Most of the people have been here for a minimum of 15 years. The core act is Tomi Jenkins and

9

myself, Tomi was one of the first members. I was 20 at the time, and he was 18. Now we're in our 50s, so that gives you an idea how long we've been doing this. I had several acts in which I was involved with before the formation of Cameo.

This is what we enjoy doing, and we have a list of steps. It's amazing to us the longevity of this act, and we are known worldwide for our shows. It has been a journey, it really has. We enjoy it today because the bigger the challenge, the bigger our hearts become. And with that, that's what Cameo is about. For us, it's about the people—the direct connection. Because that is who we appreciate and thank for the years that we've been giving and doing what we love in order to feed our families and our loved ones.

Is there any particular significance for the name "Cameo" or is that just a name that you chose?

Larry Blackmon:

It depicted what I felt we needed. It was finally called gem or stone, and you hear about cameo appearances? Well, everyone in the act was a cameo, and is. That's why we chose that name. Before we signed on as the New York City Players, but Polygram had the Ohio players, and they didn't think that was a good idea, so we changed our name to accommodate what was needed at the time. I thought it was refreshing, and I still think it's refreshing.

Making original music can be very spontaneous, especially if you're in a group. Who gets credit for the bass line, or the guitar lick, or the drum riff? How should the writing and publishing credits be divided? For young groups who are starting out as inspired musicians, what are some business tactics that they should be aware of when they collaborate with other musicians?

Larry Blackmon:

That's a very simple question. Get an attorney. These people go to school to study law and that's what they do. You make music, you're an artist. And that's what you do. You pick somebody who you can trust and develop a relationship and deal with it. I don't care if the rest of the group is using one attorney, and if that's the way. There are certain choices you have to make at a certain time. Just always have the paper checked. I've always dealt from a position of having a deal with everyone's best interest, and if you expect to be a group that has lasted as long as we have, then you must look after everyone as you do yourself as much as is fair. If people are not contributing on that level, then that's too bad. But call it what it is. If you're going to sign something, then you have to have it checked. I know collaboration is not a dirty word. It's a good word, actually. I enjoy collaborating with my associates because you never know what's coming out. So that's not a bad thing. That's not a bad thing at all.

Many times artists get in the studio and they're practicing, and a new song comes about during the process. Later on they have to figure out the splits on it. There's not always a previously arranged agreement. What do you suggest then?

Larry Blackmon:

It's always better to do that up front. We had a process that worked well for us. I would do the A&R and I would pick the songs. There would be people upset at times because I didn't pick their songs, but the song didn't work. But that's pretty much the process.

Keep your notes and remember who did what. At the end of the evening, write your notes down and go to the people that are present and say, "This is what I remember happening. Does anybody have any other input or whatever?" It is what it is. It's not complicated.

What would you say if there's some young kid out there who has pulled a few of your licks down on their iPhone and they're just going to throw in some of your samples and put in some more beats and rap on it. What should they be doing before they put that music out?

Larry Blackmon:

That is considered sampling music if somebody is using some of or part of somebody else's music. What I don't think is fair is that they should get full rate as a writer if it includes someone else's music. There should be an adjusted rate for that.

The reason why it's not is because record companies would take the property from the artist, and they would want to make as much money from it as they could. That's the only reason why they get full rate for nonsense music. Trust me, if it is one cent of somebody else's music, then it is nonsense. I think people should get a full rate for an original composition. If someone uses part of that in their composition, it should be an adjusted rate. But, that's not the way it is. And that's okay, but if you use any of my music, you're going to pay.

Contact:
Twitter.com/CameoNation

Dr. Westbrooks:
What impressed me about Larry's analysis of the group Cameo is that he recognized the moment they were about to become a success. While at work listening to the radio, their song "Rigor Mortis" played in the world premier slot, which played twelve times a day. He knew, as if being called, that it was their time. He walked away from his job and into stardom. They were not an overnight success; they had put in the work. It was an example of preparation meeting up with opportunity. He also understood the power of radio airplay. Cameo has experienced both the bright side and the dark side of the music business, but they survived and are still performing to this day.

CHAPTER THREE

JONATHAN BUTLER

Artist, Writer, Producer

"You are your own CEO. Be diligent about your business."

Not all dreams of making it in the music business begin in America, Jonathan Butler provides insight on how he ventured from Cape Town, South Africa, to the United States with a burning desire to be in the music industry. He achieved success, which includes recording twenty albums, multiple Grammy nominations and the hit singles "Lies," "Sarah, Sarah," "Take Good Care of Me" and "Falling in Love with Jesus." He offers this advice.

Jonathan Butler:
First of all you have to believe in what you have inside of you. If that gift is inside of you, then always find a place where that gift can flourish and sow the seed where that gift can grow. Often times, you have a gift and you have a seed, and sometimes it depends on where you find it. That's where it's going to grow. So don't give up on your dreams. Live it! Life is too short. Live your dreams, and you'll be a lot happier for it.

What is most important for artists to know as far as perfecting their craft?

Jonathan Butler:
Oh, it is very important that they practice. They should also pay attention to the past. There are great leaders and mentors from the past that are around that you can listen to and that you can still learn from today. Don't let technology be the end to all of this. There are other avenues. There are musicians and artists from the past that Jazz has given to us that have great values and tones that we can learn from and

grow from. We should learn our history about what Jazz is, what Gospel is, and what R&B is. There's a lot of stops. There's a lot of music and history from the past that we can learn from today, that we can grow from today. Practice is a key ingredient. Practice makes people successful to me. Without it there is no preparation, and practice equals success. If you're not prepared, and if you're not well trained in what you're supposed to do, don't expect results. You know you're not going to get the resolve you're looking for or the success for what you're not prepared for.

What business advice would you suggest?

Jonathan Butler:

Finding a great business manager is like finding a good marriage. It has to be made for you. It has to suit you. It has to be somebody that believes in you, believes in your vision, believes in what you want to accomplish, and how to facilitate you. You are your own CEO, that's number one. So be diligent about your business. Pay attention to your business. Don't waste your money, don't squander your money. It's fleeting. It comes and goes.

Contact:
www.jonathanbutler.com

Dr. Westbrooks:

Jonathan Butler emphasizes the importance of practice. Practice is like exercising. Just as physical exercise will tone, build strength and energy, practicing your talent increases your stamina and hones your skills to perfection. Your talent is already your gift, but practice makes it your second nature. Learn from the teachers of the past, those entertainers who performed without the benefit of technology to enhance vocals and instrumentation. Their classes are always available to us at a moment's notice by listening to their music. You can watch them perform live via videos on YouTube, Vimeo, Vevo, or other video sharing sites. Avail yourself of their greatness, listen and learn. The old saying is true, "Practice makes perfect."

CHAPTER FOUR

MARQUIS HILL

Jazz Artist, Educator
Grand Prize Winner of the Thelonious Monk Institute of Jazz
2014 International Jazz Trumpet Competition

"This love of jazz and the history of the music was engrained in me in the fifth grade. I want to do the same thing for upcoming students so that it's a cycle that keeps getting passed down."

Marquis Hill is an accomplished trumpet player who started playing at eleven years old. Marquis is a native of Chicago, Illinois, who earned a Master's Degree in Jazz Pedagogy from DePaul University. In 2013 Marquis won the Carmine Caruso International Jazz Trumpet Solo Competition, and in 2012 he won the International Trumpet Guild Jazz Improvisation Competition. Currently Mr. Hill is on the faculty at the University of Illinois, and as of November 2014, he is the Grand Prize Winner of the Thelonious Monk Institute's International Jazz Trumpet Competition, and he is now a Concord Music recording artist.

First of all we have to say congratulations to you because you represent the artist whose dream has come true. From the pathways of someone whose been dreaming about music, to educating yourself about music, to going for opportunities that can give you more exposure, up to winning the grand prize. What was it like for you on the night of November 9, 2014, at the Dolby Theatre in Hollywood, California, before Former President Bill Clinton and Herbie Hancock, Quincy Jones, Queen Latifah, Dianne Reeves, Arturo Sandoval and so many others to stand there on the grand stage to perform and to also win the prize?

Marquis Hill:
It was actually mind blowing, of course. I'm still floating on cloud nine. It was amazing just being around that caliber of musicians and the people that were there.

15

Dr. Logan H. Westbrooks

What is a recap of all that the grand prize entails?

Marquis Hill:
The grand prize entails a $25,000 scholarship. Half of it needs to be used for educational purposes, and the other half can be used however the winner sees fit. Also the main prize came with a record contract with Concord, which is one of the most famous Jazz labels that's still around for Jazz records today.

The holy grail for most artists would be to get a record deal, or in your case to win a recording contract. The icing on top would be to do so on a label that has been made famous for promoting music all over the world in your favorite genre, which in your case is Jazz. What can we expect from your journey now that you are a Concord Music artist?

Marquis Hill:
I just want to continue to put out quality music that represents my vision and what I'm going for as an artist. I actually had three records out before this Concord record label. Now I'm just hoping that with this deal, my music can be on a higher platform. They can help me reach more people with the label. That's what I'm looking forward to. That's the journey that I plan on taking, just really creating music that represents my style and what I'm going for as an artist. I'm grateful that Concord can help me with that.

So what does this mean? Will this help Marquis Hill reach more people because he's got more people on the ground marketing and promoting and clearing airplay on radio? Does this deal mean that Marquis Hill can pack up the whole band and travel the world and stay at fine hotels and perform at other festivals and concert halls all over the world? Can you demystify what this means for you so that other artists will know the difference should it ever happen to them?

Marquis Hill:
Well, it's actually kind of hard to say what the deal will do for me, but looking at the past winners, those things have happened for them. I am hoping that it leads to those things to be honest, because as artists that's what we all want—to be able to travel and get on the tour bus and take our bands on the road and just spread our music around the globe. That's what I hope is going to happen, and like I said before, just really getting my music out there to a bigger platform of people. Concord is a

16

well renowned label, and they do have PR people and radio people that can really help push my music way beyond what I've already done. So, yes, that's what I'm hoping for, all of those things. All of the above.

As an artist, you picked up the trumpet at age eleven. At eleven years old did you have a particular passion for Jazz or was it just for music in general?

Marquis Hill:

I was fortunate to be raised by a mother that loved music from the Motown era, the 50s, 60s, and 1970s Soul music. As early as I could remember, she was playing music from the Temptations, the Stylistics, and all those types of R&B and Soul bands. I was raised hearing that. I started getting interested in Jazz in the fifth grade when I switched to the trumpet. My elementary school band director Miss Dianne Ellis is a great saxophonist who still teaches at Diggs Elementary in Chicago. She gave me my first Jazz CD, which is a Lee Morgan record titled "Candy." I went home and listened to it that night, and I remember falling in love with it. Ever since then, I became fascinated with the sounds of Jazz, the art form. So yeah, it was the fifth grade, a pretty early age.

So not only did you continue to pursue Jazz for the enjoyment of it, you also pursued Jazz and music academically while many don't see the importance of doing that. You also went as far as pursuing a Master's Degree in Jazz Pedagogy from DePaul University. What exactly is Jazz Pedagogy?

Marquis Hill:

Pedagogy just means how to teach. I got my undergrad degree from Nolan Illinois University in Music Education. I actually went into college wanting to teach, and I still have a passion for teaching. Someday I will get back into that. Right now I just really want to focus on the performance aspects of it. But, in my eyes, teaching, educating, and performing all go hand in hand, especially in an art form like Jazz where the tradition is passed down orally. So to be a great performer, most of the great performers are great educators. My degree in Jazz Pedagogy helps me and gives me methods on how to teach.

Explain the benefits of not only being a great performer but also by being educated.

Marquis Hill:
In this day and age, to be a Jazz performer it's almost impossible to make a living at it. You need to have some other type of income. A lot of the great Jazz performers today also teach at a university to supplement their income. That's kind of the brutal truth of it. I went into it wanting to teach because I was taught, and it was engrained in me—the importance of education. This love of Jazz and the history of the music was engrained in me in the fifth grade. I want to do the same thing for upcoming students so that it's a cycle that keeps getting passed down.

Let's talk about life on the competition trail. When it comes to Jazz, with so many artists and players in the spectrum, how do you identify a unique tone or a unique vibe that is all your own?

Marquis Hill:
I think for me, it was just the fact that I was raised listening to so many different types of music. Even to this day I love Jazz, but I listen to Hip Hop, I listen to Soul music, I listen to R&B, Country, Classical. I listen to all types of music. I was fortunate enough to be exposed to such really good music at a young age. I think that my sound and my approach to composition and the way I play is just kind of a melting pot of all the things and the different genres that I have been exposed to.

Let's speak about the merger of academia and artistic culture. Because of that, we do have the Herb Alpert School of Music at UCLA. Because of that, we have the Thelonious Monk Institute of Jazz and so many more. What words do you have for institutions like this in terms of encouraging them to continue to thrive not only for you but for other artists who are coming up?

Marquis Hill
I salute and shout out to institutions like that to keep the traditions alive. We need more of them to keep the spirit of the music alive and to keep passing the traditions down. The great thing about the Thelonious Monk Jazz Institute is that they have artists like Wayne Shorter and Herbie Hancock. These are the pioneers of this music. They helped create it. They are the greats and their hands are passing down this knowledge to the students. That's the history of this music. It's an oral tradition. It needs to be taught orally and passed down from generation to generation, and institutions like the Thelonious Monk Institute is amazing. My vote is to keep doing that. Keep spreading the good word.

Now that you are an official Concord recording artist, what can fans expect from your brand new album?

Marquis Hill:
I am actually in the process of trying to figure out the concept of the record, but I would just say for fans to expect Marquis Hill. As I said earlier, I have three other previous projects available that I am very proud of because they are my life experiences summed up into music. They can expect to hear Marquis Hill.

Contact: www.MarquisHill.com
Twitter.com/mhilljazz
Facebook.com/marquis.hill.393
Facebook Fan Page: Marquis Hill Blacktet
Instagram.com/mhillmusic

Dr. Westbrooks:
Marquis Hill is an example of a Jazz artist being influenced by great Jazz artists at an early age. Also at an early age, he knew he wanted to be an educator. He was very fortunate to be able to experience both, because, for him, the two are intertwined. Marquis Hill will be able to meld his new flavor of Jazz with the traditional flavor of Jazz and stay true to the music. Now that he is signed to Concord Music Group, his music can reach a broader audience and keep Jazz alive across the globe and throughout the ages.

CHAPTER FIVE

KASHIF

Artist, Writer, Producer, Filmmaker

"We need more people who love the music and are willing to honor the process, and a part of honoring the process is knowing your history."

Kashif is an award-winning songwriter, producer and artist who was born in Harlem, New York. He is also an author, director, documentarian and a music icon who has produced and/or written chart topping smash hits for Whitney Houston, George Benson, Barry White, Lil' Kim, Evelyn "Champagne" King, Will Downing, Dionne Warwick, Janet Jackson, Johnny Kemp, Glenn Jones, Al Jarreau, Meli'sa Morgan, Mariah Carey, Kenny G, and Monica just to name a few. When we interviewed Kashif for this book, he was in the midst of working on a ten-part documentary about the origins of R&B music and its global impact.

Do you think that it is important for young artists to study or understand the history of music?

Kashif:
I think that anyone who is aspiring to be a part of any industry who is not familiar with the greats that came before them are most likely to be very shallow and probably not that in depth or talented. When we study our history, that's where we learn the foundation and the fundamentals of the music and the music game. I would even say that if you're not familiar with your past, it probably means you're not that much into music. You're more into being famous and making money. We don't need any more people like that in this game. We need more people who love the music and are willing to honor the process. A part of honoring the process is knowing your history. That's just basic, and I don't care what kind of career you're choosing.

If you're choosing to be a doctor, then you need to go back and study the history of medicine. At least to some degree, you need to understand the fundamentals, because if you don't, you're not going to be a very good doctor. The same applies to baseball, the same to bowling, and the same to becoming a radio announcer. If you don't know any other radio announcers, then you can't name the radio announcer greats and why they were great; then you won't be able to take that apart; then you will never be a great radio announcer.

It's assumed the information from this book will hit basically three kinds of audiences—the music industry aficionados, those who are novices to the industry, and those who are figuring out how to reinvent themselves. Kashif also offers career advice, guidance, consultation and all of the above in helping people define who they are and what they can do in today's industry. He further discusses his services in this capacity.

Kashif:
Kashif University One on One – What we offer is music training, because everything begins with the music. That would be song writing and producing. Then I offer career path development—the things that one should do to develop their career and move it in a forward motion. Again, it's about education. People think they can just jump into this game, and most people, I think, are motivated by money and fame. I pick those people out real quick, and if I feel that someone who wants to be a part of Kashif University One on One is just into it for the premier of fame, then I'm not interested in working with them. If they are interested in the art of it all, then from the art comes the excellence, and then comes the money and the fame.

I keep 20 clients worldwide. The reason why I keep 20 clients is because if it is more than that, I don't have time to give them the quality education that I provide. You can go to my Facebook page and put in Kashif Saleem. Hit me up there and I have discussions. It's literally five stages before you actually get to the music with me.

1) The first stage is an evaluation. I want to see what it is that you are interested in doing.
2) Next, we do a mission statement.
3) Next, is an action plan, which is a career path development plan.
4) Next, we create a schedule for what you're going to do by certain dates, in order to get through that first stage of emerging as a new artist, new producer, songwriter in your career.
5) Lastly, we focus on the product or the performance.

I think it's sort of a unique program that really focuses and forces the aspiring songwriter, producer, or artist into really thinking about their career and the stages of what to do with the assistance of someone who has been there and done that.

Assuming that there are still some record deals out there, what can an artist do these days with a record deal? And for those artists who do not seek or will not get a record deal, what can they do to manage their careers?

Kashif:

Record deals are very different now than they were back in the day. From the inception of the record industry, moving forward from the 1990s and early 2000s, there are not that many record companies out there or A&R (artists and repertoire) people, or even situations where record companies are even looking for people.

What they're looking for are people who already have careers that are developing. They're looking for the guy who has been out there on the street who has made his mix tapes or made his CD and they're out there peddling, or they're looking for the guy or gal who has a million hits on their YouTube page. They're looking for somebody who has already done the work. Then they can swoop in and take a piece of everything that has anything to do with your career or your life in entertainment. They're looking to make those kinds of deals.

Quite frankly, by that point, if you already have a million hits, what you need is a marketing or promotional company. Nowadays, most people can do music for the first time on the Internet and through sharing files with friends. It's not the radio anymore; radio is becoming less and less important.

The one thing that record companies in the past had dominion over was radio stations, radio play, and the brick and mortar stores. Now there are fewer and fewer brick and mortar stores, and fewer and fewer people are buying CDs. So any music that's being sold for the most part, the majority of it is being sold on the Internet, which you can do. So you don't necessarily need a record company for distribution on the Internet, and you don't need a record company for radio play on YouTube, or Vimeo, or any of the other outlets. So to be honest with you, the record companies are really a publicity and marketing firm now. They're asking for more than ever, and giving you less and less. At least before they were printing up the records and distribution. They had the marketing and they had the publicity. They had all those things, and now they don't have dominion over all of those things.

Now I think the role of the record company has diminished in terms of the significance to the artist and what artists don't have access to. But, now they're asking for more and more. They want a percentage of everything that you do that has anything to do with entertainment or anything that sort of unfolds as a result of your entertainment activity. It's very different.

For the benefit of those who are yet learning about this industry, what is the percentage that the record companies are asking for in exchange for the investment that they make into developing the artist's career?

Kashif:

Those are called 360 degree deals, and I don't know because I haven't done any of those 360 deals, so they don't apply to me. I just know that they're asking for more now. When I was with Arista, they got a piece of my record making, just a piece of me for recording for them. And every time the recording would sell, then I would make money. They didn't get a piece of my songwriting, they didn't get a piece of my other businesses, just a piece of when my record sold. The majority shares—because during that time I was getting 15 percent and they were getting 18 percent—so it's either in that realm or more. But, these companies are making a percentage of everything that the artist does now.

So if the artist starts a clothing line, they want a piece of that. If the artist is in a movie, they want a piece of that. If the artist is in a collaboration with another artist, they want a piece of that. It's called a 360 deal. They have less to do and they wait until you're already successful in some form, and they want a piece of more things. I'm not a big fan of the 360 deals, and they've become just a marketing company.

I think the artist now should have the bigger share, and the record company should have the smaller share. It's almost as though they're now the hired hand, yet they're walking as the hired hand and still want to rule everything.

Is there a moment or an event that you can share that was your career highlight, or at what moment did you realize 'I have made it!'

Kashif:

That's an interesting thing because I don't think like that. That's not my mode of operation. I enjoy the moments as they come, and the wonderful moments are numerous. I'm also not a person who sits around and sort of rests on my laurels and think about the past. And then there are moments that I enjoy thinking about the past. Like when I performed for the first time at Radio City Music Hall. That was fun and that was a highlight. There's so many of those moments, and life is so full of wonderments and peaks and valleys, that I'm just grateful all the time. I tend to stay right there in the middle. I tend to look into the future and grab a hold of the challenges at hand rather than looking back and swinging on successes that have been. I'm just built that way. I'm more excited about the possibilities of what's coming in the future. You know, future projects and what might happen as a result of producing this ten-part series, *The History of R & B Music*. I'm more excited about that than I am about the past. The past is great and wonderful, and it certainly gives the sense of satisfaction that I can do this or anything that I choose. That's just who I am.

Who has influenced you the most artistically, and who has influenced you the most as a businessperson?

Kashif:

Artistically, there is a wide variety of individuals. From Louie Armstrong from my trumpet playing days; to Barry White as an artist; to Quincy Jones as an arranger and producer; to Earth, Wind & Fire; to Art Tatum as a piano player; to McCoy Tyner as a piano player; and to Duke Ellington as an orchestra leader, arranger and artist. I've been influenced by all of them. There's a wide variety of these individuals, and as you can see, without history, there's no way I could have the career and continue to prosper.

Had I not had these super heroes and beyond that, I would not have had such an interesting life. Dr. Martin Luther King, Jr., Gandhi, Leonardo da Vinci—these are all my heroes. So as I move through life, I look back and reflect on more of them—their careers and what they've done. That's what fuels the fire in me. And that's what keeps me fresh and ready to do the things that may not have been done before, or to put it in a slant or to give it a new life. That's the big answer to that question.

So are we understanding that someone's artistic influences and business influences can be merged into one?

Kashif:

All of those influences are beneficial to me. I have an interest in science. I have an interest in technology, of course. I'm fascinated by Steve Jobs and his accomplishments. I'm just as fascinated by Bill

24

Gates' business savvy, but also by his philanthropic philosophy in his giving and in his sharing. There's a methodology employed, because he hopes to make the biggest impact in the areas of providing medicine, health care, and overcoming poverty and the lack of food and the lack of education. He is not calling it giving back, he is now living his purpose. I don't give back, I don't like that phrase so much—giving back. It's so over used in the entertainment industry, and so many artists and public figures use it as a photo opp.

For me, it's not about a photo opp. For me, it means I'm living my purpose, as this is why God put me on the planet. When I'm doing any of my work around education, advocating for youth in foster care, advocating for young people who are interested in the arts, I'm not giving back. I'm living my purpose; that's why I was put here. To me that represents a stronger and deeper commitment.

To reach me you can go to the Internet and type in Kashif University. The reason I don't get too specific with, "You can reach me at this number and that number" is because folks have to go out and do the work. If you're not willing to go on the Internet and do the work and hunt me down and find me, then you're probably not the right person for me. I have parents who are calling me or finding a way to get in touch with me for their twenty-year-old kid. Well, I'm like, "I'm not interested in talking to you wonderful parent. Have your not-so-grown twenty-year-old kid do the work. Have them reach out to me."

I'm big on all of us being responsible once we reach a certain age, being responsible for our own successes. I think that it's important, especially for anyone trying to get into the entertainment game, that you are responsible for you. Any place where you are in your life, you are responsible for you. You create your own reality.

Contact:
Facebook.com/kashif.saleem
Twitter.com/Kashifcreative

Dr. Westbrooks:
Kashif emphasizes knowledge and education about the music business. He has experienced the old music business model and has comfortably transitioned into the new model. Kashif encourages not just artists, but everyone, to become knowledgeable about the music business or whatever business you're planning to be a part of. Kashif wants artists to understand how to take advantage of the reversal of roles within the industry—when the major labels did everything for the artists and took the lion share of the profits as opposed to now when the artists do

everything for themselves, the lion share of the profits should go to the artist. When artists understand this, they are able to take control of their career path and be responsible for themselves. He operates under the premise that knowledge is power. In November 2014, Kashif was inducted into the R&B Hall of Fame as a Living Legend.

CHAPTER SIX

JAY KING

Artist, Writer, Producer, Label Owner

"You can't just say I want to make money. You've got to say, I love music."

Jay King brings a wealth of industry experience as the founder of Timex Social Club and Club Nouveau. At just 24 years old he formed his own label and landed the number one R&B single of 1986 with the song "Rumors." The effort amassed 3.5 million in sales.

As a multi-faceted producer, musician and artist who continues to thrive in the digital age, what do you have to say to artists who are entering or re-entering the music industry?

Jay King:
Read, study, and learn. Constantly ask questions. I'm still learning today. I learn every day. You can take advantage of everything that's in front of you. There's so much information that's in front of artists today that we didn't have years ago. You can go to Google, and you can find out anything.

You can read, and don't just go by what you read the first time. Challenge what you read. I don't just take to what I read, I challenge it. I want to find backup information on it. I'm not going to just take what's given to me. And you've got to love it. It's got to be passion in your heart for it. You can't just say I want to make money. You've got to say, I love music. I love music, and I love the creative process. You've got to know that you're responsible for the vibration that you put in the world, more so than any time before. Artists used to be able to say, "Well, I'm doing this because my record company is making me do this." Artists can't say that now, because most artists are their record company.

So you're responsible for the vibration that's out here. If you don't think that music has a direct reflection on society, then you're a scarecrow and you don't have a brain. It is an influencer. It influences people. It's a game changer, it can change mind sense. Music is a real vibration that can console the universe. So you've got to be responsible for the vibration, and you've got to make sure that it is as close to being

27

positive 1,000 percent of the time if you possibly can. If you do that, the rewards will come back to you a million fold. And you'll make money doing it, but not because you set out to make money. It's because you set out to love it, because you love what it is that you do. When you love what you do, the passion from it will earn you money, because it's from a genuine spot.

Our desire is to reach the young artists, the young executive, as well as the young engineer. Many times nowadays the artist is the entire company, or the artist and a small group of people. So with that, we asked Jay for his guidance in understanding each job position in reference to the total success of a music entity.

Jay King:
The more you have an understanding about what it is that you're embarking on, the more likely you're going to be successful and the more likely the people around you are going to be competent. It doesn't mean you have to be a genius at it, or you have to know it inside and out. But you have to have a competent understanding so that the people who represent you, represent you competently. When they don't, or when they can't, or when the wrong person is headed their way, you see it coming a mile away because you have a competent understanding of the business as a whole.

As an artist today, you can't afford not to. As an engineer today, you can't afford not to understand. You've got to understand that it's more than just turning a knob. You have to understand the sonic part of it, too, because now, if you're an engineer, you're probably going to do the mastering also. And if you're the engineer, you're probably going to do additional production. If a guy you're using is not going to work, you know that sonically it is because there's too much noise on it, or it's not clean or it's fuzzy. As an engineer you've got be able to make that call and then explain to the guy what it is. So I don't care what the job is that you're doing, because there is so much information out there, you get the opportunity to study, love, and execute the plan that you're putting forth. Whether it's recording a record or putting a budget together.

Here's what I think the difference in the business is today. Before, a manager did the managing, an artist did the performing, a writer did the writing, a producer did the producing, and an arranger did the arranging, and all of these people made this whole machine run. Those kinds of budgets don't exist anymore, and the profit margins just aren't there. So the more you understand the process, the more economical you can do it without losing quality and without losing integrity.

How important is it for anyone to get their agreements in writing early into the process?

Jay King:

The earlier the better. Most problems arise because people fancy themselves as friends, and they build a business foundation on friendship. You can't do that. Friendship is friendship and business is business. If you guys are really friends, you're going to respect that and understand it. And you guys are going to respect your friendship a lot more by getting the business out of the way.

I'll give you a simple example. A young lady I know wanted to book Club Nouveau for a show; this just happened recently. She booked us, and normally when I'm booked, the promoter pays for the airfare and the hotels, and they're paying us a fee for the performance. In this particular instance, they didn't have enough money to pay for airfare and hotels, and the fee wasn't as high as I wanted it to be. But, because it was for a city show and it was free for the community where the people weren't going to be charged, we did the show. So we're getting ready to do the show, but before the show happens, I have to call her like I do with all my dates in advance and get her my rider so that she can make sure we will have the equipment that we need and everything. And then I ask her about the plane tickets and hotel, and what airport me and Val— my sister and group member—are flying from.

She said, "I'm not responsible for that." I said, "Of course you are." And she said, "No, Jay, I'm not, you're responsible for that." "I said I never do deals like that." But because I represent Karen White, Cameo, Larry Dunn, Darius McCrary, and I do a radio show, and I write books, and I manage independent labels, I forget just like everybody else. She said, "I'll send you the agreement." She sent me a copy of the agreement with my signature on it. I called her back and told her that she was correct and that I would take care of it today. And I took care of it.

Just think had I not had an agreement with her, had I just worked it off of a handshake. I would have gone back to what I normally do, which is that I don't normally book flights and book hotels. I just don't do that. Ninety-nine percent of the time, the promoter does that. In this particular one percent, I did the opposite of what I normally do. Had I not had a contract, this would have been an issue and possibly a fight that was unnecessary, and I would have been wrong. But I would have sworn that I was right, because I would have gone by what I normally do.

I say all that to say this, when you have a contract, it's not because you don't trust people. It's so that everybody can remember what was agreed to, so there won't be a problem.

Contact:
http://www.jayking.me
http://www.twitter.com/theclubnouveau
http://www.facebook.com/jayking3

Dr. Westbrooks:
Jay King puts an emphasis on passion. Passion compels you to act from your heart and soul. He feels that if you're in the music business, it's pertinent that you love music, that you live it, that you be enthusiastic about it. But, being passionate doesn't mean forget everything else and focus only on the music. It means applying an intense desire to understand every aspect of this business because it is now up to the artists to be responsible for themselves more than ever before. Passion fuels your desire to succeed in this business. Being passionate means loving the music, but also loving yourself enough to know, grow, establish, and maintain a successful music career.

CHAPTER SEVEN

JOANNE MCDUFFIE-FUNDERBURG "JO JO"

**Former lead singer of the Mary Jane Girls,
CEO of Shameless Hussy Productions**

"You can't let what you do become who you are."

Joanne McDuffie-Funderburg is a vocalist, choreographer, and composer, who is also the CEO of her own production company Shameless Hussy Productions. She was the lead voice on classics such as "Candy Man," "In My House," "Boys" and "All Night Long," which were produced by the late great Rick James. Jo Jo tells us how she got started in music up to the time she got signed with Motown Records as one of the Mary Jane Girls.

Jo Jo Funderburg:
I came from a musical family. My maternal grandfather was a choir director and a vocalist who also taught voice. I never met him; he passed away before I was born. I was told by my great aunts and my mom that we got our talents from him and that he was the original part of that DNA. My mom was a vocalist. She sang in the choir and she played piano. I can't remember a lot of her playing as a young child, but I do remember the first song she taught me, which was "Precious Lord" because I had to sing it at a funeral. I think I must have been about 12 or 13 years old at the time. I started singing and listening to her and listening to my dad. My dad was a dancer; they both danced. From my understanding, they both danced when they were younger and that's how they met. My Mom was a 'PK', a preacher's kid. Of course, back then you weren't supposed to be doing any of that. I'm guessing my dad was the bad boy. They met and they ran away from Buffalo, New York, to get married in Erie, Pennsylvania. They were married for many years and they never got divorced, though they separated. There were five children, and I'm number four from the five of us.

We all did something. We all liked singing and dancing. This was a common thing at home. I didn't discover it was something different until I was asked to sing something when I was about 12 or 13 years old. People said, "Oh my God, how could you sing like that?" It wasn't a big deal because we all used to do it at home. I got into a few talent shows at the age of 15. I was still trying to sing. That's when I met my son's father. I'm not real comfortable about this, but I might as well tell my particular story.

I got pregnant at 15 and had my first child, which is what really pushed me to sing even more because I didn't have any money. He decided he didn't want to participate. Looking back, I can see we were both very, very young. I guess he felt like he didn't have to help. His lack of participation with me and my son pushed me, and the only thing I knew how to do was sing. I grabbed a wig, I grabbed some makeup, put it on and tried to look older. At the time there were a lot of clubs in the city of Buffalo that you could work in. I took my little sneaky self in the club, and I could make 15 bucks a night on open mic night if I was better than everybody else. You could win first prize, second prize and that kind of thing. By the time I was 19, I was known pretty well in the area as a Jazz vocalist. I sang Jazz, and, of course, I sang what is known as Top 40, which means songs that appear in the Top 40 on the Pop charts. That's how I started singing in the clubs, I needed diaper money.

When did you make your way to Los Angeles?

Jo Jo Funderburg:
I had been singing in the clubs for a long time. I quit school, but I went back and finished my high school courses. I then went to one of the local colleges, the State University of New York at Buffalo. While I was there, I met a couple of people from the Stone City Band (Rick James' backing band). I met Levi Ruffin, Jr., and I met his wife Jackie Ruffin in the college Gospel choir. I knew them. I also knew some of the bass players and lots of musicians from where I worked in the Jazz and the Top 40 bands.

I wanted a better job, so I went back to school. When I graduated, I had a job that was part time, but it turned into full time at a record store. One day while I was working at the store, Rick James came in with his entourage, and I knew the bass player. The bass player and I grew up two blocks from each other. He said, "Yeah, man, this is the girl I was telling you about." At the time, Rick was looking for new background vocalists. He looked at me and kind of sized me up a little bit and asked, "Well, can you sing?" I said, "Yes, I can." He said, "Well, give me your phone number, and I'll give you a call because I'm holding auditions." I'm like, "Okay fine."

He held the auditions in the basement of his home where he was building his studio at the time, so I had to walk through construction material. Basically, all he had was a board in the control room of the studio. This was a couple of days after I'd given him my number that I went to his audition. I sang flat out cold. He kept saying sing, so and so, sing so and so, and most of them were old Motown hits. I did most of them a cappella. He said, "Look, I like your voice. I think you would be a great addition to my background vocalists." At the time they were called the Colored Girls, but he said he was going to call them the Mary Jane Band. He said, "What I intend to do is start a group like Prince has done." At the time, Prince's protégée Vanity 6 was out, and Vanity was very hot. He said, "I'm going to start a group, but for right now, I think you would be a great addition to our organization." So I started out as a background vocalist for his tour. I believe it was the last part of the Street Songs Tour.

I believe it was in 1979 when I came to Los Angeles and did a couple of albums. The first one that I worked on was the *Throwing Down* album. That was the one that had the Temptations song on it titled "Standing on the Top." That was one of the first really big songs that I sang background on "Standing on the Top." Between 1979 and 1982 I sang background for Rick James on all of his tours and any of the albums that were done during that time. I was actually bi-coastal. I had an apartment back here in Buffalo, and I had an apartment in Los Angeles. I was back and forth quite a bit.

At some point, the Mary Jane Girls' concept fully came to life. Walk us through some of the high points of that experience. Then talk about the flip side of it because, as we know, everyone's journey and pathway in music is different. There is a certain climate that seems to take place with groups. At some point, there almost always seems to be a certain departure with lead singers and groups.

Jo Jo Funderburg:

Goodness, where do I start with that? Okay, Rick's background vocalists at that time were called the Mary Jane Band. The other two girls departed, and I started on the initial demos. Because there was no longer a group, he said we were going to start a solo project for me. I recorded the songs "Candy Man," "The Boys," "Prove It," "Musical Love" and "On the Inside." Now, all the time he had a concept for a group. He took the project, at some point, to a few other record companies such as Epic Records, Columbia, and Motown. I believe that they ended up having a bidding war for the demos. They were thinking that it was an actual

33

group. I believe he told them that it was a group. He sold those concept demos as a group, but he really didn't have a group. So he had to find girls. I really can't speak on where they came from, but what I can say is that there was no nationwide search or audition as the public was told. I met Cheri one day, and a week or so later I met Candi and Maxi. I was told these would be the women in the new group that I would be working with.

So you are saying that Rick James sold the Mary Jane Girls as a concept. He created an audio representation of this group, and you were a part of the singers on this particular demo?

Jo Jo Funderburg:
I was. I sang lead and background on the demos.

Did you sing all of the background parts?

Jo Jo Funderburg:
No I didn't.

So the other singers on the demo were not on the album cover and not the singers that the public came to know as the Mary Jane Girls. Is that correct?

Jo Jo Funderburg:
Yes. Well, we won't mention them because I don't have the authority or permission to use their names.

For clarity, Mary Jane Girls was a concept before it was a physical group. In selling the concept, Rick James compiled a demo, and you and some other singers (whom we cannot mention) were a part of the audio demo. When it was time to put a face with the voices, then Rick James went out and selected some other girls who created the image for what we later accepted as the Mary Jane Girls, but all of them were not the original singers.

Jo Jo Funderburg:
I couldn't have said it better myself.

The Mary Jane Girls not only became music icons, but style icons as well.

Jo Jo Funderburg:

There was a lot of that going on. At the time, if there was going to be a talent show, everybody wanted to be the Mary Jane Girls. And, oh my goodness, we were style queens. Fashion in the 1980s was awful. Seriously, it was so bad that it was good. As far as being style icons, we styled ourselves. The socks with the high heel shoes was our thing. The stockings with the hole in it was our thing. The little baby doll brush was for Cheri. My hair was braided, and the whole biker girl thing was for Maxi (performed by Kim Wuletich). That all belonged to us, we all did that. Actually, that was Rick's concept. He said that once he decided what he wanted, he found the girl to fit that part. One girl he wanted to be like the rough biker chick. That was supposed to be Maxi. He wanted one of the girls to be glamorous and sophisticated. That was Candi (performed by Candice Ghant). He wanted a Lolita type. That would have been the group member named Cheri (performed by Ann Cheri Bailey) or Corvette (performed by Yvette Marine who replaced Cheri). And I was supposed to be the 'round the way girl' from the hood. What do we call that, ghetto fabulous?

Were you also intended to be like the female Rick James?

Jo Jo Funderburg:

Yes, yes. Well, this is what he said. Other people have since even said that I tried to call myself the female Rick, but I never said that. They basically took it way out of context. They said that I was self-proclaimed. And I said, "No, I never proclaimed myself to be anything." This was the concept that Rick had for each girl. Everybody was cool with it until I said what his concept was for me. I was supposed to wear the leather, and I was supposed to wear the braids. I was like, as I said, the ghetto fabulous girl. When it came to me it turned into something else, always.

You guys hit a stride and it was fun. It really was a great era to experience. Please give young people some insight who might currently be a part of a group or have some curiosity about what it was like to be part of a group and to work with somebody who's really big and famous. What were some of the ups and downs?

Jo Jo Funderburg:

I can give it to you from my perspective and from what we were doing at the time and from what was going on. I hope that someone can be able to gather something from it, and I can only give you my experience.

My experience working with Rick James was great—the work and the creativity, that whole grind. When I look back on it, I'm like, "Oh, my goodness, we worked so hard." Some people would pass out if we told them how hard we worked. When we weren't on the road, we were in the studio. When we weren't in the studio, we were on the road. At the time, Rick was very creative and he was very innovative. It's hard to be an innovator or trailblazer in any day and age. He was a trailblazer when it came to his particular type of music, which he didn't call Rock & Roll. It was a combination of Rock & Roll and Funk, and he called it Funk & Roll, that was his coined name for it. He was the creator of that and the creator of everything that was the concept for himself, the concept for his band, and the concept for the girls.

I enjoyed the work because it was new to me and I have always been very, very interested in music. I came from a musical background, not from just being a vocalist, but I also learned songwriting. I was in the studio a lot, so I saw how a song was made from the beginning to the end. I saw the drummers lay their parts down and the bass player and the lead guitars and the horns and I saw the songs mixed and mastered. I got the chance to see all of that, and I am so grateful for that experience. Yes, it was hard. It was a lot of hard work. It was a creative place where everybody goes. All people are creative, but in speaking of my personal experience in working with Rick, we went to a place. You could see the results. We went to a creative place, we worked very hard. We came back with our gifts, and we shared it with the rest of the world. And I can't say one bad thing about that. I am so thankful to God that I was able to be a part of that.

Other people have this other thing where they saw the ugly side, because it became public. The business lends itself to that. In creativity, unfortunately, you sometimes have to be a train wreck. Now a days, especially for African Americans and pretty much everybody—I shouldn't say just African Americans—when you're very creative and very talented, there also has to be a bad side. You also have to have some darkness with you. Unfortunately, some people really, really do. For the most creative ones, sometimes we really do have a dark place and I saw some of that with Rick James. I saw some of it. I don't know what it was. All I know is after a while, I saw him start to deteriorate. I didn't know why. My question is, if you have all of that and you're so creative and so talented, and you go to that creative place and you come back with this wonderful gift, then what's wrong?

You've shared very heartfelt, respectful, and honest comments about your experience with the late great Rick James, but it is a known fact that for many, unfortunately, drugs and drama plague the industry, and so often end in an early death. How did you avoid this?

Jo Jo Funderburg:
Honestly, it was only by the grace of God. I have been around. Where I grew up, while on my way to school, the pimps were outside and the drunks would be outside sleeping. On your way to school you would see that as a child. I didn't grow up in a charmed neighborhood. It wasn't Beverly Hills, and it wasn't Brentwood or whatever. I didn't grow up like that. I saw a lot of things. I saw a lot of people. I knew a lot of people who did things like that, and I saw how it made them act very early on. I was scared. I'm going to be real honest with you, I was afraid of that. I don't know why, but I thank God that I was. I was afraid of drugs. I'm not going to tell you that I didn't drink. I'm not going to tell you that I didn't, at one point, have friends that I was around and that maybe everyone once in a while would try all of the mixed drinks, or every once in a while sometimes we would smoke a joint.

I'm not an angel. I would never tell you that I never did it, I just didn't like it. It didn't sit well with me because I couldn't concentrate. The first example was smoking. I did smoke before, but I couldn't concentrate. I was afraid that it would dry my throat out, and it made my throat sore. I was afraid that I wouldn't be able to sing if I did that. The same thing was true with alcohol. It dried my throat out so badly, that I would be dizzy. Basically, for me, I really wasn't that interested in it, because I had tried it. I was not interested in the drugs. When I got to a point where I started to see massive quantities of cocaine, and massive people doing it and parties and drinking, I just wasn't interested in that.

The party thing, I was also afraid of because I had an incident that happened in my family. One of my sisters went to a party when she was 14 years old. She was maybe dancing with someone or whatever the case might have been, and someone chased her out of the house and killed her. That incident was always in the back of my head, and it was always a fear. I'm not a frightened or scary person like that, but that was something that stuck in the back of my mind.

So I never was the party girl. I wasn't a stick in the mud either, but I wasn't the party girl. And, I really, really wasn't interested in drugs. When I got around the environment where it was plentiful, I was working. Of course, people would stop and smoke some weed and they would do whatever. Usually after that, sometimes the work would shut down and I would say, "Well, can I go back to the hotel? Can I leave? You know I'm really not into that." It got to a point where people would not do that around me. They used to make fun of me and say, "Oh, you go to church and you read your bible and you do this and you do that." I would say, "Yes, I do." They made fun of me, but I didn't care. I'll personally tell you, I don't believe God wanted me to do any of it. He made me disinterested; I had no desire. When I saw how crazy it would make other people act, it convinced me even more not to do it. I was afraid.

What would you say to a young or a vulnerable person about what they can do to steer clear of the drugs and the drama?

Jo Jo Funderburg:
You have to be spiritually grounded. You have to know who you are and whose you are. That, for me, is number one, first and foremost, and just have the backbone to know that this is the music business. Big "B" and small "m." You've got to know the business aspect of this and that's the other part. If you have no knowledge and you can't read a contract, please don't walk into this. Because the first thing somebody is going to do is, they want a record deal or they want to sing. Don't put your voice on anything until you know what you're doing—until you know something about this business as a whole.

Learn the business as much as you learn your craft. That's the only thing that I can truthfully say that will help them to be grounded and know who they are and what they have. As far as talent and creativity, that's all fine and well, but you have to know the business aspect of it. If you don't know the business, don't get in it because it will eat you up and spit you out.

Another scenario that we see throughout history is, when there is a group and there is a lead singer, almost without fail the lead singer moves on. Sometimes they both survive as separate entities and many times they don't. What has your experience been like since parting ways with the Mary Jane Girls? When you are a part of a group and you are the lead singer, how do you know when it's time to go? How do you keep harmony with your group, and what are the legal entanglements?

Jo Jo Funderburg:

Generally speaking, you're signed to a contract. You all sign your name one by one, which means for a certain period of time you have to do certain things under the terms of the contract. Now what goes on behind the scene is a whole different animal. If you have one person who is singing lead, after a while the other people—and I can only speak from my own situation—perceive that you are receiving favoritism. Which, it is and it isn't. From my perspective, it's like I was qualified to do this, which is why I was chosen to do this part. Our problem with the Mary Jane Girls was that we had different ideas of what success was supposed to be and how to achieve it.

I had already done the demos and was designated to be the lead vocalist or the lead person, but everyone else wanted us to be all four in the same, the same in everything. They also wanted to make sure that we were all paid the same amount of money. Well, that didn't sit well with me because I was doing the brunt of the work on stage and in the studio. They decided that not only were they supposed to make the same amount of money, but they were extremely insecure. If too many beautiful women are in a room, then somebody is going to want to be more beautiful. Somebody is going to want to be more this or more of that, and then there's going to be a problem.

I was with people who were extremely insecure about who they were and what their role was. Of course, we had people around us who were also seeing that, and they fed into that and were trying to make everybody insecure. I was not insecure about what I was supposed to be doing. They made me extremely uncomfortable as the lead. I did not leave because of that, I left because I was promised something, and I didn't get it.

I found out that everybody was making the same amount of money, which I really didn't think was fair. It would have been fair to me, for example, if everybody who was supposed to be the Mary Jane Girl on the face of things, if they were singing background the way they were supposed to be, then I wouldn't have had any problem with that. Because it would be like, you're singing this part and you're singing that part, and I'm singing this part, and I'm also singing lead and I'm also singing background on some of the parts. I wouldn't have had any problem with that. None of them were singing background. There were other people singing background for both albums, and I took issue with that because with any group there is always a reason. In this particular instance, I wasn't being treated fairly for the work that I did. Like I said, there was the animosity that normally happens between women such as the infighting, the backbiting…the ones who think they're more special

39

than others. I'm trying to explain this so that it doesn't seem personal. I would presume that this goes on in any group.

You've seen other groups break up. You've seen the Supremes break up. You've seen the Temptations break up. You've seen En Vogue break up. You've seen Destiny's Child break up. They are no more. I don't know why they broke up, but I would suspect it was because of all of these being female groups with the exception of Motown's legendary Temptations. I would expect that the Temptations had two lead singers at one point. They had Dennis Edwards and they had David Ruffin. I don't know why the male part of that happened. The female thing is a whole totally different animal. Men know teamwork, women don't. Men can be on opposing teams playing football or basketball, and they can talk about each other's mamas and wives, trash talk on the court. After the game, they can say, "Great game man, let's go have a beer." Women can't do that. We aren't wired like that. You can't say something about my man, my kids, my weave or me because then it's on and crackin.'

What are your suggestions for any artists to be able to land on their feet and survive beyond their heyday or career highpoint?

Jo Jo Funderburg:
I was flipping through the television one Sunday, and I caught Bishop T.D. Jakes. He was saying that you've got to work with what you've got left. No matter what it is, no matter what kind of job it is, if it didn't work out. It could be a marriage, it could be relationships, and you walk away; you have got to work with what you've got left.

Speaking in particular about what we do in the music business; in the aftermath for me, we didn't breakup because we weren't successful. We broke up because of internal problems. I took what I had left. I made an assessment of what I had left. I'm still making an assessment of what I've got left and what's usable and what's workable. You've got to leave your ego out of it, because this lends itself to drama. To me, the ego is a part of the drama. Now that's not saying you've got to totally dispose of your ego, because you've got to have some sort of an ego in order to do this. But, you can't let it be the be-all and end-all in control of you.

Because you are a person, you have to know that you are a person outside of what you do. Do not let what you do, become who you are. Jo Jo of the Mary Jane Girls is Jo Jo of the Mary Jane Girls. I am Joanne McDuffie-Funderburg, the person speaking right now. And, yes, there's that other entity. I'm not saying that I have a split personality, but you can't let what you do, become who you are. I never did. I knew what

I did for a living, and I got mad in the beginning when it was over, but I was doing temp work. I said, I can go and get me a job. It might not be the kind of money I was making, but at least I know I'm going to get paid. Ain't no shame in my game. To this day, if I can do that, I will do that. I will go to a job, a temp agency, the department store Marshalls or TJ Maxx. I will go to Ralph's (grocery store), somebody's going to hire me.

Your current project is "Shameless Hussy." Where can people find it, where is it available?

Jo Jo Funderburg:
The "Shameless Hussy" project is available on iTunes. It's also available through CD Baby.

Contact:
www.JoJoUrbanDiva.com
Facebook.com/JoanneFunderburg

Dr. Westbrooks:
Jo Jo respects and loves creativity, and she appreciates the whole creative process. So in an industry where everyone is creative, how do you make yourself stand out from the crowd? It's done by understanding the significance of innovation. Rick James was an innovator, and Jo Jo witnessed it first hand as a part of the Mary Jane Girls. He basically sold a concept that later materialized just as he envisioned it. He also created his own genre and coined a term for it—Rock & Funk. Jo Jo is following the same path by staying the course through her decades in the industry, but also re-inventing herself to remain relevant by adapting and presenting new music to the public. She is a very creative person, but also grounded in reality.

CHAPTER EIGHT

DORIE PRIDE

Singer, Songwriter, Musician, Author

"Never give up! No matter what anybody tells you, no matter what you hear or don't hear, or what you see or don't see, never give up."

Dorie Pride is the owner of Pride Fire Music. She is a singer, songwriter, performer, and author, and was inspired to write songs by Grammy winner Ray Parker, Jr. As a native of Detroit, Michigan, Dorie was exposed to a hub of artisans who quickly took note of her lyrical gifts. Among them was Joe Jackson who chose Dorie's songs to be among Janet Jackson's first recordings ever. The list also included Johnny Mathis, LaToya Jackson, the Whispers and more. Early in her life and career Dorie met her soul mate and collaborator Kamau Seitu, an extraordinary guitarist, writer and producer as well. They continue to work together and on separate projects. Dorie's journey as an artist has included many record deal offers that went sour, including one from the King of Pop, Michael Jackson's MJJ Records. Dorie openly shares her brushes with many big breaks, and how she finally stepped forth as an independent artist.

Dorie Pride:
I got into the music business through a very dear friend of mine who initially saw my talent as a writer. My career prior to that had been as a model. He said that you really have a great gift for words. You should really start thinking about writing songs. You could make a lot of money, and so I thought, *"Writing songs?"* I always wrote poetry, and I always loved words and communicating, but I never thought about it in that light. When he said I could make a lot of money, I said, "Hmmm, okay, maybe I should give it a shot." I started writing songs, and that friend was Ray Parker, Jr. He was the person that opened that door for me. The blessing was also that Ray Parker had given me a lot of insight into the music business, having moved from Detroit, Michigan, where we were neighbors. He showed me what the music industry was all about by going to the studio and watching great people like Quincy Jones. You name it and I saw it. I thought, *"Wow, this is really cool."* But, I never

thought about being connected in the music business in any way other than just being a fan and enjoying and loving music. But, once he put that seed in my heart, I thought, *"This could work!"*

I started writing songs by writing lyrics, and then in comes Kamau Seitu who liked what I was doing and he said, "You want to work with me? I have some tracks. You want to try some lyrics to it?" "I said, absolutely." One thing led to another, and I honed my craft. The next thing I know I was getting a call from Joe Jackson saying, "We saw some of your work. My daughter LaToya is working on a new CD. We're trying to get our daughters into the music business, and I like your work. I want to use some of your songs." LaToya Jackson did two songs. The songs that we wrote for LaToya, Michael loved them also because he heard her practicing them. He would go around the house singing them.

Now, fast forward. Joe Jackson comes back to us saying, "My baby Janet is on TV and we're trying to break her into the music business. You got any songs for Janet? I think that you're a really good songwriter; you write great lyrics. They are nice and clean, and I want to get my daughter out there. You got anything?" I said, "Yep, we got some stuff for her." We ended up working with Janet Jackson, and it was our songs that got Janet her record deal over at A&M in her early career. It was actually her debut. The songs that we wrote were "The Magic Is Working" and "Too Young to Fall in Love." Because we didn't have a big name, the song "Too Young to Fall in Love" got dropped off the album. A more well-known duo, René & Angela, had a bigger name, and they got that slot (to have multiple songs on the album). We ended up with "The Magic is Working" on her first album, which was written by Dorie Pride (PRIDEFIRE MUSIC) and Gene Dozier (Proud Tunes Music).

I can remember when Janet was first in the studio singing. She had such a little voice, and she was so shy. She would send everybody out. She'd turn off the lights, and she'd be in the booth in a little corner singing. I actually have the draft of her singing "Too Young to Fall in Love." That song actually ended up on the TV show at the time called *Different Strokes* (which starred Gary Coleman, Todd Bridges and Dana Plato). She ended up singing the song on that show because she played the girlfriend of Todd Bridges' character, and she'd sing that song to him. I still get paid from that, which is wonderful. So fast forward again, and I'm really writing songs, and I'm enjoying it a lot. Then came the Whispers. Then came Johnny Mathis. He is the most incredible person. I love him. He is so precious, so classy, elegant and down to earth. I remember something that he said to me that will stay with me as long as I live. We were in the studio eating and about to have champagne. He popped the cork and he said, "This is to you! What would make you give your babies to me, because you call your songs your babies." The name of the song that we had written for him was called "Here's To You." I said, "Are you kidding? You are Johnny Mathis!" That's just how kind and humble he is, that he would say something like that to me. That song is yet to be released because Gene Page, who was the arranger and producer on it, produced it so that it was too long to go on the album. It will eventually come out because the amount of money that they put into it was monumental. This was back in the late 80s or early 1990s, but I do have a copy of it.

Move us up to the time when you had various opportunities to be signed by major record labels as an artist.

Dorie Pride:
I have had at least ten record deal offers over the years. People would love my work. They would love my words, voice and melodies, but every time it came time to sign the contract, there would always be something in there that would make me have to back away. I was like, *"God when is it going to be right because I can't sell my soul."* That's kind of what it felt like to me. I'm a real artsy person, and I'm not Vanessa Williams. I'm not a Whitney Houston type, and I'm not Toni Braxton. But, they would want to put me in that category because of the way that I look, they wanted that type of thing. That just wasn't me. Then they wanted me to write the type of songs that they saw as being very popular money makers. While I am into that (achieving popularity and making money) I don't want to sell my soul for some money. That's kind of what it felt like.

With the last deal that I was offered, Michael Jackson was one of the people that wanted to sign me. I was blessed to have a photo shoot and my music was playing in the background as I was preparing for the photo shoot. The late Bill Bray and Betty Bailey were in the studio picking up some pictures of Michael. Bill was Michael's godfather and he asked, "Who is that?" The guy said, "That's Dorie Pride. She's an artist, and I'm doing her photo shoot. She's in the back now." We met, they became my managers, and we put together a team. Michael was going to sign me. All was going well. They sent me to New York. It was a wonderful three-day magical time in which I felt like I was a queen, because everything in that magical moment was there. The limousine took me anywhere I wanted to go, and it was just wonderful. The end of that deal was when it came time to sign the contract on the dotted line. My managers gave me the contract and I thought, *"Here we go again."* Michael loved what I was doing, but I couldn't do it. They now wanted me to be an 'around the way girl,' kind of Hip Hop like. I'm like, "Me? No, I can't do that."

I had to go to New York to meet with a certain executive. They had been courting me to meet him. Bill and Betty were very smart, they loved the music. So they decided to shop the music around without putting my picture on it. They sent the music over to the UK. The main guy there loved it, and he would drive the countryside every day listening to my music. He especially liked my song titled "Life is Just a Color TV." He was like, "Wow, this girl is phenomenal. She's like a Bob Dylan. This is like a top ten Pop hit! We have got to get her signed." Betty and Bill told me this. They didn't know what I looked like, they just loved the music. So, I'm cool and really happy about that. Michael's label was distributed by Epic, 550 Music and the Work Group. They wanted to sign me in America and then take me to the UK because it would be more money involved, so all of this other stuff also came along with it. I had people that came from London who were friends with Michael in order to make the deal sweeter. Everybody comes in and everybody is really happy. The main guy was there from London, and I'm the last one to come in. Then they look at me and I say, "'Hi, I'm Dorie Pride." Then all of the color went off of the man's face, because all of a sudden I wasn't what he thought I was. On the music—if you listen to it—I'm androgynous sounding. You don't know if I'm a man or a woman on some of the songs, or if I'm Black or White, you just don't know.

Judging by the look on the man's face, I guess he thought that I was probably White. Then when that deal did not work out, I was like, "God, what am I supposed to do?" Every time I'd get close to something or get ready to sign something, I come close and it all falls apart.

Finally, it came to me that I'm supposed to do this myself. Once I got it into my head that I was going to do this and form my own company to do what I wanted to do as an artist, I felt good about that. *Life is Just a Color TV* became my first CD because I found myself, and I didn't have to compromise. They kept saying for me to just get in there and get your first hit, and then maybe on your second album you can turn it around. But, I was smart enough to know that when you get into the record business, how you start off is how you finish. You're not going to be able to go from being one kind of person to being who you really are on your second CD. You may not even get to the second CD because that's just the way the business is. Here I am now and all of these things that I wanted to say, sing and express from my heart are poured out on that CD, I'm very proud of it, and I don't have any regrets.

In 2014 I released my sophomore CD called *Love Will Find a Way.* The blessing is that had I not gone through what I went through, I would not have what I have now. I'm playing guitar, I wrote most of the songs, the music, melody and lyrics with the exception of two cover songs. One was George Harrison's "Something" and the other was Bob Marley's "So Much Trouble in the World." Kamau Seitu, my husband, my producer, my love and extraordinaire guitarist wrote the bridge on "She Never Asks" and he wrote the music on "Cheap Thrill" and another one. As for the rest, I wrote everything else and played guitar. I feel really blessed because had I not gone through all those things that I went through, I would not have pushed myself to learn how to play in the way that allowed me to write the music from my heart that I wanted to say on this CD *Love Will Find A Way*.

So here I am in Atlanta, working my way back to L.A. I am grounded and I love my life. I love what I do. I have no regrets. I have no sorrows. Everything brought me to this place where I am now. From it, my spiritual journey (which is interwoven with my music), brought me to a book that I have just finished called *Spirit Talk, Soul Walk*. It's spiritual contemplations of my life in the last 20 years. I am blessed to be able to share that journey on paper with people who want to come up higher within their spiritual selves. I am moving towards that rainbow in the sky that my dad always said was around me. As he was making his transition, he made a picture for me with a rainbow over it. My mother also looks down on me from the heavenly realm. I am happy, blessed and empowered. What I have gone through helps me to be able to help other people to take the next step.

My new project *Love Will Find a Way* impresses the story of mute voices, the people that you see on the street who are suffering. You don't hear those stories, but they are there. I talk about 9/11 and the Hurricane Katrina disasters. That's where *Love Will Find a Way* came from. It's a vision that allows me to be able to put back into other people's eyes, ears, and hearts to get them to see what I see in my eyes every day. Hopefully, I can connect them with my heart and my purpose as a storyteller who wants to evoke and promote emotion from people so that they will go beyond themselves and see that when they think it's a difficult life, there is someone else who is suffering even more. My grandmother often said, "I once cried because I had no shoes, then I saw the man who had no feet." That frames who I am and the mission of my life.

By sharing your story and the other stories in this book, we want to lay out guidelines for today's artists and industry professionals. Can you provide a three-step guide for someone who might be where you are right now?

Dorie Pride:

The first thing that I would say is NEVER GIVE UP! No matter what anybody tells you, no matter what you hear or don't hear, or what you see or don't see, never give up. That's the first thing. The second thing would be to believe in yourself so much so that nothing that anybody would say to you can derail you from your purpose. And the third thing I would say is hone your craft. Be the very best that you can be. Practice. Do everything that you can possibly do to make yourself the very best that you can be. Have faith in God that He will lead you to where it is that you are supposed to be, on time and in divine order, which goes along with the very first thing that I said—to never give up. When you are trusting in God and you know that He has you in His hands and you're doing all that you're supposed to do, then the bottom line is that you're going to get where it is that you have to go because God is faithful and God is true. If you believe that, and if you believe in yourself, then it's impossible to fail.

Contact:
DoriePride.com
Facebook.com/4doriepride
ReverbNation.com/doriepride

Dr. Westbrooks:

Dorie Pride focuses on perseverance. In spite of setbacks and obstacles, Dorie believed in her gift and her talent. Refusing to compromise her integrity, Dorie realized that she did not fit comfortably in the traditional music industry model. Rather than give up or not be true to self, she became an Indie artist, which enabled her to call her own shots, sing the way she wanted, and to present herself as she saw herself. She remained steadfast in her efforts, albeit outside of the purview of the majors. Dorie urges everyone to not give up and to keep believing in yourself and your dreams. It's true that in this business you have to be strong and able to withstand possible disappointment.

CHAPTER NINE

STEPHANIE SPRUILL

Founder & CEO of Spruill House of Music—
School of Voice and Artist Development

"You have to stay in the game, because it changes all of the time."

Stephanie Spruill is the author of *17 Points of Longevity in Show Business: Staying Focused on Your Vision.* She has been in the industry for over 35 years. She has amassed over a hundred Gold and Platinum records and has worked with Mariah Carey, Aretha Franklin, Quincy Jones, Simply Red, Michael Jackson, Julio Iglesias, Enrique Iglesias, Whitney Houston, and many more. Stephanie elaborates on her career and what it takes to establish and maintain longevity in the business.

Stephanie Spruill:
The people that I've worked with are Julio Iglesias, with whom I toured the world for five and a half years and sang duets. One of the major duets I sang with him was "As Time Goes By" when we performed at the White House. I've sung with Whitney Houston, Mariah Carey, Tina Turner, Barbara Streisand, and Aretha Franklin. That was me singing on the chorus of Aretha's hit "Jump to It." I've been in this industry over 35 years. I've done just countless albums with Barbara Streisand and also her movie, *A Star is Born.* I sang prominently on Donna Summer's "Bad Girls" hook, also "On the Radio" and just countless songs with Donna Summer, Diana Ross and Billy Idol. I worked with him for all of his albums such as *Mony Mony, White Wedding*, and just about every one of his albums.

I also worked with Simply Red and Luther Vandross. Luther and I had an amazing time as background singers back in the day before he became a big star. It's a long list. I worked with Tom Petty. I toured with Talking Heads and then I also worked with Michael Jackson. I was the choir director for the song "Can You Feel It" on the *Triumph* album by the Jacksons. I remember when Michael called me at three o'clock in the morning. He said, "Stephanie, I know you have the choir of 45 voices, but I need you to really bring into my consciousness some children. And I want them every race, creed and color." So I'm thinking, *"Not at three*

48

o'clock in the morning. Michael is calling me to change up my game plan."

However, I rose to the occasion. The next couple of days when we had to do the session, I had an amazing choir with children of every race, creed, and color. That's when we did, "Can You Feel It," which was a major hit for the Jacksons.

I sang a duet "Beseme Mucho" with Placido Domingo. I sang "La Vita Loco" with Ricky Martin, and I've done some step out stuff with Enrique Iglesias. I've known Ricky since he was nine years old, because I toured with Julio for so many years. Maurice White of Earth, Wind & Fire was the producer on one of my albums. On the Country side, I also worked with Kenny Wayne Shepherd and did a lot of background for him. If you remember the Gino Vannelli hit "I Just Want to Stop," I did the arrangements, and also I sang on all backgrounds. And Glenn Campbell, yes, I was a Rhinestone Cowgirl. So I go all the way back to Country star Glenn Campbell, Pop star Olivia Newton John on her song "Let's Get Physical," to Juan Gabriel. I helped produce all the vocals on that.

I worked with the Brothers Johnson on "Strawberry Letter 23," and I also worked on a lot of Quincy Jones' records. That is just to name a few of the artists that I've worked with on the stage or in the recording studios. I've toured the seven continents several times. I've performed for the Queen of England at Royal Albert Hall and at the White House on three separate occasions. I've performed for the King and Queen of Spain and for the Emperor of Japan. I am a songwriter. I've written hit songs for Jon Lucien, Najee, Vesta, David T. Walker, and also I'm a songwriter for a theme song for Salma Hayek's movie, *The Velocity of Gary*.

However, I now have an artist out who I manage and produce named Chanel Loran. She's only twelve years old, and she has a record out on iTunes called "Hush, Shut It Down." It addresses cyber bullying and it's amazing. I'm also one of the writers with Ellis Miah and Chanel on this song. I have a school of voice and artist development, and that's what I am. I'm an artist developer. I'm giving back everything God has bestowed on me back to my community because they need people like myself with all the skills and all the work that I've done for the past 100 years, ha ha.

I came here with this skill that they need us to give back. They don't have this training now in public schools. When I was coming up playing cello in the orchestra in school, I could go to the music department at my junior high or high school and go in the music room and just write my name down and check my cello out. In many places they don't have that now. So we need people like myself to give back to our community.

With such an outstanding career, you bring expertise as a performer, artist developer, vocalist, arranger, producer, and now as a manager. First, let's identify the importance of an artist developer in general and then lay out the specifics of what you do, how you do it, and how future artists all over the world can connect with you.

Stephanie Spruill:

When I identify the market of being an artist developer and being an artist for so many years, and having my own record company, I felt that there was a niche that wasn't being met. Like they did at Sony or Motown and so many labels, they used to develop artists. They had an A&R (Artists and Repertoire) department, they don't do that anymore. So I saw and identified the market, and I just jumped on it and by doing that, I saw what I did for myself, by developing myself with skills and techniques that you need in order to be successful in this industry and to have longevity. That's when I started my school of voice and artist development.

Everybody is trying to reinvent themselves. They need skills that they thought they had or skills that they have, but they let lie dormant. What it takes is for the people to know—whether they are beginners or in this industry for a while like Meagan Good and Sinbad—they must advance all of the skills that they have and bring forth new skills, whether they are a singer, orator, writer or a dancer. All of those are skills that need to be developed so you can have longevity in this business. My artist development plan is "17 Points to Longevity," and it starts with confidence. We can't do anything in life, let alone show business, without confidence. We must focus on being engaged in the right things to do in this industry and with our physical and emotional well-being. Oh, that's a big one. And, of course, don't skimp on your vocal training. A lot of people come with a great voice, but it's not a skill. They don't have the techniques in order to have longevity. They get hoarse easily, so I also show and teach how you can have vocal maintenance. I just don't teach you how to have the best vocal runs in the world, you have to have vocal maintenance, because when you're out there on the road for five months and getting hoarse, you have to really know how to use your voice properly.

Of course, education and versatility with your skill, and knowing how to have a stage presence are also important. A lot of people can sing, but they don't have stage presence. They don't know how to engage their audience and how to put their audience in their pocket so that when they finish that performance, they're going to buy your CD, they're going to go on iTunes and purchase or download your music.

You have to really engage people so what you have out there and what you show and emit on stage, on TV or on your record, it is out of your authentic self. You're not trying to be somebody else. It's okay to take some things from other people, because nobody knows everything. Aretha Franklin, Sarah Vaughn, and Ella Fitzgerald, they're my idols. So, of course, I learned from them, and that's what I give to my students. You learn from every aspect of life because that's what it is. Show business is a part of life. Show business is not just for the business of show business. Show business is for everybody, because what we have to do is show people what we have going on in order that we generate business. That's why I have a lot of business people coming to me to learn my method. This is my method. I talk about business savvy, about self-marketing, because no one can market you better than yourself. In my artist development school I teach how to self-market yourself, how to network, how to use those industry contacts that you make and let them work for you.

It's all about staying in a positive, spiritual, and healthy environment, as well as having a global awareness. Additionally, you had better learn another language. I don't care if it's Chinese, Japanese, or Spanish. What I try to impart to my people is Spanish, because three quarters of the world speaks Spanish. So jump on that. I have an album in Spanish. Thank God I was brought to a man like Julio Iglesias, with whom I toured the world for five and a half years. It showed me that the entire world loves not only English, but also Spanish. So we must open up our mindset to a global awareness because it is just one world, and it's God's world. Hallelujah my book is also faith based, because I don't do anything without the Lord being in front. The name of my book is *17 Points to Longevity in Show Business: Staying Focused on Your Vision* by Stephanie Spruill. It is an e-book as well. It's on Amazon, it's on iTunes, CD Baby, Rhapsody, and everybody who does e-books.

Just how do artists get started wherever they are? Perhaps they've been the local singer at a local venue, or maybe they sing in church or in school or feel like they have something and the world is calling them. Where do they go? What is the science of getting started right where you are?

Stephanie Spruill:

You said that they've already started because they're singing in clubs or at schools, so the process has started. As an artist, you must continue to believe in yourself. It is so important because the periphery will come into play, so you must stay focused on your vision and not someone else's.

Other than that, visit my website www.spruillhousemusic.com, and you will find a plethora of information that can help you to jumpstart your career. Now for questions such as: How can I get started? How can I take my passion for performing to the next level? How do I start a business plan? All of that is in my book *17 Points to Longevity in Show Business*, but I'm just going to tell you to keep your nose to the grind. Stay positive, stay competent, keep learning new skills, keep learning new songs, and start writing, because that's what it's all about! You want to make some money? You become a writer. And you say, well, I can't write like Dianne Warren, but most of us can't. However, it's your story, and your story may be the story that somebody wants to hear. So I think you should just keep doing what you're doing. Keep believing in yourself.

You can Skype with Ms. Stephanie via Stephanie Spruill on Skype of Spruill House Music. And read positive books that will uplift you and educate you toward finding out what you want to do, and just do it. Like the Nike sign, just do it. Just jump in there with both feet. Don't let up, because you can't. You have to stay in the game, because it changes all of the time.

Keep an open mind, and also use your social media. That's the biggest thing going. Keep your eyes open. You guys have social media now. I didn't have this in the beginning, so I had to work it. God has been good to me, and I have worked it, and I'm giving it all back. But this social media really works for you. You just Google any and everything, and you can find out any and everything. In fact, more than you even want to know. You guys have so much at hand. For those who are in the industry feeling a little bogged down, reinvent yourself.

Read my latest article that was in the *Music Connection* magazine, go online and get it because they keep you abreast of what's happening or *The Music Business Registry* by Ritch Esra. You can find out these things. They will keep you abreast of what's happening in the business, NOW. Today, not yesterday, but today. It's all about reinventing yourself. And, it's okay because what you're doing, you're going to bring all the things that you've learned and all the things that you're doing into this new reinvention. That's what we do. We reinvent ourselves daily. So don't be afraid of it because it's there waiting for you to find your other passion. I always say, when we find what we love, we are happy. However, when we do what we're good at, we are at peace. That's a peace that passes all understanding.

I'm here for you because we all need to go to the next level. I was with the Young Saints, Tommy and Evelyn Freemen, I'll never forget them. My first gig was with Danny Kay at the White House, for the Duke and Duchess of Windsor. I said, "I want to be like them, because they were the shoulders that I stand upon—Tommy and Evelyn Freemen." If anybody needs Ms. Stephanie, I'm here for you when you need me.

Contact: In English or Espanol
www.spruillhousemusic.com
Facebook.com/stephanie.spruill
Twitter.com/stephaniespruil

Dr. Westbrooks:

Stephanie Spruill takes an all-encompassing approach toward success in the music business. She recognizes voids and confidently steps in to fill them. When the old model was transitioning, most labels dropped A&R. Stephanie knew how important and necessary A&R is to an artist, so she began doing artist development. She knows just how important vocal training is, so she teaches vocal training. She knows just how important it is for artists to understand the business side, so she has written a book about it. When things change in this industry, she changes right along with it focusing on needs that must be met. This makes her invaluable to clients, which ultimately benefits them and the listening public. Through natural talent, skill, training, belief, and confidence in herself, Stephanie has transformed from being just another good singer to becoming a one-woman operation with the mechanisms of a major label.

THE PUBLISHERS

INFORMED SOURCES

Maryann Johnson
Kevin Ross
Bill Speed

CHAPTER TEN

MARYANN JOHNSON

Director TV Music Administration
20th Century Fox Television

"You have to write songs and music. You have to own your publishing and constantly study and do research to stay relevant in the field."

Maryann Johnson has spent over thirty years working at 20th Century Fox, with her more recent years as Director of TV Music Administration. Songwriters and publishers who are fortunate enough to get their music placed in film and television shows can earn enormous sums of money from what is called synchronization rights. While many musicians and artists seek fame in the spotlight, many are content to write and produce great music for soundtracks, musical scores, jingles and features in broadcast productions, and they are paid very, very well. Maryann provides insight into this lucrative side of the music industry.

What are your great success stories in the music industry?

Maryann Johnson:
Working with my favorite rock band and watching all of their albums go Gold and Platinum.

How have you seen the industry change?

Maryann Johnson:
There are fewer creative people running record companies.

What was good about this change?

Maryann Johnson:
Not a lot.

What was the downside of this change?

Maryann Johnson:
Most artists sound the same because most music is slick production with voice enhancement. Back in the day we were taught how to write songs, you had to have a verse, a bridge and a chorus.

What cautions would you provide to others about staying relevant (or current) in the music business?

Maryann Johnson:
Learn how to write songs. If you write lyrics, collaborate with someone who plays an instrument. Before you begin your career in music, you should read Donald S. Passman's book *All You Need to Know About the Music Business* (9th Edition, Free Press). You need to know your rights as a recording artist, a songwriter, and a music publisher. You have to research the Internet and industry publications to find out what is current and what is selling in the marketplace.

What must any artist, music executive, producer or lawyer know about selling, marketing, and/or collecting royalties on digital music?

Maryann Johnson:
Regarding digital music, well, music is music. Make sure your stuff is copyrighted worldwide because people can use technology to alter or steal your music creations. Join a performing rights society. They track and license use of your music. Also, with the Internet, there are companies that can monitor airplay and music being used around the world. When you are new to the business, publishers want to take all of your publishing rights, or part of it, or if you are savvy, your legal people can negotiate so you can keep your publishing and pay them an administrative fee.

Where do you think the future of the music industry will take us?

Maryann Johnson:
Everything will be over the airwaves or Internet and no hard product. There will always be music and, I'm sure, some type of videos.

What is the best way to make money in the industry today?

Maryann Johnson:
Self-publishing, self-publishing on the net, sell your stuff on iTunes, etc. License the songs and music you own to others, and use it in commercials and other avenues.

What is your answer to the standard question: What advice would you give anyone who wanted to be successful in the music business?

Maryann Johnson:
You have to write songs and music. You have to own your publishing and constantly study and do research to stay relevant in the field. And networking is the key. Join the industry organizations and go to events. Take your product and network as much as possible.

Dr. Westbrooks:
Maryann Johnson stresses ownership, ownership, ownership. Write your own songs, publish your own songs, capitalize on licensing and sync rights. It's the most efficient way to benefit from your creativity. Also, if you own 100 percent of the song, you get 100 percent of the money. Ownership presents an everlasting flow of revenue from your work.

CHAPTER ELEVEN

KEVIN ROSS

Owner, Radiofacts.com

"Constantly reinvent yourself, and get as many skills under your belt as you can. That way you will never stop working."

Kevin Ross' career extends from stints in programming and production in broadcast media to distributing his own trade publication called Radio Facts. He has worked across the country at KKBT, KACE, KJLH, KDKO, Mesa Blue Moon Recordings, R&R (Radio & Records), The Urban Network, and now Radiofacts.com, which he has owned and operated for 18 years. Radio Facts is distributed daily to programmers nationwide. Radio Facts consists of news related items in the radio and music industry, as well as featured advertisements on music stars and radio personalities. It is a viable tool for marketing new music to programmers, as well as staying abreast of what is going on in the industry.

When did you get into the business?

Kevin Ross

I was 19 years of age, and I worked for Turtles Records on Old National Highway in East Point, Georgia.

What are your greatest success stories in the music business? How have you seen the industry change?

Kevin Ross

My greatest success was to start my own business, which I have now been doing for 18 years. Yes, the industry has drastically changed. Radio consolidation has spread to consolidation in all areas of the industry, which has changed the entire industry perspective. Radio and record professionals are required to do several jobs since the industry has been slashed by at least 70 percent since 9/11.

What was good about this change?

Kevin Ross

A lot of the 'game' and the B.S. is gone. Everyone has to justify their positions and their expenditures by going the extra mile. There were some great people who were booted out, but there were also a lot of people who were just lucky who probably should not have been in the industry. In addition, because of consolidation, older industry people have gotten to stay longer. Most urban radio program directors are over 40. This would not have been the case 15 years ago.

What was the down side of this change?

Kevin Ross

There are no more record label events, which made the industry very exciting and it was a way for the industry to connect physically. The labels drove the industry with record release parties, conferences and events, but they don't spend the money that they used to since most of the radio stations are now owned by corporations. It makes perfect sense. They don't have to appeal to, let's say, 20 program directors from 20 different companies anymore. One person pretty much makes the decisions concerning music airplay now, and there is no need to do industry events anymore.

Would you like to share any horror stories?

Kevin Ross

Probably the greatest one was when I once worked for a Program Director who was very jealous of the staff. He was not as talented, and he targeted those who were better announcers than he was, which was pretty much the entire staff. He used his power to manipulate us, passing us over for promotions, not handing in our time sheets and doing a lot of dirty illegal deals. In the end, the station failed miserably and it was no wonder. The other one was getting the dream job at KKBT in Los Angeles. It was the first station that I worked for that was not Black owned and having to deal with massive corporate racism. I understand why they did a lot of what they did now, but they did it all the wrong way.

What cautions would you provide to others about staying relevant (or current) in the music business?

Kevin Ross

Constantly reinvent yourself and get as many skills under your belt as you can. That way, you will never stop working. I learned that lesson by mistake. I started off as a singer, then a DJ, then a record promoter, then a Rap editor, then a Program Director, then voiceover and now an industry trade publication/site owner. I've worked consistently for 28 years, and I've seen people who could only do one thing and last five years. Also, make sure you surround yourself with the right people. Always, and I mean always, watch how people treat others behind their backs. It's a guaranteed truth that they will treat you the same way behind yours. Trust is everything, and when it comes to competitive industries, it's often very hard to find.

What must any artist, music executive, producer or lawyer know about selling, marketing, and/or collecting royalties on digital music?

Kevin Ross

The answer is in the question, know how to do it. The more you know, as I stated in the last question, the better off you are and the longer you will last.

Where do you think the future of the music industry will take us?

Kevin Ross

I think the day will come when radio gets the shock of its life and Internet radio will explode. It will be available in cars and everywhere else. The radio corporations are in dire financial straits right now, and it's going to get worse. I think radio syndication is killing urban radio. For those of us who listen to Internet radio now and then try to listen to commercial radio, the difference is extreme. Commercial radio sounds like a lot of clutter and talk. I also think artists will become more business savvy as they are now and become more than artists. They will understand the power of marketing their brand and making deals with not only the labels but consumer brands.

What is the best way to make money in the industry today?

Kevin Ross

Working for yourself and understanding how to do the business side of the industry.

What advice would you give anyone who wanted to be successful in the music business?

Kevin Ross

The advice that I got was so antiquated and ridiculous. Things like, "Keep your mouth shut and your ears open." Truth be told, had I done that, my career would have been over years ago. My theory is more along the lines of, "A closed mouth doesn't get fed." You have to be aggressive in your career or you will leave it in the hands of others. And that means you may wait a lifetime for nothing.

Radio Facts has a dedicated section for other aspects of music publishing which may be accessed here:
http://www.radiofacts.com/category/music-publishing/.

For daily industry related news and information visit radiofacts.com.

Contact:
kevin.ross@radiofacts.com

Dr. Westbrooks:

Kevin Ross stresses entrepreneurship. He started off working in a record store, then he became a singer, then a DJ, then a record promoter, then an editor, then a Program Director, then a voiceover artist, then owning a trade publication. He continued to morph through growth, but also out of necessity. Kevin understands the value of 'getting in where you fit in,' which has kept him relevant and successful in today's music industry.

CHAPTER TWELVE

BILL SPEED

Trade Publication Editor, Music Video Programming Pioneer

"We need to spend more time mentoring the next generation of people and making sure as older folks from the industry, we understand the technology and not be intimidated by it. We need to embrace it. We need to give as much of the knowledge that we can to the next generation and it'll help them go forward."

Bill Speed was the first Black editor at the popular industry trade publication R&R, which stands for Radio and Records. In the early days of music videos, and before Black artists were a mainstay on MTV, Bill was a pioneer video programmer at BET, helping to launch trailblazing platforms such as *Video Soul* (hosted by Donnie Simpson), Soft Notes (a Jazz formatted video show), and This Week In Black Entertainment. Speed was instrumental in introducing Sade to American audiences, and he also created the first ever recognized Rap and Hip Hop charts for the industry trade publication titled *The Gavin Report*. Speed's intrigue with the industry began when he was just 15 years old and continued when he became a broadcaster while in the Navy. It has sustained throughout his personal and professional life. Bill took us on a historical journey that spells out the business side of how live performance transcended into video popularity that equaled worldwide success for musical artists.

Bill Speed:
I realized that I was really destined to do production writing. My partners and I went on to create a radio format because Black radio at that time was still a little bit behind times from general market radio. Having seen Black radio up front and close, I realized there would soon be a need for general market Black radio. So we began to create what was called an automated format, meaning there was no live disc jockey. The music was picked, the voice tracks were laid, and we got a lot of attention. This was in the mid-70s, in 1976 or 1977.

Then in 1977, I was approached by the sales manager of a trade publication called Radio & Records. By this time, I'd gotten a previous reputation for producing commercials—spots for record companies, tour spots for artists like Parliament and the Funkadelics. They were looking at adding a new section to the R&R magazine. They had every music genre represented, except Black music. They liked what I was doing, and they approached me to be the editor of this newly-formed section. It scared the daylights out of me, needless to say, because I already had a decent syndication thing going on. We were into about six cities at that time, which was a lot. I went to work for R&R as the first Black radio editor. About a year and a half later, Westwood One came out with the Budweiser show, which was actually the first urban-geared syndicated radio show. My partners and I had this little show that was getting a few markets, but we were doing well. I'm with R&R, you know, being the editor there. By the way, I was the first Black person from the industry to write for an industry trade publication.

It was major. I had no idea at the time how powerful it was until after being in the job for a while, you start to get the idea that this is something special here. That's during the years that I met Logan Westbrooks. We were both on the Grammy screening committee. The screening committee was where we'd picked which artists were going to be considered for Grammy nominees.

I did Radio & Records for five years, and it was great. I left because there was another technology that was starting to emerge. What I wanted to do was produce music shows. MTV had just come on the air, and it was a hot new thing. I'd seen videotapes before, but it wasn't known to the general public. It was just an industry thing to promote an artist. At that time, when they introduced new artists, they would literally take them door-to-door. Promotion persons would get on the road and take them from one radio station to the next, and they would be interviewed on air. This video thing captured all of that without the travel and headaches of dragging somebody around. I'd been talking about this in certain circles, and, mind you, I'm still at Radio & Records as the editor of Black music, Disco, and Jazz, which was still very much alive. That was three formats and a lot of real estate for a new editor.

A friend of mine named Frank Washington was a lawyer at the F.C.C.—Federal Communications Commission—in Washington, D. C. He knew of a guy who was putting together the first Black television network—BET. R&R had a Washington bureau that was watching all of the legislation that was going on for broadcasting. Being in Washington, most of the young Black lawyers who worked at the F.C.C. were all around my age. Frank arranged for me to meet Bob Johnson, who was the founder and then president of BET. Johnson approached me to come to work for BET in Washington to help them create programming for this new Black network. They were already on the air, but they were running old movies that were Library of Congress movies. He wanted to get into original programming, but he didn't have a relationship with the music entertainment business, nor did he know his way around Hollywood. That's where I came in. I was probably very high profile in both worlds—music and print. The television thing was kind of interesting. I had seen videos, and I knew that was the future. Also once you've seen groups like Parliament, the Funkadelics, or Earth, Wind & Fire, or the Commodores or any of the other big bands, your imagination would talk to you and say basically, *"What would this look like on videotape?"*

I used to go to the Washington bureau of R&R at my own urging because there was a lot of legislation going on. There was a minority tax certificate, which was a big deal at that time. There were a lot of payola hearings that were geared primarily towards Rock & Roll radio, but it was starting to filter into the Black side of radio. Frank, Fred Cooke, Tyrone Brown, and people like that were all lawyers at the F.C.C. We became friends. I wanted to investigate on my own, because, primarily, the news would come about the payola finger pointing at the Black radio stations, but not at Pop radio stations as much. They were mainly saying the Black guys were taking money, when, in reality, it was the White guys who were really taking a lot of money.

I invited them to start coming back and forth to Los Angeles so they could see for themselves what the industry was all about. I forged a relationship with them. Frank was the one who pulled me aside and said, "Listen, you ought to talk to this guy Bob Johnson. He's starting this new network, and I think you would be a perfect fit for him." I said, "No, I don't want to leave L.A. I've got a great life out here. I'm in Los Angeles, and why would I want to go to an unknown Black network?" BET hadn't even began to be anything, because they were running these movies that were classic Oscar Micheaux movies, but no original programming. So with my production skills and my eye for detail, I thought about it, and I said *"Hmmm, videos and movies, this could be something."*

He told Bob about me and me about Bob. Bob contacted me and invited me to come to Washington to have a meeting with him face to face. I went to Washington, and it looked like a small operation to me. I thought to give up what I have in L.A. for this is a big deal. He thought with my contacts, my writing skills, my production skills, I would be a great fit for them. It took him about seven or eight months to convince me. At a certain point, he called back and said, "Look, we want to have you, tell me what you need to get here. I agreed, and went to Washington late July of 1983."

Video Soul debuted on BET late that September. It was either late September or early October. I sat down and wrote out this script and came up with the concept with music videos to be *Video Soul*. Donnie

Simpson was the local air personality here in Washington along with a woman named Sheila Banks. Sheila Banks was on WETA, which was a public PBS station. Donnie was the program director and morning man with WKYF. Bob had basically wanted Donnie to be the host and Sheila to be the co-host. I'd known Donnie from radio and he knew me from R&R in Detroit and Cleveland and all that, so it was a perfect match.

We wrote the first five shows, produced them, and the first one was a complete disaster, because the timing of a music video is very different than programming a record. A record usually ran between three and a half to four minutes long, and videos were a little bit longer. By the way, they were not concept videos at that time, most of them were just performance videos where artists were standing on stage with a captured concert footage or whatever. I got off the airplane from Los Angeles with 100 videos in my bag. I sat down and mapped it out, we did five shows. The first one ran a little long, but that was okay. Now, here's an interesting twist, too. Because my job entailed creating programming, they assigned me a secretary. That secretary was Jamie Foster Brown who is now the publisher of *Sister 2 Sister* magazine."

Jamie was my assistant because I had so much going on. Her job was to help keep the balls in the air. *Video Soul* was a hit out of the box. It was a blowout. At one point the video show itself was becoming so huge that we had to come up with other programs like it so that one show wouldn't stand out. The original programming at BET, at that time, was college sports. A guy named Jim Felton was over college sports. We had a woman named Cathy Stanley who was over Public Affairs programming. There was another woman named Bev Smith who was doing news.

We had a newscast and *Video Soul*, and we tried to put everything we could in there. The show was a hit as I said, so I sat down and created four other shows that could run around *Video Soul*. The thought behind that was to keep the list of viewers connected to the station. In other words, when *Video Soul* came on, people were going to watch. When it went off, people left. So we had to come up with more shows. I came up with a show called *This Week in Black Entertainment*, which was a forerunner of what an *Entertainment Tonight* show would look like. The news was focused on showbiz, sports, and all of that. We had billed so much Jazz music in Washington, and the Jazz artists were creating a lot of videos, too, so we created what became *Soft Notes*.

Soft Notes was a visual version of *Quiet Storm*. The *Quiet Storm,* which you know was Grover Washington, Freddie Hubbard, and Miles Davis, people like that. We ran their videos. We put this string of shows together and that became the original programming for BET. While I was at BET, I did a lot of interviews for a lot of magazines. My name was pretty well circulated, so I was invited around 1984 to go to Saint-Tropez, France, to be a part of the first International Video Music Festival. That was where all the video programmers around the world were invited to this one place. We all got there, and it was like a Grammy sort of thing. We picked the best programming, the best producers, the best artists, and that's when I first saw a concept video. In that video there was a French guy who was 14 different characters within these four minutes. He was the flower; he was the stop sign; he was the policeman on the street, all while this song is playing. Again, my mind is saying, *"Oh my God, I can imagine George Clinton being all these various characters!"* So I came back and told everybody about these concepts.

While I was there, the video guy from Sony records asked me if I wanted to meet this new artist that they were considering bringing to the U.S., but they weren't sure if the act was going to work. I said, *"Okay let's take a look."* So we went to the club. The clubs in Europe, by the way, were two levels. There was a dance floor level and another level where you sit upstairs and eat and watch the dancers. I see this Black woman with this White guy sitting at a booth, and I'm thinking they're a couple. We go to the table and sit down. He introduces me, her name was Sade. I met her, we talked, she wasn't very talkative, but her partner was. They were thrilled that somebody from America was going to be involved with their music possibly coming to America.

Of course, I gave them a thumbs up, and the rest is history.

When I got back to the U.S., they sent me a copy of the Sade video, which was "Diamond Life." It was a concept video that I had seen all through Europe while I was there. If you get a chance to look at the original version of "Diamond Life," it's almost animated. They're singing, but it looks like a 1950s beatnik style set. They had cardboard instruments, and they were characters in this video. Well, that concept caught on in America. By this time we were against MTV in the ratings. We beat MTV in every market we were on against them because MTV would not play Black artists up to that point. Anyway, my years at BET were quite a success. I loved it and it was fantastic. I thought after meeting these people in Europe that I could create programming for them, because the one thing I kept hearing over and over was, how can we see American Black artists on our shows? I'm surprised record companies hadn't had that type of relationship, but they did not.

So I am proud to have been a big part of introducing Sade to the U.S. market. After that trip, I came back to BET. Now we're starting to get visuals from everywhere. A guy I went to high school with managed a group called Midnight Star and a group called the Deele, that included Babyface, Antonio 'L.A.' Reid, Daryl Simmons, Stanley Burke, Carlos Greene, Darnell Bristol, Kevin Roberson and Steve Walters. He managed these people, and he would always tell me, "I've got these videos of them in performance. Would you be interested in any of them?" I said, "I don't know. Let me know, send me something." So he sent me a one-hour concert of Midnight Star. They had the hit "Freakazoid" at the time. I sat down with Bob and laid out my vision for both concert videos and concept videos and how I thought it would benefit our new network.

After my success at BET, I left with the thought of creating my own programming for European TV. I created a show called "American Airplay." The show did extremely well, but what happens in programming is people want to buy a block of shows at a time. They want to buy 10 or 15 episodes. I was broke trying to get up enough money to produce a number of these packages, which I just didn't have the money for. Right after that I had to get a job in the real world. I was offered a job, once I made myself available back to the print world, to come in as managing editor of the *Urban Network*. I came in and replaced Gary Jackson who had left. I came to the *Urban Network,* and I stayed at Urban Network for three years.

I was then approached by some old radio friends who worked for another magazine in San Francisco as the department head. By this time Hip Hop and Rap and these sort of genres were getting to be huge. They were the love of America at that time. So I took the job at *The Gavin Report* because I could create the actual first industry charts that could chart Rap and Hip Hop music, which I did. We created it, and it was a big celebration. I had worked in the Bay area as a college kid, and now I'm coming back as a so-called big-time editor. I brought Rap charts with me. I stayed at *The Gavin Report* for a number of years and did extremely well—big conventions, met all the big stars, Tupac, Snoop Dog, Easy E, all of them. I met all of them during that period.

Then, I had another offer after I left *Gavin* to go back East to work for Chrysler doing marketing. They were starting to go after the ethnic market to buy their cars. So I was doing marketing for Chrysler for a couple of years. Right around that time, Keith Clinkscales, had helped to create a magazine called *Vibe*. *Vibe* wasn't being well accepted in the music business because they were thought of as the bastard child. A lot of people in the industry didn't embrace *Vibe*, though it was huge on the streets. Keith would come to *Gavin*, so I could introduce him to people around the business. Years later, Keith left *Vibe* when it was sold. He and his partner Lynn Burnett started their own publishing company called Vanguarde. They owned a couple of titles, they had *Heart and Soul* from Bob Johnson. They had *Honey*—a local magazine sold around New York. *Emerge* became *Savoy*, that was another one of the publications, and *Impact*, the magazine that I ran. This was my first job as Editor-in-Chief. I ran the magazine, and I ran the convention. I did that all the way up until 2002, and then I kind of retired because technology had taken over. The Internet had come into being and the music business collapsed.

A very rich history lesson is revealed in your story, and technology has emerged that has put some veterans askew in terms of figuring out how to remain viable. However, we also have millennials and digital natives who are entering the industry for the first time. They have no idea about anything that you've just shared. How can the knowledge of old school and new school merge to come up with a plan for today's young or emerging artists?

Bill Speed:
I think the most obvious opportunity with people like Logan and myself who've been around and have seen the many changes, is to teach classes, create textbooks, and go on lecture tours. We can keep the tradition of the old-fashioned way of communicating. That's the only way that we can tie the old and the new together. Not only just the lecture tours, but these things should be recorded so that when you sit in front of a class of kids who have no idea, they can look at the face, they can look at the pictures, and they can get an understanding from the horse's mouth, if you will. Therefore, with that, maybe they can take the best of the old, implement it into the newest technology, and it'll live forever.

One of the benefits of digital media is that now at your fingertips, you can reach the world at lightning speed. Due to social media, self-publishing platforms and online video channels, we don't even have to go through a network to see the artist's latest video because we have a blogosphere now. So in many ways it is empowering to individual artists and independent artists, but what do you say about the value of creating good old-fashioned relationships with established industry publications?

Bill Speed:
Well, that would be ideal. We have become such a 'pad' living society, and I'm sure that's where iPad and iPhone come in to play. We still have to talk; we still have to communicate; we still have to speak with those that are coming up. We need to spend more time mentoring the next generation of people and making sure as older folks from the industry, we understand the technology and not be intimidated by it. We need to embrace it, we need to give as much of the knowledge that we can to the next generation, and it'll help them go forward.

So are you still available as a consultant, a producer or industry professional in any way?

Bill Speed:

Currently, I'm building a two-fold project called Urbananza, which is a combination of urban and bonanza. Basically, it is an expo type exhibit that showcases the latest technology, holograms, and things of that nature along with video towers where people come to this sight, they walk through. It's a vendor village where you can buy everything from beats, to headphones, to the latest recording equipment, to the latest digital information, and that sort of thing. But, you've got to have entertainment in there as well. I'd like to think that we're going to come up with the first Cirque du Soleil type presentation also. With that being said, the second part of this thing is going to be all of the exhibits are going to break up into their own separate tours. I want to take time and money to build an institution, somewhere hopefully in the Carolinas, that would be like a Smithsonian style education center. Where people can come and see costumes from Phyllis Hyman, to see James Brown's cape or they can see holograms of Tupac in concert. That and an amusement park backdrop. It would be like a Walt Disney World where education and entertainment mix. We're not quite ready to make it public yet, but the curious can still contact me through email the old-fashioned way.

Contact:
billspeed7@hotmail.com
Facebook.com/billspeed3

Dr. Westbrooks:

Bill Speed was a pioneer in the beginning of the music industry transition. Already an established writer, he helped usher in Black music videos through BET. Ever the pioneer and visionary, he's now working on another concept that will showcase the latest music and video technologies as well as highlight music history, education, and Black music legends. Bill quickly grasped the power of entertainment as a spectacle, and his new project will integrate an interactive approach that will educate as well as entertain.

THE INSTRUCTORS

INFORMED SOURCES

Paul McKinney
Stephen Herring

CHAPTER THIRTEEN

PAUL MCKINNEY

Instrumental Music Director at Stax Music Academy
and The Soulsville Jazz Ensemble

"Versatility is the key to longevity."

As a child Paul McKinney was ushered into the music industry as part of his father's band the Alvin McKinney Trio. Throughout his high school years he was selected to play in several honor bands and went on to the University of Memphis where he earned a Bachelor of Arts in Music Education and a Bachelor of Science degree in Recording Industry Management from Middle Tennessee State University. Paul later studied for a Master's Degree in Jazz Studies before joining the staff of LeMoyne-Owen College as an instructor of trumpet, trombone and clarinet. McKinney also directs the James M. Harris Orchestra at the historic Metropolitan Baptist Church. He is an instructor at the Stax Music Academy in Memphis where he is the Music Director for the Stax Academy's Rhythm Section and the Soulsville Jazz Ensemble. Paul guides us through his task of training young musicians at the legendary musical oasis known as the Stax Music Academy in Memphis, Tennessee.

Paul McKinney:
As Instrumental Music Director I have several tasks, which most people at a non-profit usually have. I am responsible for teaching the Stax catalog.

The Stax catalog consists of music that was recorded between 1957 and 1975 on the label formerly known as Satellite Records. It was founded by the brother and sister team of Jim Stewart and Estelle Axton. Al Bell became co-owner in 1968. Artists signed to the label included Booker T. & the M.G.'s, Otis Redding, Rufus Thomas, Carla Thomas, the Staples Singers, and Isaac Hayes. The Stax label produced world-renowned hits such as "Respect," "The Express," "Sitting on the Dock of the Bay," "Shaft," "Try a Little Tenderness," "The Funky Chicken,"

"Gee Whiz," "I'll Take You There," "Respect Yourself," and many more. This is the catalog that you are referring to?

Paul McKinney:
Yes, and with that being our home base, I also teach Music Theory, Western Music Theory, and Jazz Theory because we have multiple ensembles at the Stax Music Academy, which is an afterschool music program.

Let's dig a little deeper into that, because this book is going to be not only for people who have been in the industry for a while, it will fall into the hands of people who are just embarking upon their music careers. So can you briefly give us the history of the Stax Music Academy as it relates to the legendary Stax music label?

Paul McKinney:
The Stax Music Academy was formed in the year 2000. Stax Records actually closed and was shut down due to bankruptcy in 1974. A group of people in the late 1990s, including the legendary Willa Dean Parker, decided they wanted to redo this area—this neighborhood that's called Soulsville. If you had an opportunity to see what the former record label looked like between 1974 and about 2000, it was just desolate. It looked terrible. It was just a rundown building at that point. This group of people formed a foundation called the Soulsville Foundation. They started the Stax Music Academy, which was to be an afterschool music program for getting the next generation ready to learn Stax music and Soul music from other professional musicians—some of whom were former Stax record label musicians and singers.

We encounter a lot of aspiring performers and musicians, and many of them have aspirations of making it big in the industry. And we know what it's like to have that type of a dream. What would you say to those musicians, and how is it that you are instructing your students and musicians everywhere to prepare for a lifelong career in music? Also how is that different from just going for the big dream or the overnight sensation?

Paul McKinney:
First of all, everybody in this society, in general, has a short attention span and short patience. Everyone loves playing the lottery, everyone thinks they are going to win. I think it's up to $425 million

now. Everybody wants to get that quick fix. Everyone watches the TV talent show *American Idol* and thinks they can be an overnight sensation. They think Justin Bieber was an overnight sensation, but he's been singing for a long time. What we try to do is simply educate our students in a manner where they can become the most versatile musicians that they are capable of becoming, because versatility is the key to longevity. With that being said, yes, we're teaching Soul music, but we're also trying to make sure that the students are all fundamentally sound, and they can read music, write music, and write their own songs. They can understand how to publish and copyright their own music. They understand how to record their own music, so they can understand the physics of sound, like a professional engineer might. To make a long story short, we introduce them to multiple aspects of the music industry so that they can have a choice not just of the music industry, but of the different genres of music. Our students are exposed to Classical, they're exposed to Soul and they're exposed to Jazz. All these variations are really important for them to see that these are the steps that you have to go through in order to learn your key signatures, in order to write music, read music, and also to use your ear. They understand that it's not as quick as it always seems when all of a sudden somebody wins on *American Idol*.

You mention the importance of Soul Music. Do you believe that enough is being done to preserve Soul music and its history?

Paul McKinney:

No, I really don't. I do not believe enough is being done to preserve it, but I am extremely excited to say that the Stax Music Academy is certainly on that path in helping to create the next generation of Soul communicators. We believe all of these young people will be the keepers of the Soul flame. That's why this place is so unique in that, at any given moment, Eddie Floyd may come by to mentor students, as he has in the past. Bettye Crutcher, who wrote Johnny Taylor's hit "Who's Making Love," and well over 300 other hits, may stop by. The Hodges Brothers who recorded at Hi Records, and who did "Love and Happiness" and all the Al Green hits are frequent guests. Guitarist Steve Cropper and singer/songwriter William Bell have also been back. We've performed with Dr. Mable John. That's the connection in terms of understanding how to relate to and perform Soul music; it's to simply be mentored by people who have done it like Carla, Marvel and Vaneese Thomas (daughters of the late Soul legend Rufus Thomas). All of these different artists have come back at one time or another, and they continue to give continuously. Mr. Kirk Whalum is now the Chief Creative Officer. Students have access to him and to me, as I've been in music now for 40 years. I started at the age of three and I'm 43 now. I was blessed to play with people like Rufus Thomas, Bobby Blue Bland, Kirk Whalum and many others. Students who have access to musicians who played that music, who are also church musicians, begin to get an understanding of how to play that music.

Describe your musical legacy and then provide encouragement or guidelines for those who were also born into musical families.

Paul McKinney:

Well, I was blessed to be born into a musical family. I was the youngest child of two. I have an older brother—Dr. Alvin McKinney, Jr. He is a saxophonist, a music educator and a fabulous musician. It's all because of our parents. They met in the music department at Lane College in Jackson, Tennessee. My Father grew up on a farm in Denmark, Tennessee, which is right outside of Jackson. He really didn't have an opportunity to play music while he was growing up. He was a late teenager going into college before he even had a chance to play a lot. He played piano, and he had such a desire to do it that he absorbed everything. Now let's fast forward to my brother Alvin. He started playing drums at about four. He's four years older than me, so when I came along, he was my idol. He was my hero and everything my brother did, I wanted to do. If he had on blue shoes, I had to have blue shoes. So if he was playing an instrument, then that was the key to get me to do it also.

My father played in a band. Actually, he'd played in several bands. In the 1970s he was playing with a band called the Memphians. They were an outstanding cover band. They played behind soul man Syl Johnson and a lot of great artists. They toured the South at that time, and they were one of the best cover bands in the city, if not THE best. They were going back and forth with battles against the Bar-Kays. They had a musician in the group by the name of Preston Shannon, who was a very, very young guitarist at the time. He is now called the King of Beale Street. But, he was a learning musician at the time. They had other great musicians—the bass player Julius Bradley was best friends with Willie Mitchell (who produced Al Green's big hits) of Hi Records. They had an outstanding band.

So the members of the band would come by the house when my brother and I were growing up. My dad would say, "You know the boys are starting to play drums." And they'd say, "Oh really, let me hear ya'."

74

My brother would jump on the drum set, and he would start going at it. They would say, "Hey Paul, come on and play!" I was so shy I would run and get under the bed. They offered my brother a dollar. They offered the dollar because my brother was doing his thing. When I saw that I said, "Well, may I have a dollar?" And they said, "Well, you'll have to come from under the bed and play." So I came from under the bed and started playing.

By the age of five, we were starting to do private functions. We were playing for weddings and festivals, and we began entering talent shows. I was playing all kinds of smaller percussion instruments like bongos, and maracas, and tambourines, along with drum sets. We were singing as well. We grew up as 1970s babies. We sang everything from "Ring My Bell" to "You Light Up My Life," you name it. We can do Captain and Tennille and all of that stuff. I just loved all of that music. The Eagles and Michael Jackson were naturally included as well. I was singing "Ben" and all of that early Michael Jackson stuff. We really got heavily involved in it. It was one of the most wonderful times of my life. We were on television shows. People were painting us as the 'next' I don't know what. I don't know who we were supposed to be, but we had a group and the group was my father on piano, my brother playing drums and singing, I played drums and sang, and we'd alternate on the drum set. I'd play all of the percussion stuff and eventually we graduated up.

When we got to the second or third grade, we started to play piano, and eventually I picked up the electric bass at seven. The first song my dad taught me was "Slide" by the group Slave. That was only on one string, and you can still be funky playing on one string. He taught me the strings. He did not teach me how to read music at that time, formally like on the staff because I was seven. He taught me the notes of the strings. I was playing a four-string bass. It was small, and it was not a professional size bass. I think it was a little smaller than that. It has a G string, D string, A string and an E string. And, of course, he taught me about chromatic movement. He was teaching me half steps. At that point, he was using the piano to teach me. He would write the song out by the letter names. And then, of course, I'd listen to the song to learn the rhythms. That's how we learned. We just listened to the records and used our ears.

I didn't get the formal training in terms of reading a staff until I entered Hillcrest Jr. High School in the seventh grade. Then I picked up the trumpet and started playing trumpet in the band. My dad did another really cool thing. He was teaching summer camp, and at the end of summer camp I was with him almost every day. He told me to go in the instrument room and pick out whatever instrument I wanted to play. And I did. Up until that point, as I mentioned earlier, everything my brother did, I absolutely followed him lockstep. My brother picked up alto saxophone when he hit junior high. He was four years older than me, and he'd been playing alto sax. So we'd been doing gigs where now Dad's playing piano and my brother's playing alto, and I was playing drums then began playing electric bass. I picked up trumpet by the time I got to junior high school. That was the first time we'd done something separate.

I almost forgot to mention we had begun a small acting career when we were at the Theater of Memphis. I don't quite remember how we got started with that, but this was a little bit early, probably in between that five to eight or nine-year-old range for me. A guy named Moses Peace was acting, and so we had the Peace family at our church as well. We got into acting, and we did three or four plays there. I know one was *The Last of Miss Lincoln*. The other one was *A Midsummer Night's Dream*, which was at the Theater of Memphis. That was a special opportunity. We really had a great time doing that. The reason why that came to mind was because from that opportunity of acting we got a call to do a commercial.

We got a call to do a commercial for Church's Chicken in 1977, I believe. I'm seven years old, and what happens to all seven year olds is that they start losing their baby teeth. My two front teeth came out. Naturally, in a chicken commercial, the producer asked which one of us two boys is going to bite the chicken and look right into the camera. I smiled, and of course, my two front teeth were gone. My brother smiled and they said, "Oh, good! We're going to use you." I told them that I could bite it on the side. But, they chose my brother. Rufus Thomas (Memphis artist who recorded "The Funky Chicken") was the lead actor. That was the first time I had the opportunity to meet him and share with him. He knew my dad, and my dad knew the Thomas family.

Going forth, in junior high I played trumpet. I basically put the other instruments down once I picked up the trumpet. I began taking private instructions on trumpet, and I got to be pretty good. By tenth grade I went to the Overton audition, the only school of arts in the state of Tennessee. By my junior year I was section leader, and I began making all the regional bands and made All State. I was considered the best trumpet player in the state by then and playing Jazz as well. Then I went into the University of Memphis and got a little bit of music education. I thought about teaching, and I said no. I saw my Father teaching and felt that it was not for me. I went and pursued a second degree, a Bachelor's in Recording Industry at Middle Tennessee State University. I completed that, and ironically I went into teaching.

Right after I graduated, I had an opportunity to tour with Bobby Blue Bland for almost a year in 1997. That was an amazing opportunity, and I learned so much from him in terms of how to play music. As an example, I was back stage with him and he said, "Look, I want you to play something for me." I didn't know why because he had heard me playing. I had been touring with the band for a few months. I played this little Jazz riff because I'd been studying Clifford Brown and all these great Jazz trumpeters. I was used to playing a bunch of notes really fast, you know just all over the place. Then I played this one bluesy thing and he said, "Oh, yes, that's it!"

People didn't know it, but he was a Jazz aficionado. He loved Jazz, and he mimicked his style off of Nat King Cole. They called him the Frank Sinatra of the Blues. He had this really smooth, but very articulate style, which is uncommon in Blues singers. When I played this really bluesy lick, he said, "You know people want to hear something soulful and meaningful." I learned from him not to try to play so many notes, but what you can do with one note or two notes or a short phrase. He was a master at that. So listening to people like Bobby Bland and Kirk Whalum helped me to evolve my style into being a more soulful player.

After touring with Mr. Bland, I started teaching. I taught for about seven years, and then I decided to go back and get my Master's Degree in Jazz Studies. I completed that, and that's when this opportunity at the Stax Music Academy became open. At the academy's website you can learn more about the history of the Stax Music Academy and how we train future professional musicians.

Contact:
Paul McKinney
www.staxmusicacademy.org

Dr. Westbrooks:
It's very refreshing to know that young people are still learning to play instruments and read music. I was afraid reading music was going to become a lost art because technology has made it so simple for people to make music and record without knowing how to play. A lot of the music in some of the new songs is actually just beats and samples and not full-fledged music.

To see a new generation being taught to play the Stax catalog is awe inspiring. The Stax catalog is rich with phenomenally orchestrated musicianship and classic songs with eternal appeal. The Stax Academy is simply going back to the basics, which exercises the true foundations of music.

Another beautiful aspect of this program is the original Stax artists returning to give new generations a sense of what it felt like to be a part of something bigger than themselves.

CHAPTER FOURTEEN

STEPHEN HERRING

Educator, Performer, Music Consultant

"I made a conscious decision to pursue both performance and education so that I could actually share, or do what I was teaching to the students and show them how it was done."

Stephen Herring grew up in Alabama and Virginia, and attended Berklee College of Music in Boston, Massachusetts. He majored in performance, with a concentration on the saxophone. He earned degrees in Musical Performance and Music Education and relocated to Los Angeles to work in music publishing and music licensing. Stephen specializes in the placement of songs in film, television, and advertising projects. As a consultant and industry professional, his emphasis is on music law, artist representation, artist development and music clearance. He is affiliated with the Musicians Institute in the Artist and Career Services Department. Stephen recalls what motivated him to pursue a degree in music education as opposed to being only a performer.

Stephen Herring:
Originally, I felt very strongly, after working with private instructors and my band director in high school, that I didn't want to just be a teacher that was not able to also do what it was I was teaching, which was music. I wanted to be able to perform and show people what I know as a performer and an instructor as well. So I made a conscious decision to pursue both performance and education so that I could actually share or do what I was teaching to the students and show them how it was done.

Starting with that, I took that same logic from when I became a performer and an educator that I would also need to know what it would take to stand out from the crowd. I found that people that really make an impact in this industry aren't necessarily the best people. Many people who were really good who I played with and grew up with never actually pursued the business. They had the talent, but they didn't have the knowledge that separated them to get into the business. They didn't understand how to break into the industry. They did not understand how to share what they learned effectively as a teacher. They couldn't monetize what they were doing. That's why I pursued education and business along with my performance. I would be well rounded, and could actually stand out in the crowd because I would know how to promote myself correctly. I would know how to share what I do with other people.

What are the realities of bridging the gap for the artists who are promoting themselves, and the songwriter who is hoping to get their music placed in a project where they can make money off of it, such as a song in a movie or TV?

Stephen Herring:
The difference is that in the last ten or fifteen years, the expectations to push your music forward is not on the backs of the record labels, or even a publisher. It's on the back of you—the artist personally. Every song of mine that I was able to get placed or place for someone else, it wasn't hand delivered to me by a record label and recorded, and mastered, and ready to go. The artist themselves, found access to get the material recorded to a broadcast level quality on their own. For that you need a really close knit circle that is hard to get into.

What it really is, is getting your recordings together and getting them good. A lot of licenses might even take a song that's better recorded than a song that's better before it's recorded. Because having that quality, being able to produce at a high level content equal to that of record labels breaks you in. Some of my songs weren't my best songs, but because I was able to record with home studio technology, and had friends with resources who had engineering capabilities, that is what broke me into TV shows like *Shameless,* where I had songs that I wrote or was featured on. There are several Fox sports placements that I had with my own material, and also the other thing I think really makes a difference is, the Music Supervisor really takes a big risk when they put a song in a TV show. They don't know who you are. They don't know if the song is correctly copyright protected. They don't know if the song is featuring any samples. So what music supervisors for TV shows do is they rely on publishers to clear and make sure that these songs are safe to use, and that creates a trust relationship with the publisher. That's why it seems like a close knit circle.

Music Supervisors only have a handful of people they can trust in the industry to deliver the music. Otherwise, if a supervisor just picked up a song off the streets just on a CD, they don't know if a producer on that song owes money to someone, or if it is registered correctly with the performance rights organization or not. That's how you break into that circle. It's about having recordings that are good enough for a publisher. Then the publisher shares their personal connections, and have shown enough trust in your material to then engage the trust of that supervisor to then get you through.

Is there still such a thing as being in the right place at the right time for today's singer-songwriter? And what is that right place? And what is that right time?

Stephen Herring:
There are general ways of answering that question, and there are some specific ways that I'll give you as well. Yes, it is extremely very much possible. In fact, this happens very often that an artist is in the right place at the right time. I would find a band with an incredible song, and almost always it would be right at the same time where the perfect TV show was coming out for them. For instance, there is a show called *Plain Jane*. The day before I got the show, as a matter of fact, the artist who wrote the song "Plain Jane" had given me a heads up that they were going to be writing a song with the same name and they were going to give me a rough mix. So I already had it available, and I was able to tell that person, "Hey, instead of working on the other ten songs in the album, why don't you work on the title track 'Plain Jane'? There's a show coming out next week looking for a theme song."

There is definitely a right place and a right time as far as timing and as far as physical location. When a music supervisor or a record label is looking for a band, they're not just looking for the right song at the right time. They are looking for the right band that will advance their career. Essentially, if a music supervisor finds a band like Arcade Fire, then their profile as an A&R (Artist & Repertoire) consultant is going up in the industry. If they can see the band, feel the band, hear the music, get the press kit, see the photos, and get the whole package by seeing them at a showcase, it's like doing a week worth of A&R work.

Reps will go to places like the Viper Room or Marley Malone's in L.A., for instance, and look for those bands. In fact, the Lumineers was a band that opened for my band and was picked up from Marley Malone's because they would play weekly, Monday through Thursday when a lot of industry representatives would come down. So yes, it is definitely very possible to be found. It's just a matter of knowing that sometimes the major venues we hear about—the bigger names—are not necessarily the places where the industry hangs out. It's a lot of the smaller, more petite clubs like the Hotel Café (a popular Los Angeles night spot for new bands) and places like that where professionals in the industry seem to lurk a little bit more.

What are the geographic hotspots? By this we mean, what other places in the United States or around the world might be good places for bands to play to get noticed by industry professionals?

Stephen Herring:

It's interesting that in the United States, it's now a good idea to look away from the three major cities that are most closely associated with music, meaning New York, Los Angeles, and Nashville. There's still a lot going on there, but a lot of the newest stuff is coming out of Ashville, North Carolina. There's some really great bands coming out of the New England area, and the Boston area, as well as Portland, Oregon, and San Francisco.

It is these sort of satellite cities and other areas where we are finding all sorts of talent. In Detroit, actually, and in New Orleans, they both have really committed themselves to revitalizing their cultural image. Some of the bands we sourced from Detroit were incredible and really hidden gems. So that's the thing about the United States. Internationally, there are major hotspots like Toronto and Montreal, and a lot of great bands are coming out there in Canada. Nowadays, looking even in the South, there's some new music coming out of Brazil and Mexico, and a lot of the Latin American, Central, and South American countries that have a lot going on as well.

The cool thing is now since there's YouTube and a lot of online methods of distributing music, it doesn't really matter where you are. It matters that now instead of having to wait for a record label to pay a lot of money to get your CD made and put into a bunch of record stores, you can go on YouTube in any city and put your music up, and you'll find success in that way as well nowadays. Even in Europe, there's opportunity pretty much in any city. Actually, the more remote your city is sometimes the more people like it because it seems newer and fresher. People are coming up with new ideas that aren't on the radar, and so there's not like geographical central points any more. They're kind of all over the world, so don't feel like you have to move to the major cities to break in.

Why is it vital for people all over the world to be able to pick up their instrument and play their songs and sing?

Stephen Herring:

There's an experience I had recently where we played in Italy, and it was so incredible to see their reaction. I'm used to playing a lot in Los Angeles where there are many, many bands, but this is a city that does not have a lot of bands from other countries coming through it at any time, so this was a big event for them. The rewarding thing for the performer, and why it is so important that people have to continue to create and play and perform, is because this reaction that we received was over the top. We were literally flooded at the end of the show because the audience loved it so much. They could vicariously live through us.

We all admire rock stars performances, because, in a way, we all want to feel like we can be that and have that experience. So, we play an important role as musicians, to inspire people, to move forward and to give them a life lesson, and to share in their own way, and to share their own art. I think one of the most inspiring things I've seen is watching other artists who are watching other good concerts bring out new ideas and new concepts. This is what changes my perspective and makes me a better saxophonist and a better performer. It's still critical. Nowadays, with our standards of music, it is very different. It's not just the standard Pop, hip music anymore. We have music that's cross cultural, and you don't have to be afraid of your ideas anymore. You can put something on YouTube and get it out there, share what you think is music, and you can find fans and find people who identify with that. It's so important that we, as performers, identify and share and make our presence known in the industry, and in the world, so that other musicians can be equally inspired to pursue their dreams.

How important is it for musicians to come out of their musical caves or creative tombs to take a formal step in being educated in music? Please describe also what you do at the Musicians Institute.

Stephen Herring:

Music and musicians are naturally collaborative. You can have a guitar and sing and write your own song, but really everyone has to learn to work with other musicians and other players in order to get their music shared in the world and get it orchestrated. That's something different about our industry. Musicians naturally learn to work with each other to move each other forward.

Something that is critical to opening people up to that kind of collaboration are musical institutions, including the Musicians Institute, College of Contemporary Music. It makes it possible for you to join a larger body of musicians who can help you change your perspective and inform your music to become more creative and also help you. You may have that idea for the song, but you don't have the bass player, or the audio engineer to help you create your idea, or you just don't have that knowledge. You can access that knowledge yourself and merge with others in the industry who already have that knowledge, and that's how you push your craft forward.

Another thing that separates you and gets your music heard and gets you out of your cave is networking. One thing that happens when you join a musical institution or college is that you have now entered a family of other people who are also going to move in different ways into the music industry as either performers, or engineers, or business professionals. Now you've built a whole network that will allow you all to rise up together and work with each other, so that when you are now a gifted songwriter, someone that you knew in college is also a well-known publishing representative, and now you have a relationship that can carry you forward. That brings you, not only out of the cave, but into the spotlight.

How do readers get in contact with you?

Stephen Herring:
A great way to directly connect with me would be my website www.stephenherring.com. That has a lot of my performance credentials and the other facets of me as an entertainer and songwriter as well. For the purposes of college, I would state that the Musicians Institute website would be the best place for you to learn about all types of music careers, pursuing careers and making that angle, that's www.MI.edu. For me as a licensing consultant, you can contact me at either location. That also ties together with everything I do.

Contact:
stephenherring.com
MI.edu

Dr. Westbrooks:
Stephen Herring understands the significance and importance of networking—be it through music collaborations or with business connections. Stephen is a total package, meaning he is both creative and business oriented. Education and knowledge as well as talent are key to an artist's success, and organizations like the Musicians Institute are there to help artists advance themselves musically and professionally.

Stephen acknowledges the shrinking global village and urges artists to share their music with the world via YouTube or similar video sharing entities. He thinks artists should just get their music out there and let the public decide if they're interested or not since the opinion of the gatekeepers has been minimized.

The Marketers

Informed Sources

Michael Corcoran
Dan Weiner
Thornell Jones
Michael White

CHAPTER FIFTEEN

MICHAEL CORCORAN

CEO, MusicSUBMIT LLC

"Get your music to the small guys, the Internet stations, the bloggers, the guy who's always hanging out at your local music venue. These people are the new mavens and connectors, they are the grease in the music discovery wheel."

Michael Corcoran is the CEO of MusicSubmit.com, an online music submission company that submits new music to radio stations around the world for airplay consideration. He started with the company in 2005 as the Marketing Director. He describes how he helped a startup digital distribution company develop and grow. Michael lays the non-traditional framework that artists can take advantage of in today's music world.

Michael Corcoran:
In 2005 I joined MusicSUBMIT—a small music startup—to help organize the company, develop its services, and grow the business. The greatest success story in the music business in the past fifteen years is the removal of traditional barriers that prohibited unknown artists from getting heard. The Internet and the music services that sprouted from it have combined to democratize the process for unknown artists to be heard and distributed, allowing them to grow their fan base and sell their music completely on their own.

What was most beneficial about this change?

Michael Corcoran:
Artists can skip the traditional 'record deal' and take control of their own careers. In the past, a record deal was necessary just to get recorded. Now, with the costs having come way down, artists can record on a small budget and distribute on a smaller budget. The result is more music for everyone.

So now artists have more options and responsibilities, but what is the downside of this change, or is there a downside?

Michael Corcoran:
Now, there is more music for everyone. This also means more lousy music for everyone, and it's hard to get through the clutter. But, at the same time it also means more good music for everyone.

The music industry has a reputation for both fairy tales and horror stories. Would you like to share any horror stories?

Michael Corcoran:
Paris Hilton recorded an album and so did Kim Kardashian. When anyone can record an album, just about anyone will try.

What cautions would you provide to others about staying relevant (or current) in the music business?

Michael Corcoran:
You really have to be even more original than ever these days, because there is so much competition out there. It's been said for ages to "be original," but never truer than today. It will only magnify in years to come.

What must any artist, music executive, producer or lawyer know about selling, marketing, and/or collecting royalties on digital music?

Michael Corcoran:
They must know a lot. Digital music is close to eclipsing physical music (CDs) in total sales across the music industry, and it's much more complex in terms of marketing the music and collecting royalties than selling CDs in a retail store. In 1995, you had FM radio and retail record stores, and that was about all there was to it. Now there are download royalties, digital streaming royalties and YouTube, just for openers. The digital music business is literally a global business. So you have, not only, multiple U.S. performance rights organizations to deal with, but different rights organizations all over the world. To properly monetize your music and make a living as an artist, you need to be on top of all of it.

Where do you think the future of the music industry will take us?

Michael Corcoran:

It is anyone's guess, but I suppose we'll see even more choices for fans to consume music in the way they want it.

What is the best way to make money in the industry today?

Michael Corcoran:

As a musician you should treat your career as a real business and keep track of everywhere your music can be found. And don't forget to tour.

Here's the standard question. What advice would you give anyone who wanted to be successful in the music business?

Michael Corcoran:

Write songs and record them, then get them in the hands of the new tastemakers of today. No, not the A&R guy at Columbia. Get your music to the small guys—the Internet stations, the bloggers, the guy who's always hanging out at your local music venue. These people are the new mavens and connectors—the grease in the music discovery wheel. If your music is to be discovered by the masses, or at least an audience that can support your career, this is the way it will happen.

Contact:
michaelc@musicsubmit.com
www.musicsubmit.com
MusicSUBMIT LLC
New York, NY
(917) 512-2958

Dr. Westbrooks:

Michael Corcoran speaks about artists being in control of and responsible for their own careers. An artist no longer has to wait for the rare opportunity of getting your song heard by someone at a major label. Today, there are almost unlimited resources to get your music heard. But, the fact remains that it's still up to the artists to do the work. The difference is that now you have a much better chance to find your niche market or even reach a wider audience. To do that, you still have to have a product that has that special something to catch the attention of the listening public. Remember that listeners have a discerning ear and they also have options, so artists should try to present their best efforts to the public.

CHAPTER SIXTEEN

DAN WEINER

Vice President for the Western Region of Pandora

"What the business is today is probably going to be really different in 18 months, and then it's going to be really different from that three years from now."

Dan Weiner specializes in sales management, branding campaigns, mobile sales, web sales, audio sales and video. He has worked in digital and traditional media with Fortune 100 brands in multiple verticals, such as Toyota, Sony, Budweiser, Mercedes-Benz, HP, Bank of America, Macy's, Ford, AT&T and much more. Weiner recalls how he got into the sales side of radio and ultimately landed his position at Pandora, formerly The Music Genome Project®.

Dan Weiner:
I got into the radio business after having spent five or six years in equipment sales. I was in radio sales for 18 years for AM/FM radio with Clear Channel and CBS. There were a lot of mergers. I managed a sales team that sold oldies formats, Classic Rock, Rock, Pop, sports, play by play, Smooth Jazz, you name it.

In 2008 I switched because it was pretty obvious that the factory was exploding in the media business, particularly with radio. Things were changing to online. They were changing because the economy was making advertisers feel like they had to be accountable for anything that they spent advertising money on, show a return on their investment and a cause and effect. Traditional radio still suffers in that regard. Rather than chasing the money, I went to where the money was going. So I went online. I was with Myspace, which obviously had a pretty deep music and artist relationship. That was the origin of Myspace. It was really to help fans connect with fans. I was there for a couple of years and then Pandora started to call. It seemed like the perfect combination for my digital background and my radio and music background. So I've been here for four years, and it's providing everything that personally I wanted and everything professionally for the clients I work with. I believe in the cause. It's a really good mission.

Trying to create a musician's middle class was the reason behind the Music Genome Project. There was a way for people to discover music when they were not signed by a label, or when they were not a Mariah Carey, but they had really good pipes and they could sing. They just weren't getting the support to get airtime on traditional radio. So that's the mission of Pandora, and it works really well for the consumer. But, typically, when things work well for the consumer, they can work well for advertisers. Obviously, that's why I'm here.

How would you speak to that aspiring artist or aspiring music industry executive who may still be in college right now? All they know is that they like music, and they know there is some relationship between radio and music. They don't, however, understand the mechanics of that relationship.

Dan Weiner:
The mechanics are changing really quickly every day, and the one thing you can say for sure is that it's not glamorous. It's probably not what a lot of people would perceive it to be from watching certain movies or reading *Spin* Magazine. It's a tough business and it's been getting tougher over the years because their margins have changed and people are not buying music like they used to, if at all. If the digital edge has created a way for people to illegally share all kinds of music, it's a problem. So if you're looking at getting into the business of music, I think there's a lot of different ways and different avenues to get into it. I just think it's really important that you get into it for the right reason, because, if not, the days that built the Capitol Records building in Hollywood are way, way in the rearview mirror.

So if you want to do it, it just depends. If you are a musician, then you should follow your passion and your dreams and have a plan B. If you're into music and you like music, then it could be a fun business to get into, I would say. What is really important is to define what that fun really sounds like verses a job, and try to get an internship—paid or unpaid—so that you can get a little closer to it. Just understand that what the business is today is probably going to be really different in eighteen months, and then it's going to be really different from that three years from now.

The business is changing at lightning speed, and I think the way people consume music today verses three years ago is just a different world. You also have to be prepared for that if you go in the business because working at a terrestrial radio company three years ago verses today, you're doing a lot of different things that didn't exist. All of a sudden, you're supporting personalized radio and online radio when your company previously said that it's not a real business. It's a nifty feature, but it's not a real business. Now when you look at certain companies they're hedging their future on successfully migrating their audience from an AM/FM shtick to some form of personalized or online or mobile radio.

Can you explain for the novice or lay person what the Genome Project is—what it means and how it relates to Pandora?

Dan Weiner:

Pandora has actually been around for close to 13 years (at the time of publication). It's taken a couple of different pivots in our business model, but the music genome has been consistent throughout that entire span. It's basically a bunch of trained musicians who listen to music, song-by-song, track-by-track, artist-by-artist, and analyze it against up to 450 different music attributes. Everything from gravelly voice, electronic drum beat sounds, country twang and more. There are literally 450 different musical attributes that are associated with a track, and these professional musicians who are college trained (a lot of them are from the Berklee College of Music), they're analyzing each song. The idea is that it doesn't matter who the artist is. They don't analyze it based on how many downloads or albums the artist has sold. They analyze each track on the basis of the musical sound. The idea is that every song is connected through some genomic relationship that can enable you as an independent artist (John Doe) who has got a really good song with a really nice sound that is on par with that, and, in theory, can be played right alongside or right after a John Legend or in between a Miles Davis song. Or depending on the sound of your voice, could be right there and available for the music lover to discover your music the way that traditional music and radio really doesn't offer.

So how can someone who wants to get into the business or to maintain themselves in the business be most prepared for the challenges that there are now?

Dan Weiner:

I think you've got to be real flexible, and you're going to have to really work super hard. Network like crazy and be persistent. You're going to hear a no or two. The founder of Pandora was told no probably somewhere up in the neighborhood of 600 times as he went around trying to get financial support for this project. I think just like he was told no hundreds of times, musicians are probably told no hundreds of times and that they weren't good enough to be on this label or that label. I think you've really got to be persistent about it. At the same time, I think you've got to be ready to pivot. And you've got to have a plan B in the background so that you don't starve.

What is the most encouraging situation that you can remember as a result of being a part of Pandora?

Dan Weiner:

I can't really tie up that one particular thing, I can just tell you that consistently every day the greatest thing about what I'm able to experience by working for Pandora is that people really love Pandora. For the most part, it's a brand that has gone from sort of semi-recognition to unilateral love and appreciation. I just love to hear people tell me their personal antidotes about an artist that they discovered on Pandora that they'd never heard before. And I get to hear those stories every day. So that's something that keeps me waking up every morning.

Contact: www.Pandora.com

Dr. Westbrooks:

The Music Genome Project is an example of the new music model creating amazing opportunities for unknown and Indie artists to be discovered. Pandora's name has become synonymous with radio, and is one of the top streaming services. This works out great for consumers and advertisers. The downside to this is that the artists—the music creators—are still on the losing end of the streaming method of music delivery. I think more needs to be done to give a more equitable share of streaming revenue to the artists. Hopefully, that will be the next big change in the new music model.

CHAPTER SEVENTEEN

THORNELL JONES

Chief Strategist, Fortress Marketing

"Start at the Internet and work your way out from there because the Internet is the place where you can reach the most people fastest at the lowest premium cost."

Thornell Jones, Jr., is the visionary behind Fortress Marketing —a marketing and consultancy that has been instrumental in grooming the careers of Jill Scott, Brenda Russell, Mike Phillips, Jeff Bradshaw and more. His history in the music industry includes positions at Capitol, Mercury, Motown, Giant, and A&M Records. In our interview we learned of Thornell's history in business and finance, and how it fortified his career as a highly coveted marketing guru.

Thornell Jones, Jr.:
In 1998 after doing stints at several major record companies, I realized it was probably time to hang out my shingle. The mid '90s was the beginning of the wave of consolidation in record companies, and I found myself moving from job to job as companies consolidated and started to get rid of urban product management positions. I figured that there was enough business out there, and I could consult people on marketing and getting their records into the market place.

It was ironic that my first interview for a consultant position was when I was hired by Jerry Greenberg, President of MJJ Music. He was the former President of Atlantic Records, which was responsible for all that great music that came out of Atlantic Records in the '70s. I was off to a very good start. It was in that period of time that my passion was in the area of developing third party relationships with artists and record companies so that I could find potential sponsors and cross-marketing partners to expand the marketing opportunity for artists.

Early on when I was first at Mercury Records, they thought I was crazy trying to find corporate partners to work with because that kind of thing had been reserved for superstar acts. I said, "No, I think we're at a place now, especially since the mass marketing techniques of the '70s and '80s had gone away, we were kind of moving into a niche marketing era." I realized that if you could find companies that were targeting the same folks as you were trying to target, you could leverage the third party's marketing dollars with yours. You could target the same audience and have tremendous results. So cross-marketing and doing sponsorships have been the cornerstone of my success with marketing artists for many years now.

It takes a team to build great brands in the industry whether it be a music label or an artist. What are the names of some of the artists and companies for whom you have worked?

Thornell Jones, Jr.:

I actually came into the music business a little late. I didn't make the decision to pursue a career in the music business until my mid-20s. I came out of college—I went to Wesleyan University in Connecticut. I had a degree in Economics with a concentration in Corporate Finance and a minor in Music. Because I studied economics, I spent a year trying to find a job in the world of investment banking and that did not pan out. I got really frustrated. The people of Bank of Boston thought I was too 'colorful.' I laughed at that because I was trying to get into the entertainment finance division. I said, "Okay. Well, I guess you don't know who your client base is." Needless to say, I ended up opting to go to work for IBM in a technical marketing role as assistant engineer. I did that from 1984-89. In 1987 I went on leave of absence and went to business school at UCLA.

I moved from New York to Los Angeles and decided to study marketing and entertainment management at UCLA. I figured me being here in L.A. would be a great way to jumpstart a career in the music business. I was a frustrated musician. I spent my entire college career performing with bands, writing songs and in the creative entity. For some reason—and it probably had to do with a lack of support from my family—I didn't pursue a career as an artist, which probably was the best decision. But, at the time I felt that I should go figure out more about the music business that would help me with my own career. I packed up all my stuff and moved out to L.A. where I started studying marketing and finance.

I said to myself that I was absolutely not going to get a job in finance. I felt like I had put that part of my life behind me after my first internship at CEMA, which at the time was the name of Capitol Records Distribution Company (CEMA consisted of Capitol Records, EMI Records, Manhattan Records and Angel Records). I had done marketing research for them that turned into…well, you know, business is business for them. They appreciated it, and all of a sudden I had human resources looking for a job for me. I wound up in finance once again against my original intentions. I was a senior financial analyst at Capitol Records at an amazing time. One of my jobs was to count the recording expenses, but I was also responsible for tracking shipments. At one point during the *Please Hammer, Don't Hurt 'Em* project, we were selling 100,000 records a day. I was totally excited. Capitol was an interesting experience for me because even though I was a financial analyst, I used it as a training program for me to learn the business inside and out.

I understand it's a pending business. I understand that everything we do is on the margin. So even when I'm coming up with marketing models, I'm thinking in terms of return on investments and how my marketing impacts profitability. Ironically, I was passed over for the Capitol Manager Training Program at the time, but I spent a lot of time in Business Affairs. Part of my job was analyzing contracts and the return on investments. I had some special projects for the Executive Vice President of the company, and I would go around and talk to the different departments. I would talk to A&R; I would talk to A&R Administration; I would talk to Sales, Promotions, and Marketing. I would go in and have these conversations and ask them questions about their job. I would use this as an opportunity to really learn about the record company structure and who did what, and things of that nature.

After about a year and a half, I had some family situations. My dad had heart problems and I wanted to move back, so I started looking for a job on the East Coast. A lady named Gwen Franklin, who worked in sales at Capitol, had taken a job as VP of Urban Marketing—the new Rhythm and Black Music group of Mercury Records. While I was in school, I would send her my projects and ask for her feedback. When I started looking for a job on the East Coast, I was really hoping I could transition into marketing. Sure enough, I went in for a casual meeting. The same day that I had a meeting with her, I had an informational interview with Miller London, who was at RCA at the time. Two days later, she called me and asked if I would like to come work for her as her assistant. Here I am faced with this opportunity to get into the marketing department. So I left my management level job at Capitol Records as a Senior Financial Analyst with an office in the Capitol Tower with a view of downtown L.A. I moved to New York to be in this cubical sitting outside of Gwen Franklin's office answering phones and helping manage the interns.

I'm one of the people who always sails out of the box, so I was very fortunate that we had a team of really visionary, exciting out-of-the-box people. We were all really spiritually based, which would always come back as a theme for me in my career—making sure that my decisions were always spiritually based. It was a great team of folks, and Mercury was just trying to reboot its Black Music Division. Ed Eckstine had come over to be the president of the label and the Black Music division, and the division was run by this guy named Tony Anderson. When Ed came over he brought Wing Records with him. We had Vanessa Williams, Tony Toni Tone, and some new guy no one had ever heard of yet named Brian McKnight. We had some Hip Hop acts; Black Sheep was one of them. We had Diamond and the Psychotic Neurotics and several others. We had a deal with Chemistry Records for marketing and distribution.

So here I am an assistant in the marketing department. As you can imagine, the big wigs were running the acts that were making money. What was not making the money at the time in the network was these Hip Hop projects. I started doing work with kind of a deep dive with these Hip Hop acts starting with Ultramagnetic MCs who had a charismatic lead rapper whose name was Kool Keith. I made a big stink one day after seeing the show. I was thinking, *"We have to do a better job."* I did one of the most naive things anyone could do, but I did it anyway. I wrote this letter basically slapping my entire team on the wrist for not giving these Rap artists their due and giving them their proper attention. The head of Artist Development, Jackie Rhinehart, said, "'Thornell's right. What do you think we could do?" I came up with some ideas and she said, "Okay, let's try them!" We did, and they were working. People were saying things like, "Oh, okay, he might know what he's doing after all. He might have something here."

Within just 24 months, I was actually promoted from being an assistant to being product manager. I was two years into my marketing career, and I was the product manager for Tony Toni Tone's *Sons of Soul* album. I wrote my first marketing plan that was worth a million dollars. It was really a blessing because Ed Eckstine actually saw something in me. He would call me into his office, and we would sit there and think of advertising campaigns. We would talk through what the marketing should be on certain projects.

I really appreciated the kind of attention I was getting, because, like I said, I came into the business a little bit late. A lot of people were already doing college radio and retail stuff when I was still in college, and I was 30 years old by the time I made it into the marketing department at Mercury.

How did you make it back out to the West Coast after Capitol Records and the Mercury Label?

98

Thornell Jones, Jr.:

In 1994, I actually left Mercury Records. I was recruited away to come to work for Cassandra Mills, the new head of Black music for Giant Records. She had great success with Jade and the New Jack City soundtrack and Color Me Badd. She actually had Hammer signed to the label, which was kind of ironic. She hired me away from Mercury, and I came to work for her at Giant Records. It was a great opportunity. It was there that I did my first soundtrack, which was marketing for *The Inkwell* soundtrack for *The Inkwell* movie. The cool thing about that is I had a chance to work with Disney and to really see how meticulous they are and how professional they are. It really kind of set with me that if they're standard bearers in the industry, then this is the way to set the benchmark for the way that things need to be. That experience only lasted a year, because they closed the Black music division down almost exactly one year to the day that I came on board.

I found myself without a job, but I was fortunate enough that six weeks later I was hired by Motown Records as a marketing manager. While I was there, I was responsible for Diana Ross and her *Take me Higher* project, for Johnny Gill, for Blue, and for a group called Impromptu who were signed to the MoJazz Label, which was run by Steve McKeever. He went on to found Hidden Beach.

After Mercury, I was hired to work at A&M Records. At A&M I was responsible for all their Black music roster including Ann Nesby, Sounds of Blackness, Mint Condition, and some distributed label artists, including Takea and Billy Porter, who recently won a Tony Award for his performance in *Kinky Boots* on Broadway. While I was at A&M, I realized that what we were doing was developing campaigns and driving campaigns across various channels. So I developed a marketing method that would be become known as what I call The 6 Channels™.

While the rules have changed over the years, fundamentally they haven't. The 6 Channels™ are airplay, retail, press, videos, consumer/lifestyle, and the Internet. I would say to start at the Internet and work your way out from there because the Internet is the place where you can reach the most people fastest at the lowest premium cost. So after my stint at A&M, I started my own company—Fortress Marketing. My first client at Fortress Marketing was at MJJ Music—Michael Jackson's label underneath Epic Records. Working with Jerry Greenberg, who was the president, was an amazing experience because he really understood business. He also, in his experience, understood Black music, which was ironic because he was a Jewish man.

In 1999 I was really frustrated because I was getting a little tired of this kind of record company round table. I decided I was going to turn my attention towards developing sponsorships and cross promotions on behalf of artists. I made a cold call to the vice president of marketing for Reebok, and I realized that they were having trouble connecting in the market place. Adidas had a brand identity, Nike had a brand identity, but Reebok had kind of fallen off. I recommended that they start doing some lifestyle marketing efforts. She explained that they had positioned their company on performance, and if it didn't have to do with performance like athletic performance, performance on the court, or performance on the track, etcetera, then they weren't going to market too well.

Six months later she called and told me that they were kind of shifting and that she had an opportunity for me to help develop a mall tour around their engagement with Nickelodeon and Kid's Footlocker. I was able to put together this mall tour with Tatyana Ali, who was one of the artists on MJJ Music, and another artist from MJJ music called Male Authority. We put together the Southern California mall tour, and it was a huge success. But, at the end of the summer, I had spent so much time working on this tour that I hadn't generated any new business.

I had a chance meeting with Steve McKeever at this hamburger joint called Mo Meaty Meat Burger. He invited me to come in for a meeting, and I was very excited because he had just signed one of my favorite artists, Brenda Russell. She hadn't put out a record in like twelve years, so I went by to hear this record. This was in October of 1999, and I was so blown away. I started doing my marketing churning of ideas. I just started doing stuff, and eventually we came to an agreement for me to work for him on this Brenda Russell project and form a strategic relationship where my offices were based out of Hidden Beach. I would work on their projects, and I would do my independent stuff, and it could all be hunky-dory.

A chance meeting at a hamburger stand re-connected you with Steve McKeever, the founder of Hidden Beach Music. Under the new partnership, you were instrumental in branding Jill Scott, Mike Phillips and Jeff Bradshaw when they were newcomers. What were some of the key elements of your strategy?

Thornell Jones, Jr.:

In January of 2000 Steve McKeever asked me to take a listen to another record that he had. I had been hearing music around the office. I hadn't really done the deep dive on the project yet, so I took the record home. I came back and said, "This girl is going to blow." Of course, that was Jill Scott. Hidden Beach was a small company with a distribution relationship with Epic Records. Because we were an independently-owned company, we controlled the show. We controlled the money and, basically, we knew that we had something with Jill. We knew there was going to be an audience with Brenda, but the company hadn't officially been launched. So on June 1 of 2000 we executed this huge launch party for the entire industry. There were like 2,200 people that came to Santa Monica where our offices were at the time. We had a case with Brenda Russell, Mike Phillips, and Jill Scott, the first three signings on the label. The Jill Scott campaign actually started in March of 1999. She went out on tour with the group the Roots and performed the song "You Got Me," which she wrote but Erykah Badu sang. It was the beginning of the *Who is Jill Scott?* campaign.

At the time, we didn't know that was what the album was going to be called, but they were handing out cards trying to drum up interest in this woman who was singing this song that everybody knew. It worked because people did start asking, "Who is Jill Scott?" There was even a piece that she does, "My Name Is J-I-L-L S-C-O-T-T," that appears on her album. When it came time to finally name the album in the spring of 2000 we said, "Why not just call the album, *Who is Jill Scott?* Sometimes you kind of stumble into brilliance. Sometimes people say, "Oh, that was something that was really strategic that you laid out," etcetera, but, often times, it is just the thing that makes sense.

Jill had a very deep album. We had been releasing singles at that point in July of 2000 when the record came out. We had been releasing singles to mix shows and to the underground for over a year. It was the single out with rapper Common, it was a couple of mix-up singles like "Love Rain" and "Getting in the Way," which became the official first single. But, even Epic thought that the marketplace wasn't big enough to release the record. I had a heated conversation with the head of marketing at Epic at the time who told me that I knew better, and I shouldn't be foolishly releasing this record and that there was so much potential. But what happened was, the record came out the first week, and it did more (in sales and airplay) the next week, and did more the next week. By the fourth week, we're doing 20,000 units a week. It sat there for ten weeks before I was finally ready to pull together a video, which launched over Labor Day weekend. It went up another 10,000 a week until Christmas. By Christmas, this record that came out in July was Gold.

Over the winter break, radio host Steve Harvey was introduced to the record while he was hanging out with his friends playing cards. He came back in January talking about, "I love this girl. I'm going to play her on the radio. I'll give her time whether the Program Director says I can play it or not!" He was the first person at a mainstream R&B station to actually play the record. We had success at Urban Adult, but he was the first person at a mainstream R&B station to actually play it, and he wasn't syndicated at the time.

Hidden Beach has always had a commitment to quality. This is one of the reasons why I have stayed with Steve and been in the trenches as long as I have. When I was at A&M records, I realized they were making a left hand turn down a path they really didn't understand. I also realized at the time that I was doing some soul searching. I realized that I only want to use my God-given gifts to uplift good and to put positive messages out into the universe. When I knew what was happening at A&M, I was disappointed because it was my favorite label as I was growing up. It went from the Carpenters to the Captain & Tenille to Janet Jackson to the Brothers Johnson to Quincy Jones to Brenda Russell.

So much wonderful music had come out of A&M, and here they were making this left-hand turn into gangster Rap when they did this deal with Ice Cube and Shaq and some other folks. It didn't fit right with my spirit. But, when I started working with Steve, I realized that he and I not only went to the same church, but we have very similar values when it came to spiritual principles and quality of music. We just had a commitment to quality and a commitment to using our gifts for positive good. Our initial roster, as I said, was Brenda Russell, Mike Phillips and Jill Scott. Mike Phillips has phenomenal talent. In fact, that is one of the cornerstones of Hidden Beach. No matter how hot the record is, the artist has to be able to perform it live. The artist has to be a real artist. They can't just be studio confection. Mike did that from the very beginning.

Over the course of ten years, we had people come and go, but that was also the strategy of the label. To create a home for artists to come and make those records that they couldn't make anywhere else. Like if Stevie Wonder wanted to come and do a Jazz record, he could come and do that. Darius Rucker, one of the biggest vocalist of the '90s came to Hidden Beach and did a Soul album because he wanted to do a Soul album. He was known for Rock music, now he is on percussion music, but he was known for Rock music. Now he's known for Country music. His album with Hootie & the Blowfish sold 18 million records. But, he wanted to do a Soul record, so he came to Hidden Beach and did a Soul record.

Bebe Winans ventured out and put a couple records out through the label. And we had the privilege of putting out two Obama related compilations. One was the "Yes we Can" compilation that has the music from the campaign. Then came "Change is Now," which is the official presidential inaugural collection on DVD with speeches from the campaign and inspirational songs from the campaign cut together from pieces of the speeches. It is an amazing piece. There's a whole other story that goes along with that. I'd just like to say that I'm proud to have been a part of that piece and to help create that piece of history.

What are three things that an independent artist or label must do in terms of their company structure?

Thornell Jones, Jr.:

The first thing I'd say is that the growth of independent music has been extraordinary. That is definitely as a result in the growth of technology. When I left IBM, I told them there was going to be this real growth in the music business. The opportunity was there. I really want to work in this space. Help me find a job in this space, otherwise you'll be left behind. They told me, "Oh, no, no, no." I said, "Oh yes, yes, yes." I promptly submitted my letter of resignation.

Technology is definitely at the root of this entire shift. In the ten years between 2000-2010, we went from releasing about 65,000 albums a year to probably about 100,000 albums a year. I don't know the actual statistics, but what that means is, there is a lot of clutter out there in the market place. When talking about independent artists and independent labels—remember Hidden Beach is an independent label—we do have distribution, but we are an independent label. We control our own destinies because we own the catalog, and we exploit the catalog and various distributions and licensing. So it can be done.

It starts out by surrounding yourself with a committed team of folks. Obviously, looking at just the artist level, you have to make sure you have someone who can advise you in legal concerns. As an artist being in a bubble, people might think they can put a video on YouTube, and they will become famous and rich all of a sudden. There is really no shortcut for hard work, which means that you have to get out there and perform. You need to have a manager and/or an agent who can help you find gigs so that you can actually perform. I want to say that you have to have some kind of marketing person who has some facility with the web and innovation through technology, whether it be mobile or some of the web-based applications for pushing out music.

A good marketing person probably has some facility in all the six channels. I would have to say they should have a knack for working with artists and labels in a resource constrained environment. That's 'corporate speak' for not having a lot of money. They should have skills in all the six channels from writing and issuing press releases, to managing and expending, to how to grow your Facebook fan base. Those are probably just three things for independent artists and independent labels.

Start out with a strategy and surround yourself with the people who can help to bring that strategy to life. If you really do not know what the strategy will be, start with that before you really release anything. There's no reason to do that. The world is not waiting for the next single from an independent artist who has no fan base. No matter how excited you are, you have to build a demand. It is really important that you take your time. One thing I will say is this, though, the music business has kind of gone back to the 1950s and 1960s. It's kind of like when you see those movies like *The Five Heartbeats* or *Why do Fools Fall in Love?* A single will take off, and you run around the country and support the single. Part of the problem with the music business was that in the '80s, the business kind of shifted to trying to sell albums to everybody. Frankly, the quality of those albums was marginal at best. The consumer got savvier, so we're back to where we were in the '50s and '60s where people would respond to singles. You have to be prepared to release a series of singles that will create a fan base before you run out there and create this whole album. It's a waste of time that takes the focus away from developing a fan base.

How would you complete this sentence? "My greatest joy in this industry is what?"

Thornell Jones, Jr.:
I would say my greatest joy is in helping the artists make their dreams come true, manifesting their dreams into reality. Taking an artist from obscurity into prominence, I would have to say that is my greatest joy.

Contact:
FortressMktg@gmail.com

Dr. Westbrooks:
Just as each marketing campaign has to have an element of uniqueness, Thornell Jones has made himself stand out from others by developing his own marketing technique called 6 Channels™. He also made the bold move of obtaining sponsorships for Indie acts at a time when that type of attention was reserved for already developed superstar acts. His personalized marketing concept and branding partnerships helped create awareness for his client's music while communicating the value of that music to the listening public.

CHAPTER EIGHTEEN

MICHAEL WHITE

Independent Consultant
Former Marketing Director at Capitol Records
Consultant for GospoCentric Records

"Everybody makes music and somebody else has to enjoy it, and that was always my job—to find the person who was willing to spend money on it."

Michael White's career at Capitol Records spanned 25 years where he worked as a Customer Service Rep, National Sales Director and Marketing Director, among other titles along the way. He was an integral force in the strategic marketing of artists such as M.C. Hammer, Natalie Cole, Frankie Beverly & Maze, Bonnie Raitt, Michael Franti, Peabo Bryson and many others. Upon leaving Capitol Records, Michael assisted GospoCentric Records in bringing the music of Kirk Franklin and Trin-i-Tee 5:7 to the masses. He gives a candid look at his career and a forecast for today's industry.

Michael White:
I was with Capitol for about 25 years—I was a Marketing Director, which was a liaison for the company in all departments with the goal of making it successful. I was also the Product Manager, or whatever the title was at the time, making sure that all of the artists' needs were met and that everything was going in the proper direction.

Was there another title as well?

Michael White:
I was National Sales Director, Regional Promotions, Production Assistant and Customer Service Rep. I went through all of the phases. I went from production to sales and then to marketing.

So now in this quarter of a century, who were some of the artists that you were instrumental in marketing and promoting?

Michael White:
I last worked with Bonnie Raitt, Dave Koz, Spearhead (Michael Franti), whom I am happy to see is doing so well these days. That was actually at the end of the rainbow. Previous to that and in other capacities, I worked with Hammer, Maze, Peabo Bryson, Natalie Cole, and just a wide spectrum of artists. When we got rid of Black music in 1994, I was working with more Folk type of music.

How is it that you got involved in the music industry in the first place?

Michael White:
A very good friend worked at Capitol Records. He worked in distribution, and he was able to keep a lot of money in his pocket. I didn't exactly know why. I told him, "Hey, I could use cash like that!" But he wouldn't hire me in distribution, and that's when they gave me a job in production. Subsequently, I found out distribution was a very bountiful place to be if you could avoid the legalities of shipping product to Japan. That's what they were doing out of that department. I did not get caught up in that bust. I ended up starting off in production. After just over a year, I was able to get into the sales office as a Customer Service Rep. I continued on from there. I've always loved music so much, and all of these things in my life stand out to me. I was very good friends with Martha Reeves. I've always had music around me, but I was never interested in being in the business. I just loved the music. Roberta Flack, who was Roberta Novosel at the time, was my music teacher in the ninth grade at Rabaut Jr. High School in Washington, D. C.

Was your job in production on the manufacturing side or on the creative side at Capitol?

Michael White:
It was on the manufacturing side, I basically controlled the presses. I was non-union and everybody who worked at the plant was union, so I had to set up what was put on the presses.

Now tell us more about your Washington, D. C., experience and how it ignited your passions in music.

Michael White:

Mrs. Novosel (Roberta Flack) was a tough teacher when she was able to show up. We had two teachers, and we always wondered why Mrs. Novosel missed so many days. It was because she was working all night. She would put us through all kind of stresses in regards to making good music. We had a really nice choir and some of the people were considered her pets. She was hard on a lot of us, and she got the most out of everybody. Let's put it that way. Subsequently, when she came to Capitol, we wanted to sign her at Capitol. We heard the album and her song with Peabo Bryson. That was when we made the re-acquaintance. That was funny because I was not one of her favorites. Meanwhile, the president of the company Jim Mazza loved Roberta Flack, and he wanted to sign her so badly. I'm not sure what happened with the negotiation, but it just didn't happen. I guess this was in 1978 or 1979.

Explain your transition from Washington, D. C., to Los Angeles and ultimately into the music industry.

Michael White:

As I said, it all came by chance and chasing a dollar. Mostly, I've always appreciated all kinds of music, so it wasn't hard to delve into the music world. When you are Black, you get slid into Black Music. There's nothing like Stevie Wonder's *Songs in the Key of Life* and Marvin Gaye's *What's Going On*. I appreciated Black Music, but some of my favorite albums are from Traffic, Yes, and Zeppelin. There were just so many acts. My friends loved all genres of music, and I did, too. Everybody makes music and somebody else has to enjoy it, and that was always my job, to find the person who was willing to spend money on it.

Having been a part of Capitol Records, also known as the House that Nat built (as in Nat King Cole), what can today's music industry learn from yesterday's music business model?

Michael White:

I think that they should continue the value of music. I sat there and I watched an eradication of music. When Larkin Arnold was running Capitol, I know that there were political repercussions, but the roster that he put together was great from Tavares, the Sylvers, Taste of Honey,

Natalie Cole, Maze, Peabo Bryson, and on and on. We also had Eddie Henderson from the Jazz side and other artists like that. I mean it was a well-rounded description of Black music. What happened in the business was that we started to not value the whole music sense of it. We became so business oriented. When I started, Steve Miller had become a hit on his third album. We would do artist development. Today there is no artist development. So what happens is you put a single out there, and the single sells real well, but there is no love towards the artist. There is no artist education. Then, if they don't come back with another hit (which is very difficult to do) they just disappear in the clouds. You can see the way the business model works and how everybody is grasping for singles, because that is how you learn to become a buyer. We all started out buying a single, then we'd buy the album, but it was also an affordable album, back in the day. It's the same thing online today, the audience buys the singles, but they don't have to know anything about the artist and that's the one thing that's missing. If somebody can bring all of that back, they'll be very successful.

Are you saying that everything that is old, is new again? There are so many ways that artists can connect with their fans, which can be beneficial, but what about artists who still lack the savvy and budget for additional marketing, promotions and even production?

Michael White:
Okay, first off, only three percent of all albums (even in the good days) sold over 25,000 records. So do you know how insurmountable that mountain is? What happens is that people think that because you're an Indie (independent artist), *"Oh, I can do things, and I don't need a big record company."* It's almost like in politics where the Supreme Court just ruled that people with money can spend it any kind of way that they want on a candidate, but if you don't have that kind of support behind you, you can't win. You need money to be able to make things happen, to bring your face to the public. That's what's going on because a lot of artists make music and then they think, *"Well, I should be a hit."* The same thing a record company does, or did, no matter what, you still have to do. You have got to do the marketing, you have got to do the sales, and you've got to do the promotion. You have to take care of the production, in whichever format. You have to do all of the business, the hook ups. It's no different than having a regular record company. But, the main thing that a record company does is that they sponsor you, which is something you can't do yourself. You can't afford to spend the mass amount of money to put you on the radio. Out of the 50 million

artists on the Internet, what makes me look for 'Joe Smith?' There has to be something that brings my attention to Joe Smith. It takes money because that is just the way of the world.

Some people who are thriving in today's industry may believe that things will never change. Are there any forecasts that you can share on how rapidly things can change?

Michael White:

We need advocates, and we need strong voices. What we had previously that actually put together Black music departments, we don't have that strength any more. We have to do it as a vigil, if we can get in and gain some strength. I see that as such a long range problem of people trying to get back in through reaching the Diaspora. I'm not sure of the glue and if we can get any of that back. I think that with independents there are opportunities. There are things that you can do on a regional or local basis that could actually blow you up. Through the Internet, you can reach the world. You just have to be able to touch them also.

What would your heartfelt instructions be for young people who want to be businessmen and women and moguls in the industry? Their desire is to be in marketing, or management, or distribution worldwide. What can a legend and a veteran like you tell them?

Michael White:

Basically, I would think that if I was coming out of college and I wanted to get involved, I would probably find an artist that pleases me, and try to work with them from all aspects. Because you know them from college and you've seen their work, I'd suggest that you adopt them. Take a little bit of seed money, and know that you're going to struggle a little bit, but start there. You know the greatest example of someone in the music business that I would recommend to anybody to read about, emulate, and learn more about is Sean Combs. P. Diddy is a phenomenal kid who was an intern for two years and then was in college and established his tag. I think that he is the role model and the blue print for how it still can be done today.

Are there any other stories where you were instrumental in building an artist's career or turning the key, so to speak?

Michael White:

I was not the turnkey, but Hammer is the smartest artist that I have ever been around. I say smartest because he was the best well planned and thought out. Three years before we released the *Please Hammer, Don't Hurt 'Em* album, he already had it done in his mind. We were travelling together on a plane, and he ran through the whole album for me from beginning to finish. That album was so strong that it went on to sell about 20 million worldwide. He always knew what he wanted to do. People just look at the bankruptcy, and that's so stupid to just look at that because now a lot of people know what that is. But even more so, Hammer had a plan. What he did was he brought in others around to help create the business aspect of it, which ultimately hurt him, but it was not because he wasn't loving and caring and didn't have a plan. There was a time when it was just me and him travelling. After that he had an entourage of 25 at the least. He took care of people, but I was there at the beginning and, subsequently, at the end of his career at Capitol Records.

Are you still actively involved in the industry?

Michael White:

I remain a part of the music industry. I mostly deal with Gospel music. That's what I've been working the last few years. I helped Vicki Mack Lataillade start with Kirk Franklin. When I left Capitol, I went and worked at GospoCentric Records for a few years as a consultant and in management. Subsequently, I have been involved with the Gospel music world in all facets since then. I remain an independent consultant, and I am always available if someone needs help.

Contact:
bmjwhitemarketing@earthlink.net
(818) 599-5336

Dr. Westbrooks:

Michael White speaks honestly about the harsh realities of the music industry. Yes, a lot has changed in terms of not needing a major to produce a product, but everything—every step—that the major labels did still need to be done (that includes Artist & Repertoire, Production, Marketing, Promotions). The difference is that now artists have to do it themselves, including providing the money. An adequate amount of money is still a necessary part of getting not just music known to the world, but also for obtaining visibility for the artist. The Internet has changed the game tremendously, but the role of money is still significant and difficult for most Indie artists to overcome. The bottom line is that artists have to create their own opportunities, but success is still possible on many different levels.

THE PROMOTERS

INFORMED SOURCES

Jesus Garber
Clifford Russell
Michael Nixon

CHAPTER NINETEEN

JESUS GARBER

**Former Executive with Motown,
A&M, Zoo Entertainment & Hollywood Records
Founder of the Jesus Garber Company**

"The business is all about publishing. It's about ownership of songs; it's ownership of product, that's what it's all about."

Jesus Garber entered the business by way of Dorsey High School in Los Angeles, California, in the early 1970s. What started out as a hobby being the lunch time DJ led into a lifelong career in the music industry. Jesus would later steer the careers of Herb Alpert, Elton John, Janet Jackson, Barry White, Ray Charles, Vesta Williams, James Brown, Shanice Wilson, Jeffrey Osborne, Sting, Jennifer Hudson, Drake, Miguel and more. Jesus tells how it all began, and how he provides guidance for those in the current and drastically different climate of music.

Jesus Garber:
My whole thing was, I was broadcasting from the main office into all the outdoor quad areas where the kids would be sitting having lunch and on the grass throughout the different parts of the campus. I was the lunch time DJ, and the kids would come and dance during the lunch and recess hour.

The 1970s was a time of great social change in America. The Motown era of Soul and R&B was merging into Disco and beyond. How would you describe the decade in music?

Jesus Garber:
During that early 1970s and onward was an exciting period in music because there were a lot of great songs that come to mind. From Aretha Franklin to Smokey Robinson's debut song by himself without the Miracles, "Baby Come Close." Rufus & Chaka Khan were hot with so many of their great hits. It was just an exciting period. Even Cuba Gooding's group the Main Ingredient was hot during that period. There

113

was also Major Harris, and Sussex Records had a lot of hit records with Bill Withers. Stax had a lot of great hits during that period with Al Green, the Staples Singers, Otis Redding, and Booker T & the M.G.'s. There was a tremendous amount of product. There were the Independents that came through there that really made a significant contribution. As you evolve towards the end of the 1970s, Disco become very pervasive in dominating the very end of that era from like 1976 to like 1981, and it peaked. But, at the end of the day, it all started with great songs, and that's why they're still enduring today.

As far as working in the industry, what types of opportunities were developed during this time?

Jesus Garber:
It was an extremely fun period because if you analyze where we are today and you go back to the 1970s and 1980s, the pattern for the consumer was basically listening to terrestrial radio. That's where you really were enlightened as to what was new and exciting. It was not a problem for you to get in your car and go to your local record shop and pick out your favorite album. The record business was thriving; it was amazing. What makes periods in a certain industry really great is when consumers are consuming your product. That's why that period was so much fun. It was obviously a reinvestment into the community, to the record shops, to the distributors, and to the one stops from the record companies because they were selling records. And what they wanted to do was keep selling records. That period we were looking at $9.98 to $12 dollars for a vinyl record, so that was a great price point and they had nothing to compete with like we do today.

Briefly describe the chronology of your career.

Jesus Garber:
I got my first job in the business from a gentleman who used to work for Mattel Toys. I ended up becoming the local merchandiser guy for Stax. His name was Jheryl Busby (future president of Motown in later years). He came to our high school, and he liked what I was doing. He started bringing artists to perform live at lunchtime, and so on and so forth. He started giving me records in excess. There were hundreds of records from the excess of what they had left over from Wattstax (a 1973 music festival named after the area of Los Angeles known as Watts that featured artists on the Stax music label) at the L.A. Coliseum. I would

give them away at lunch time. The kids were extremely excited, and these were records or songs that couldn't get played at local stations like KDAY, KGFJ, and KUTE 102, or KJLH. Those stations were tightly formatted at the time. What we would do was play a different track off the album. The kids would hear it at lunchtime and then go home and request them at those stations, and those stations were forced to play the records.

So what I did was this. I took the idea of what I was doing at lunchtime at my high school, and I started my own company right out of high school. I called it the High School Radio Network. I took 60 high schools in the city of Los Angeles and started a noon time program. I helped them with programming it and provided all the songs. The kids played the songs that I provided, and they definitely had a campaign where we started a call in to KDAY, KGFJ, KJLH, and KAGB which was called KAGB at that time and was owned by Clarence Avant. The kids would actually call the stations. So when you think of about 60 high schools, and you take a low number like 100 to 50 kids from one of those campuses calling in the stations at a certain given time. The stations were literally flooded with calls for those specific songs. It turned out really positive because when the stations responded by starting to play the songs that the kids had requested, the kids felt that they had a pulse. They said, "Wow, something must be going on. These kids like the songs, let's start playing it." So, it was very effective. That's how my first account became Motown Records in 1974.

As it ended up, Jheryl Busby helped me out with Clarence Avant. We did a weekend radio show on KAGB, which was called the "High School Happenings," and that's how I met Skip Miller, another mentor of mine, and Miller London (who was the first African American to work in the sales department at a major record company). This makes Miller a living historical figure in the music industry. That's how my association with Motown came along. One of the independent labels that I ended up working with was Source, and that was owned by Logan Westbrooks. I worked a group called Smash; which was comprised of the very young DeBarge family. This was very interesting. I took them to about 15 to 20 high schools, and we created a very nice street buzz long before street promotion was around. They were great, and they signed autographs, they performed, and they were very excited about the whole process.

I remember my contact at Source Records was a gentleman named John McCray, who worked for Logan as a promotion marketing guy. I believe that John has since passed. Logan really impressed me because it was at an early period in our industry. He did his deals with distribution through MCA at the time. That was a time when you had to know the people who built the movie business and the record business. Lew Wasserman and Sidney Sheinberg, those guys were tough as nails. In order for you to impress one of those gentlemen that you were worthy to get distribution and funding from them, you really had to have your act together. I mean not just together but super-super together. Logan was just that. He always had a great ear for music, and he's always been very serious. One of the things I would say was really a great example to me is when you do make money, you don't blow it. You invest it. Legend has it that Logan invested very well in the Crenshaw area (a local neighborhood in Los Angeles), and it obviously paid off for him. That's what you call doing smart business.

Give three or four of your most dynamic roles in the industry.

Jesus Garber:
From Source Records. I had the privilege to work with Smash in the early 1980s. From 1980-85, I was the Western Regional Promotion Manager for Motown. In February 1983, I had the privilege of traveling the entire month with the group DeBarge. So we had "All This Love," "I Like It," and "You Wear it Well." All these were great songs, and it really catapulted the artists and the group to a whole other level.

It was just such a privilege and an honor working with Motown at that time when you had Lionel Richie's first and second solo albums. The second album *Can't Slow Down* sold 10 million. Obviously, I'm a huge Rick James fan. I was on the road with him during the *Street Songs* album in 1981 and 1982 along with Teena Marie. I am a definite Teena Marie fan. We had the Mary Jane Girls and the Dazz Band. We also had the Temptations, the Four Tops, Smokey Robinson, Jermaine Jackson, Diana Ross, Stevie Wonder and all those wonderful, legendary artists. It was just such a privilege.

Now with the A&M label (owned by Herb Alpert and Jerry Moss), I was the National West Coast Promotion Manager, which was actually the territory from Cleveland all the way to the West Coast. I would say that a real pinnacle of my career was that they promoted me from National West Coast Promotion Manager to Marketing Manager. The first marketing plan I wrote was for an artist they were considering dropping. The artist had two albums, the first one sold 150,000 and the second one 120,000. I said, "Well, you know, we need to go on the road. We need to get limos, we need to have this artist in a suite, first-class air travel, and we need a bodyguard." They said, "Are you crazy? Wait a minute, first of all, we only do that for our biggest artists, which are Sting and Bryan Adams. This artist has had a decline in sales, and we are considering dropping the artist." I said, "Oh, really? I think this is a hit. I guarantee if it doesn't work at the end of the tour, you can let me go. No questions asked." The song was called "What Have You Done for Me Lately." The album was called *Control*. That is the absolute truth.

I had the privilege of really being instrumental in another artist's career, and this artist actually thanked me in his one and only book ever. He tried to hire me from Motown. Interestingly enough, I ended up being at A&M and I said to this artist, "How would you like to come to A&M?" The artist was Barry White. What was really interesting was that I had no idea that at that time he was in real dire straits financially. I saw him in the mastering room at A&M in the basement and I said, "Barry, I want to apologize." He said, "What are you apologizing about?" I said, "Well look, I know that we just offered you $350,000 for your master." This is unheard of today, but back then there were millions of dollars advanced to artists. I said, "I know how heavy that financial monkey is on your back." He said, "Jesus, you're right that that financial monkey is heavy on my back, but let me tell you something, that $350,000 is enough to get that monkey to start climbing down."

Were you responsible for bringing Barry White back up the charts with "Practice What You Preach" in 1994?

Jesus Garber:
We had before that, but it all started when I brought him to A&M. It all started there, and there's one thing about Barry White—the fact that his fan base is much larger outside of the United States. He sold in excess of a 100 million records. I had the privilege of giving Herb Alpert his first number one with "Diamonds" on the Urban chart, Vesta Williams with "Sweet Sweet Love," Shanice Wilson's first one with "No Half Stepping," and as for Jeffrey Osborne, even though he was with the group LTD, he was by himself in a solo career for a long time, but he never had a number one on Billboard until I gave it to him with "She's on the Left." Then Herb and Jerry sold the company.

I went over to a brand new start-up called Zoo Entertainment run by Lou Maglia who was over at Island Records. We did a joint venture with Philly International. I had the privilege of working with one of my favorite female vocalists—Phyllis Hyman. She had the album *Prime of My Life*, but she never had a number one on Billboard. Then with "Don't Want to Change the World, I Just Want to be Your Girl," we gave her a number one record with that and a Gold record. I was Vice President at A&M and Vice President at Zoo Entertainment, which is a BMG company, and then I became last Vice President of A&M's Urban division, under the ownership of Herb Alpert and Jerry Moss.

Anybody after that was a PolyGram company. I was the first Vice President of Urban Promotion at Zoo Entertainment, and I was the first Vice President of Urban Promotions at Hollywood Records, which was owned by the Walt Disney Company. We did a lot of work with different labels and assisted them, like Jive Records with stuff on the soundtrack for *Sister Act II*. I worked some of the *Lion King* stuff with them, *Pocahontas*, *Low Down Dirty Shame*, stuff like that. We did a lot of assisting and co-promoting with major labels. Then after two years, they wanted to pick up my option. I really looked at myself and I said, *"I don't have any Black artists signed to this company. I don't really see a firm commitment to Black music here. What I'm doing is very comfortable, and I could just continue to coast along, which is how I become the facilitator of Disney's world passage for Black radio in America."*

I was hooking people up, I'm coming down to Orlando, I'm coming to LA, and I'd get them their tickets and they were happy. I was the hook up, but it just wasn't a career move. At that time in 1995, they split the format between R&R and Billboard. Instead of just having an Urban division, because of Hip-Hop they created Urban and Urban AC. I saw Urban AC as an opportunity. There were only about 27 reporters, and I started working it. I went from a nice big office to a cubical, but I was making more money. So I was happy with that. I started the Jesus Garber Company, and I've been working that for 18 years now.

How have you seen the industry change?

Jesus Garber:

Here's the thing, I'm going to first start with my example of change and progress. I would go to a lot of conventions early on in the '70s and '80s. We had Jack the Rapper, BRE (Sidney Miller), the Gavin... it was like an average of seven to eight conventions that you had to attend annually. They were fun, and you saw a lot of people. I also saw it to be efficient because instead of traveling around the whole country, at the conventions in two or three days you're seeing everybody, and that was great. I used to call them forced vacations. Even though I was young—in my 20s—I would hear folks who were like in their 50s talk about their good old days, and how they wish that certain things would be like they used to be. They used to be more fun. I took note of that, and then I experienced that.

The only thing I could compare progress to is this. When living here in Los Angeles with my parents, it was five of us kids. The seven of us would go downtown on Broadway because there were no shopping malls anywhere, and that was the only place you could buy your clothes. So that's where we would buy our clothes for school and stuff. You had stores like the Broadway, May Company, and Bullocks, and so on and so forth. They had elevator operators. The elevator operator would wait for you to get in, and he would announce what was on that floor. All of a sudden automation came along, and it replaced the elevator operators. I have not seen any elevator operators come back. So I said to myself, *"Wow, from a business point of view—a progress point of view—once you go to the next level, I don't see any owner of any big building on the planet saying, 'I'm looking at the news and I'm looking at the plight of unemployment, and you know what, I'm really sick of this. I want to do something about it. I'm going to rip out all the computers out of my elevators, and I'm going to hire 40 people to operate our elevators. That's not going to happen."*

That is the big example that I have in my lifetime of progress. The reality is to look at what is today and what opportunities there are. The beautiful thing is that God illuminates and gives you discernment of where you should go. Fast forward to today, I think the music business is thriving more than ever. The reality is, it's really in the content. Who owns the content? Let me give you a great example. In 2012, Universal Music, which is owned by the French company called Vivendi, bought EMI Capitol. They would have not been allowed to do so if the industry was in such a destitute manner, and making no money knowing that it would hurt the core business of Universal. They thought that it would enhance the overall business by acquiring EMI Capitol.

That was very transparent, very telling, and very definitive in illuminating the story about where the business is today. The business today is all about publishing. It's about ownership of songs; its ownership of product, that's what it's all about. That's why people like Logan Westbrooks were incredibly successful. That's why guys like Clarence Avant are still successful today, because he got the publishing on music by Alexander O'Neal, Cherrelle and Bill Withers. He's got publishing, so even today he's making money. So are there opportunities? Yes. The record business is a little close to the vest about how you can become successful, because they had a huge attack some 15 years ago or so. And people said, "You know, we don't need to go and rent a professional recording studio. We can go buy Pro Tools for about 35 hundred bucks, and we could do a whole album. Instead of spending a half million dollars, I could give you a whole album for maybe about 20 thousand dollars." There were all these attacks on the industry. Then with file sharing and Napster, what happened was people were literally stealing. It's just like if you had a record shop, at the end of the day you close the shop, but through the Internet, somebody came in through the backdoor and just picked whatever they wanted. It's like they just robbed, raped, and pillaged your industry. That's what they did.

The problem is this. They had an old guard that had very closed minds that didn't want to embrace the Internet. They tried to do everything to shut it down, and it isn't going to be shut down. There used to be a time when record guys would load up a car and station wagon full of singles and they would be on the road for 6 to 12 weeks. Everywhere they saw a transmitter antenna, they dropped off a record.

At this point, I have to quote a gentleman named Dave Clark. He was one of the first African American promotion guys. I remember asking him in the early '80s at a Jack the Rapper Convention* in Atlanta, "What can a guy like you, who has experienced so much in this industry, share with a guy like me that I could take into the future without taking too much of your time?" He said to me, "If you don't change with the times, you get left behind."

It's very interesting, because I saw the evolution of phones. Some people didn't want to have a cell phone. Then I saw fax machines, and some people didn't want to be bothered with that. Then all of a sudden email came along, some people didn't want to be bothered with that, and you know what? You've got to be current with everything that is available. You have to be current. Would I say that Facebook, Twitter and all these social media outlets today aren't extremely important in commerce? I would say—not because the basic premise of those media instruments are social and gathering friends and all that—by the end of the day, I don't see them relevant and effective to selling stuff.

Say for instance, take Myspace. Myspace was a craze ten years ago. Everybody had a Myspace page. But at the end of the day—look at it this way—from a business point of view, if you had five million people on the planet hear it domestically by clicking on or checking on your page and see you jamming your song in your garage, your living room or your bedroom, they all leave you five stars or thumbs up or whatever the thing is, but not one of them called the radio station and requested that song; or say I heard this and you've got to play this; or was so inspired to say, "Look, how can I help you?" So it becomes pointless. You are what they used to call the 'barker,' but on the Internet. At the end of the day, business is about transactions. So if it doesn't help your sales, it doesn't matter. That's why Myspace doesn't mean anything today. At the end of the day, you've got to think about the people that built this business.

From the beginning of my corporate career to the end, Berry Gordy said, "It's all about the song, period." I recall Jeffrey Katzenberg saying that it doesn't matter if you are selling shoes, houses, cars, or some other product. It's all about the product. People will go out and make a great record, but they are unprepared to go spend the money to go get the record on the radio. I've seen very accomplished people that have a lot of money that would say, "Well, I just spent $100,000 or $200,000 on this record. I think it's great. I could just mail it to the radio stations, and just because of this artist's name, they'll hear it and they will want to play it. It just doesn't work that way. You have got to be represented by the right people that have the relationships and credibility to make sure that your goal is happening or achieved.

How do artists or Indie labels get to people like you?

Jesus Garber:
First of all, I am available through the Internet. All you've got to do is Google me. But, here is the one thing of wisdom that I would say to all aspiring artists. Even though they can Google the radio station, and call the radio station, and find out who the program director is, there is a certain way that business is done in this industry. When you go outside of your comfort zone, there is one thing that this industry has always been about—the one thing they are going to ask is, "Who speaks for you?" That means who in our industry, our circle, our trust, our confidence, speaks for you? If you are not in that inner circle of knowing these people, or you don't have a reputation of history, they're just going to say, "Hmm, that sounds nice, and we are going to wait and see." Then years go by, nothing happens and 'wait and see' is a polite way of saying "No."

I love the great Walt Disney quote that says: "You can dream the most wonderful dreams, and have the greatest ideas, but you need people to make them happen." I would say to any artist that you can make it happen, but you need a team around you. You need a manager, you need a lawyer, you need an agent, you need those kinds of people that are really going to positively affect the growth of your career.

Contact:
jesus@thejesusgarbercompany.com

*The Jack "The Rapper" Convention was not a Rap convention, but it was a major industry convention started by the late Joseph Deighton "Jack" Gibson, Jr., whose radio name was "The Rapper" because of the rhythmic and eloquent manner in which he commanded the microphone. In 1949 Jack Gibson assisted in launching the first African American owned radio station in the United States—station WERD—in Atlanta, Georgia.

Dr. Westbrooks:

Jesus Garber speaks on publishing. Owning your music is one of the upsides of this business. If you own the copyright, this means the money comes directly to you through several ways, primarily through mechanical, synchronization, performance, and print rights. If you choose to start your own publishing company, you will probably need help to oversee worldwide tracking of your music. If you consider signing with a publishing company, get involved only with a reputable publisher. If a writer or artist decides to take the Indie route, you will still need a team. Having a good team or a good network will free you up to continue the creative process.

CHAPTER TWENTY

CLIFFORD RUSSELL

**CEO of CR Promotions, Marketing & Media—
Former Marketing Executive with Arista,
Columbia, Epic, CBS, Sony Music**

"The music industry is a very creative industry. Those that are inspired by really making an impact should just go out there and shine. Do your best, be the best that you can be, and deliver the best that you are."

Clifford Russell has assisted in marketing campaigns at major labels such as Arista, Columbia, Epic, CBS, Sony Music and more. He has worked with artists such as Gil Scott-Heron, Dionne Warwick, Ray Parker, Jr., Phyllis Hyman, Angela Bofill, and the King of Pop Michael Jackson. Clifford and his marketing team opened the Michael Jackson BAD tour in Kansas City in 1987. It was the highest grossing tour of the year with 123 performances in 15 countries. He continued to work with the Jacksons through their three releases on the Epic label and for five solo releases by Michael Jackson. Currently, Clifford Russell oversees the day-to-day operation at CR Promotions, Marketing & Media—a full service agency he founded in 2010 that specializes in devising regional and national campaigns targeting all aspects of the urban lifestyle.

How long have you been in the music business?

Clifford Russell:
I got started in college in Chicago in 1981. My first job started at ground level. I was one of the very few that came up through the industry during that time, and I kind of went through the ranks. At that time, the business wasn't about what you knew, but who you knew. So individuals that moved around during that era in the late '70s early '80s were all about, "Hey, I want to work in the record industry, put me in this position. I need to work here, there, and the other." I got started at the ground level, which was at one of the one stops in Chicago—Sanders

One Stop. There were 5 One Stops that pretty much controlled all of the distribution of music in the Midwest.

Describe a One Stop.

Clifford Russell:

A One Stop is a distribution company that distributes music to the smaller mom & pop retail stores throughout the various cities. The product would be shipped from the major labels to the One Stops, and the One Stops were responsible for getting it out to the market via the small independent mom & pop stores. Mom & pops stores were small retail stores whose purpose was to sell music. They were located just about everywhere. At that time these corner stores were all over the place, especially around high schools and colleges. That was the responsibility of the One Stops. It was almost like a distributor point for music. So I got started at Sanders One Stop. What interested me was, I have a brother in the business named Carter Russell and he managed artists back in the day at his own record label. He ran an independent label, and I was responsible for making sure that the records were put in his trunk so that he could promote these artists through the Chicago area. Records back then were vinyl LPs and 45s. He introduced me to Runa Sanders, the owner of Sanders One Stop, and he brought me in to be able to sell music.

Not only was it a distribution outlet, it was also a retail store. The distribution stores kind of had more of like a handle, because they would get the music first. Anything new that was coming out obviously was at that distributor's location. So, Runa brought me in, and I ran one of his stores on 79th Street in Chicago. He owned two locations, one was retail and another one was a retail distribution store. I worked for Sanders for about a year or so, and I'd seen a lot of these record reps come in promoting their artists, and obviously they were like sales guys.

They would come in and pitch the distributors about what was really hot and coming out, and who was playing the record and why they needed to stock it and buy in on those releases. I was seeing all of these record reps coming in, and I thought, *"Oh wow, that looks really cool."* They'd come in any time of day. They would lollygag around and they had a really great job position that included dining out or bringing in lunch. I thought, *"Oh, wow, I want to do that. I want to be like that."*

At that time, Arista was part of that independent distribution. I was on my way to graduate out of Columbia College. I was in my last year majoring in advertising and marketing, with a sub-major in graphic design. After working about a year with Runa, one of the industry reps,

John Hall, Jr., said, "Why don't you come in and work with me? It will give you a chance to see how the business is run and kind of give you an insight on the record business." I said, "Oh great, that's what I've been wanting to do." At that point, I started out working with Arista Records/ MS Distributors. MS had a lot of various labels that they distributed, but Arista was the biggest of all. John brought me in working for Arista, and I interned while I was finishing my last year at Columbia College.

I was working in merchandising the retail stores, and it was my responsibility to bring awareness to new releases from Arista Records. That meant being as creative as possible and going into retail stores and putting up the point of purchase displays. All of the displays that you see at the retail stores, on the walls, counter top displays, and everywhere else is so that when you would go in you were like, "Oh, wow, I like that; I want that; that's who I want to get." It was like an eye contact that informed the record buyer that a new release was out, who it was by, and that it was available. All of the graphics, looks, and all of the ambience kind of went with being able to educate and bring awareness to that artist from a consumer standpoint. At that time, I was working with Gil Scott-Heron, and Ray Parker, Jr. had the *Ghostbusters* soundtrack, which was one of the biggest soundtracks during that era through Arista Records.

We had Dionne Warwick. We were also working projects by Phyllis Hyman and Angela Bofill. All in all, we had a kind of eclectic variety of music and artists that Arista represented. After Arista, I really got experienced in terms of how music is actually distributed and sold once it leaves the warehouse, where it goes from that point all the way down to getting it into the hands of the consumer, which is obviously the bottom line.

After I graduated, there were about three labels out there that I had pinpointed if I was going to continue to be in the record business. These were the labels that I wanted to work with. They were the biggest labels. One of them was Sony, at that time it was CBS Records. There was Warner Brothers, and then there was RCA Music Group.

All of the other label reps knew who was out there and doing extremely well in terms of merchandising and making a career in the music business. After that, another friend, Frank Chaplin, who was with Columbia Records at that time, said, "Cliff, would you like to cover this position? It's going to open in merchandising."

That's the same thing that I was doing with Arista, but it was with a bigger company and with bigger artists. Obviously, that was one of the labels I really wanted to be with. It was the top label. It was the number one record company during that time. They had everyone from the best of Jazz, to the best of R&B, with everyone from Earth Wind & Fire, the Isley Brothers (on the T-Neck label), the O'Jays, Billy Paul, and

Harold Melvin & the Blue Notes (all from the Philly International label). There were various labels under the Columbia spectrum, and they were very, very successful with all of their major artists.

I decided to leave Arista as an intern and work full time with Columbia. CBS was built on two labels, Columbia and Epic. Both kind of operated solely on their own, but it was all under one umbrella, which was the parent company CBS Records. At the time, I was on my way to graduating. I was about four months out. I sat down with Lou Mann, who was very instrumental in hiring me to be full time at CBS. I sat down and said, "I have three months before I graduate, so I can come in and work part time if you would allow me to until I actually graduate. Afterwards, I would dedicate my full time hours in the position."

They allowed me to do that, which was pretty much unheard of, to hire someone and let them work part time on a full-time salary. So I started off doing the same thing. I was merchandising retail stores, and the interesting point with CBS is that when I was working with Arista, many of those products came through CBS, because I didn't just work R&B. I worked Jazz, Classical, I worked Country, and I worked Pop. I worked all of the retail locations throughout Chicago. I worked the Northside stores from Rose Records to the neighborhood stores on the Southside of Chicago. There were no boundaries, and I had the chance to go in to be really creative because all of the tools were available for me. The best of the tools were available because CBS spared no expense. They spent money insuring that the artists were as visible as possible to the consumer, because that made a big awareness point, and obviously that would translate into sales. That was my responsibility, I did that for six or seven years. After that, I really made some huge accomplishments. Every year I would receive awards like the 'Merchandiser of the Year' or the 'Account Executive of the Year,' because after we left the field as merchandisers, we put another spin on the title. They made us Account Executives, but basically it was kind of the same role that we played.

What is the timeline of the history of your story?

Clifford Russell:
We're up to the mid '80s as of now. And 1987 was an incredible year because at that time, music, and in particular R&B, was THE genre of music. It was just what was happening, particularly in the Chicago market. Chicago was still considered a strong break out market. When I say break out that means that artists got 'broke' (cracked the surface of their career). I hadn't made it to L.A. I was still in Chicago during that

time. After I left merchandising, I went into promotions for Epic. It was still under the CBS banner, which had a name change to Sony Music.

The Japanese came in and bought CBS and changed the name to Sony Music, which it is today. Sony had all the labels—Columbia and then the Epic label. I then worked for the Epic label, and I got hired to do promotions for the various radio stations in the Midwest. My responsibility was to get records on the radio stations, and to get records played on the air by all means. At that time labels were selling music incredibly well, and the distribution points were really, really heavy. When a release would come out, it was a whole trickle-down effect. If it was hot, it would get on the air, it would sell, someone would buy it, and it would just keep a whole bubbling effect.

Give an example of the schematics for marketing or 'breaking' an artist.

Clifford Russell:

Not to take away from today's online elements and social media promotions, but the number one promotion vehicle to break an artist was radio. It was the quickest and fastest way to determine whether you had a record that was a hit, or if you had a record that was mediocre and just needed some additional time to develop, or if you had a record that was just not in the mix.

A typical promotional meeting would be to canvas the country. There were eight reps. We would canvas to find out where a record was breaking out. You had the Midwest. You had the South, Southwest, you got the East Coast, mid-Central. You had all these regions. We would identify the best region that we felt had the best potential to break an artist. Whether it was based on the artist having some type of history or exposure, or where they grew up and got their career started from an artist stand point. Those were all of the elements we used to determine where we would go to break an artist.

Once we identified that, we put as much momentum into that region to start penetrating airplay exposure, and doing things with the artist from the ground up in terms of promotional tours, getting them out on the road, and getting them into radio stations doing on-air interviews to bring awareness to them. Once we started getting a bite (we called it a bite like a fish with bait), we started seeing some reaction. At that point, we feel we have something we can take to other surrounding markets. It's like a signal. We started right in the middle, and then eventually we went a bit outside of the radius, and then it would just become a trickle effect.

What books are you currently reading?

Clifford Russell:
I'm reading a book on artist management and booking, as in the concert booking of artists. That's a key that a lot of artists are not aware of in terms of booking. They should know what their royalties should be, how it's all laid out, and what is important about making money from touring. The book is *How to Be Your Own Booking Agency: The Musician's and Performing Artist's Guide to Successful Touring* by Jeri Goldstein (The New Music Times, Inc. Palmyra, VA 2008).

I'm reading that, and also the 2nd Edition of *Start and Run Your Own Record Label* by Daylle Deanna Schwartz (Billboard Books, New York, NY 2003). It gives more winning marketing strategies for today's music industry. A lot of the times we're always looking at new and fresh ways. Although I have had a lot of experience in the record business, obviously there are a lot of things that I want to be able to stay abreast of and to be able to utilize those techniques to help my company see our marketing, media and promotions grow.

What advice do you have for newcomers?

Clifford Russell:
I would truly have to say believe in yourself. Believe that what you have is the best coming from you, and then compete with what's out there. It's really about being able to promote it. Promote yourself in the best way possible using all of the elements you are exposed to. I'm a very strong believer of that. It may be old school, but it's just the way I came up.

Performance is also one of the key elements of developing and breaking an artist. Today, lots of bands are what we call broken into the industry and developed, based on them constantly going out and touring and doing club sets. Every week, every day they're some place where they can be exposed to the consumer and be seen by a possible fan. You just have to continue to develop that momentum. Several individuals are going to like you and follow you wherever you may go. Not only that, then they're spreading the word—word of mouth, particularly today, is very key. You can Tweet it out, you can Facebook it out, or you can Instagram the pictures.

There are so many other elements to build your base. Or someone can build it for you based on them just coming out and seeing you perform and loving what they saw. They then go on and spread it to their thousands and thousands of fans urging them to go out and get this

CD or download because they feel it's incredible. That's pretty much where it is. To be really successful in it to the point where you've got a base and something that warrants the attention and exposure to the masses, you have to take it to that level.

Tell us about your new company.

Clifford Russell:
I decided to develop a company about three and a half years ago. I'd always done independent promotions because I have a love for music, and I have a love for artists that really want to get their music out to the masses by not going through the normal record label BS. So I developed my company CR Promotions Marketing & Media. It's a promotions and marketing company and a kind of boutique agency where I take an artist, or new artist that really wants an edge on getting out of the bubble of the whole social media medium role. I take them to radio and really get them exposed and seen and heard on that level.

My company features, or specializes, in new artist development. It's for artists that really feel they have a very unique style and sound, and they really want to get it heard by the masses. I help them sort out the various promotional strategies and markets, where they want to go and what they would like to do. Do they want to tour in that market? Then let's get them touring. Then let's get them into that market. Let's get some radio and Internet exposure. Let's see how we can get more performances, and then we start working from that. It's really traditional. It's the way I grew up in terms of breaking an artist. It hasn't changed. People, or companies in particular, have just kind of gotten away from really taking the traditional role and developing their career. What I do is go back to that traditional role and help them to get exposed.

What would you say is the greatest thing about your experience in the music industry?

Clifford Russell:
My greatest experience was when I opened the Michael Jackson BAD tour in Kansas City. That was in 1987 and 1988. Kansas City was the first market to kick off the Bad tour. That was my market, and I was obviously very excited to open and close the tour after taking a relocation move with Epic to Los Angeles. It was in 1989 when Michael closed his Bad tour in L.A. at the Forum. I had the opportunity of working several markets with Michael, but never had the opportunity to get a picture with

him because he was just not taking any photos with staff. But, on the last day of his tour, he said you all have worked so hard for me and so hard with me during this tour, I want to take this time out to take a picture. He took a picture with me one on one. Me and Michael, and I didn't ever think I would get it. Michael had the pictures framed and signed and sent directly to each individual that was on the set of the last night of the BAD tour in LA.

I worked with the King of Pop, I worked with the Jacksons through their three releases of the Jacksons on the Epic label and worked four or five releases for Michael. So I have seen the best of marketing campaigns. I've seen the best of marketing plans from a superstar's stand point. That was the ultimate. The music industry is a very creative industry. Those that are inspired by really making an impact, should just go out there and shine. Do your best, be the best that you can, and deliver the best that you are.

Contact:
www.crpromotionsMarketingMedia.com
Clifford@crpromotionsmarketingmedia.com

Dr. Westbrooks:
Clifford Russell describes how he moved around and rose up through the ranks, learning the business along the way. He had stints at several major labels and worked different genres, including R&B, Jazz, Classical, Country and Pop. The method and speed of breaking a record or artist has changed dramatically. You no longer have to drive around the country delivering physical products. The Internet eliminated the need for all that travel. And though it is also in transition, terrestrial radio—traditional radio—is still king in terms of getting music heard. As of right now, that is still the destination where artists aspire to be.

CHAPTER TWENTY-ONE

MICHAEL NIXON

President of N5 Marketing—
Expert in Street Team Promotions

"New artists and whoever is in the business, you really have to build up your own universe."

Michael Nixon's roadmap into the music industry is by way of Harlem, New York. He journeyed to Howard University, and in the early days of WHUR he was Manager of Business and Fiscal Affairs. Michael was intrigued by local record promoters who came to the station, so he moved to Los Angeles. After a stint with KJLH, he was on to Warner Brothers, Electra, and Atlantic Records and revolutionized street team promotions in Northern California and beyond. He helped strategize early campaigns for Prince, Bootsy Collins, Rose Royce and a who's who of Rap and Hip Hop stars. Michael created Rap Sheet, the world's first Hip Hop newspaper, and he was instrumental in forming the first Rap charts in major industry trade publications such as The Gavin and Billboard. Michael Nixon is currently the CEO of his own company N5 Marketing. His quest as a scholar of accounting, economics and marketing at Howard University in Washington, D.C., set the course for his career in the music industry.

Michael Nixon:
I'm from New York, Harlem, uptown 126th St. and Broadway. I went to an all-boys Catholic school in Harlem. I also went to Howard University. I worked for WHUR when it first started as the manager of Business and Fiscal Affairs. WHUR 96.3 began as a Broadcast Communications Lab. It was 1971 when it first signed on under the guidance of Tony Brown and a guy named Phil Watson. He somehow convinced the university to switch the station around with a commercial license. They agreed, and it burst out Black music as we know it now. It was the first 360 degree Black experience on FM radio. Black radio was always on AM—WOL, WOOK. WHUR birthed the Quiet Storm format with Melvin Lindsey. Deana Williams, Michelle Eldridge, Milton Allen and people from radio and from records came into play there.

I was Manager of Business and Fiscal Affairs because I had degrees in Accounting, Economics and Marketing. I trained myself to become a sales person underneath Cathy Hughes, who was Cathy Liggins at the time. She was a Sales Manager, and I became a sales person who started selling the station and making lots of money because we were a conceptual station. After our first Arbitron® rating book, we burst into a 42 market station at number five all of a sudden. So the advertising agencies that we were calling on all manifested into money.

Nonetheless, how I really got my start as it relates to the record industry was through a guy named Vernon Slaughter. He was a college rep at CBS Records. This was around the time when Logan Westbrooks was doing his thing. As a matter of fact, I think this guy might have worked for Logan. Vernon is a lawyer now.* He would come by and bring records to the station and have tickets to the concerts and t-shirts, and I said, "Dude, what is that about? How can you give away stuff for free?" He said, "It's my job!" I said, "What? That's a job? To do record promotions and come to radio stations and give away records and promote? That's what I want to do!"

As a result, I left my job at WHUR in Washington, D.C., to train for the Olympic Games in 1976 as an excuse to move out to California. I had never been to California, and I moved out there and trained for the Games. I made it to the trials and missed the Olympics by four places, but then started competing at the Montreal Games. I ran the 800 meters.

I also started working at Stevie Wonder's radio station KJLH 102.3 FM back in 1976 with the job experience I had gained at WHUR. I was working with guys like Ron McGrew and another DJ named Frankie Ross. Stevie had just gotten the station. I also somehow got an interview with a Warner Brothers sales person. They moved me to San Francisco to be the first Black music marketing rep for Warner Brothers for WEA. WEA is a distribution chain consisting of Warner Brothers, Electra and Atlantic Records. This was a whole new stem because now we're getting into the Black music thing. The year was 1977.

I worked for Warner Brothers and for Electra and Atlantic, then Electra hired me as their Northern California representative. Working there, I had Prince's first retail in-store promotion. His first record had just come out in 1977 titled "Soft and Wet." It wasn't selling anywhere except in San Francisco. It was the disco era, and sales were popping up there. We brought him in from Minnesota. He had never done anything like that, and it was amazing. One of my friends had a Rolls Royce Phantom III, and we rolled around the Bay Area with Prince to about 16 stores. There was Tower Records, Bananas Records and all of those names that Prince had never heard of for the most part. This was doing street promotion back then before street promotions were popular. No one had ever brought in a Black artist (or actually a Pop artist), but we broke him as an R&B or urban artist. No one had ever done that in the streets of San Francisco—bringing an artist to those small Black-owned record shops. I mean local artists had done this, but nothing that was off of a major label.

Break down the mechanics of street promotions. You're taking product to record shops and clubs? Spell out what types of facilities you were hitting?

Michael Nixon:

I can break that down for you. As the first Black music marketing or merchandising rep, the main responsibilities were to service all of the independent Black retailers in the Northern California area such as Fresno, Sacramento, San Francisco, Oakland, San Jose, Santa Rosa, the surrounding areas and the Bay Area. There were about 40 or 50 of them, and no one had ever called upon them before. Some local artists would go around with their cassettes and 8-tracks (CDs had not quite hit the market yet). Major labels had not yet included these smaller retailers.

I would go around to all these Black record stores and introduce myself and put displays up of all of the Warner Brothers, Electra and Atlantic artists. They would have all of these posters, and banners, and t-shirts, and I would supply them and even have all of these displays on the outside of the stores, precluding all of these big records. I'd place all of the big 1x1's which was like three feet by three feet, or four feet by four feet foam posters. We'd put them up outside anywhere near the record store. The record store would keep them up until it became a city ordinance. All of the other record companies didn't have a rep up there. Warner spooked everybody, so I owned all of the stores with all of my products. There was no space for anyone else to put anything up, except for what I had up.

I had multiple artists; I had Rose Royce, whose first record was out. I had Bootsy Collins, Prince, the Spinners, the Temptations, Linda Clifford, and Donald Byrd. I had all of these campaigns from Warner, Electra and Atlantic.

I would not say that I invented the first 'wrapped' vehicle, but I utilized a 'wrapped' vehicle. What I did was, I acquired a milk truck for about $100. It had little panels on it. I spray painted it black and outlined it with the posters and kind of glued them onto the truck. At the time, the record companies where producing these big four feet by four feet foam poster boards, and I put them on each side of the truck and on the back. I put a big double "R" on the top, and I spray painted the wheels gold so it looked like a Rose Royce full boom truck. We rode it around all of San Francisco and this was like 1978. People were like, "What is this RR Rose Royce?" We'd give out posters and t-shirts from the truck, and my sales manager and all the staff would just marvel at me doing this, because no one had ever done this before.

We were servicing the streets with the new artists at that time. We had Bootsy Collins for an in-store promotion at a legendary music store in Berkeley called Leopold's. It was THE store for the late '60s and mid-1970s. I included Bootsy in my reference for a reason because it was a monumental in-store promotion that I created, but the label didn't want to have him in there. I knew how popular he was and how big he was, but the label didn't want him in there. Bootsy was from George Clinton and Parliament Funkadelic—right out of that camp. He was so out there and over the top. Google him and get your own picture, but trying to describe him does an injustice. Nonetheless, I don't know how I did this, but Circus Vargas was in town. I convinced them to have their black panther in the store with Bootsy, because the black panthers were big in Berkeley at the time. It was like "Bootsy Meets a Black Panther." By the time he got to the store, it was so crowded, they were rocking the limo so much that we could not even get out of the car. All the kids were like "We Want Boosty! We Want Bootsy!" The whole street was crowed, and we never even made it into the store. The fans are something else. It was so incredible. I became a hero after that.

It sounds like you were one of those early promoters who was able to connect the people who loved the music with the people who made the music, and extend their experience from just hearing them on the radio, or in seeing them in concert or occasionally on television. How did you transition from grassroots street promotion to your work in the music industry trade publications?

Michael Nixon:
That wasn't officially street promotion. It was street promotion in its infant and pre-natal stages. It was just my idea as to what had to happen because I was definitely just a record executive out in the streets. They (the record company that I worked for) were telling me that I should not be doing that, and I went totally against the grain on that. I was always on the outs with them because I wouldn't conform. After that, I moved back East to New York to work with RCA and Arista. That was about from 1980-84. Then I moved back to Los Angeles, and that's when I started working at BRE, Black Radio Exclusive magazine, which started in about 1976 and is still being published today. Sidney Miller

was the publisher. That's where I met Logan Westbrooks. I became one of the sales and account executives, and I got my awakening into the trade publication world. I worked at BRE and at R&B Report, which is the Rhythm and Blues Report. That was the publication with Graham Armstrong (Rest in Peace) and Tom Cozzy. They were the publishers at that time. They were in business from about 1983-86. I also worked with the Urban Network and The Gavin Report. This is the one that really put it all out there.

The Gavin was the trade publication in the music industry that reported charts like Billboard, but got more intrinsic into charting with Alternative music and Country, Jazz and Reggae. They tapped me to help this other guy Brian Sampson start a Rap chart back in 1990. He was the editor, and I was the marketing director for the new chart. I had to sell this chart to Urban or Black music divisions at record companies like MCA, Warner Brothers, Arista, Relativity Records, Island, Tommy Boy and Select Records. The Gavin Report was a publication that wasn't considered Urban at all. Every year in San Francisco was The Gavin music convention which happened in February at the famed St. Francis Hotel. It became legendary every year from Thursday to Sunday. This was like the perennial music industry conference for general markets for Pop and Rock that put radio and records together. That's what made it so large.

As we debuted this Rap chart, we were the only outlet for the whole Hip Hop music industry back in 1990 when it was just starting to happen. Our convention (The Gavin) was the place for them to come and showcase their artists, and to have workshops and panels on how Hip Hop or Rap music was being charted. We had workshops on the different ways to use lyrics or music publishing or just discussions about the Hip Hop or Rap industry in general. The Gavin was able to bring in the new Rap music directors from different radio stations who were starting to program all the radio stations with Hip Hop music. We debuted a lot of different major artists who were just hitting the scene such as NWA, Busta Rhymes, Kriss Kross, X Clan, Cypress Hill, and Ultra Magnetic. For a lot of these artists, this was the first time that they were able to perform on a major scale because there was no outlet like this before.

The Gavin convention moved to Atlanta, then to San Diego and then back to San Francisco before ending in 2000. I had left in 1993 to start a publication called Rap Sheet. It was the world's first Hip Hop newspaper; that's what we termed it. Then Rapper Easy E dubbed it The Recycler of Rap. (The Recycler is a local Los Angeles discount sales paper). I still have those Rap Sheet publications, too. A lot of good stuff is in there, a lot of old pictures. It was great. It was the whole beginning of Hip Hop and Rap into the music industry. We had to figure out how to chart it. The reason The Gavin got me to do the Rap chart was when Lee Bailey and Greg Johnson (of Radioscope, a nationally-syndicated program) and Atty. Rhonda Dixon did the Rap symposium. That kind of put us out there as experts to a large degree, and that's when The Gavin people called me to do that.

In 1993-94 the market started getting flooded with all of these regional Rap/Hip Hop publications. I started a Hip Hop/Rap advertising agency in lieu of all of this. I was the representative for about sixteen publications around the country. In L.A. there was one called "Kronick," and there was another one was called "Underground Free Style," and in San Diego there was one called "Straight From the Lip." There was one in San Francisco called "The Bomb," and another one called "Booty Crack" (It was crazy, you already know). There was one in Seattle called "The Flavor." There was one in Portland called "Illicit Rap." There was one out of Detroit called "Underground Connection" and one in D.C. called "Mad Rhythms." New York had "Around the Way Connections." That was with Star and Buckwild. They went on to become legendary stars in New York on KISS radio. There were all of these publications. There was one in Chicago and Phoenix. I had about 16 or 17 publications in the industry.

Since I knew everybody in the music industry on the Hip Hop side, I would go and consult record companies because they didn't know how to market or advertise this record. They were like, "What do we do with them? We can't just put them in Billboard." It was all new; it wasn't traditional. So they'd adhere to my advice and place ads in publications that I recommended. I would get my commission from publications. That was when Hip Hop was blowing up and taking over. Now the promotion reps at record companies were like, "Yo, we need to hit these publications."

I was getting all of these ads, but not always the commission that came with it, because after a while the record companies began going directly to the publications. Then Billboard hired me as the first Black Account Executive. Terri Rossi was the R&B editor at Billboard, and she was very much a maverick. There were Black people working at Billboard at the time, but they were selling classified advertising and classified ads were based out of New York. She positioned it and they hired me.

As a way to get back at her and to show that racism was present, they did not give me the R&B charts to sell. By that I mean I wasn't able to get ads from the record companies for placement on the more popular pages, which were the pages with the R&B and Rap Charts, because that's what I had been trained to do and had been doing for the past five or six years. They gave me the Karaoke category, Latin, directory and music publisher, laser discs, and a couple of other categories to sell. But, instead of complaining, I decided that I would get to learn about all of this new stuff. I went straight to task with it.

What do you mean by giving you Karaoke to sell?

Michael Nixon:
They were trying to make that a category or genre in the music industry. Remember those laser discs? They were trying to make that a category also. It was short lived. There was also that mini-CD. That was another form of music that failed.

For our readers, will you clarify what you mean when you say that Billboard wanted to give you these categories to sell? Does this mean that you were to sell advertising to interest customers in buying Karaoke tracks?

Michael Nixon:
In Billboard you had different sections and different charts. You got an international section, an R&B section and so forth, and they also have different business sections. They have a music publishing section, they have a Reggae and Latin section, and back at that time the Latin Grammys hadn't even been invented yet. That's how small that category was. By this, I mean the Latin market. So I would have to go and entice different clients or Karaoke dealers and let people know where they could get their hardware, or where they could get their Karaoke machines and what the Karaoke machine was all about, and which one was better than the next one so that they could publicize and create visibility for their product. Billboard was trying to create a whole Karaoke scene or genre, and, as you know, it became a whole offshoot type thing like it is now. Laser discs failed miserably; so did mini discs.

Music publishing is a category or section of the music industry that you really have to be involved with, or have a record out, or be a songwriter and then you go through the whole processing. Unless you do that, you really don't understand what's going on. It's a real hands on and intrinsic category. I got to learn a lot because I was able to go and sit with the Leiber/Stollers (songwriting team Jerry Leiber & Mike Stoller who wrote Jailhouse Rock & Hound Dog for Elvis Presley), and the Warner Chappell people. At that time, Big Jon (referring to Jon Platt, now President of North America division Warner Chappell), I don't even think that he was working in publishing yet. He was just promoted to president of Warner Chappell. Big Jon was a promoter who has been in publishing for the last ten or fifteen years. I was at Billboard for a year, and it was crazy because the executives and even my clients all tried to plot against me.

You evolved from radio, to marketing on the streets, promoting Rap, and into ad/sales at Billboard. So then what happened?

Michael Nixon:
I left Billboard after one year. That was 1994, and I started my company N5 Marketing. It started as a consultancy to those Rap publications that I previously mentioned. I saw this one kid Ron Hill passing out cassette tapes to people in the clubs, and it jarred me because this is what I used to do at the record company. This is what was happening then. It brought everything back home for me. I knew all of the record companies and wound up being everybody's street team for every label. At one point I was working for like 30 or 32 companies.

What does all of this mean for the present day artist? We have digital media at our disposal. There is a lot of ambition out there, but there is a lot of ignorance about what it really takes. You have degrees in Business Administration, Marketing and Economics, with a minor in Accounting from Howard University. You also have a Master of Arts in Communication Management. What about young rappers today who expect to become overnight sensations in today's music game who believe that education is optional? During your high point, you not only promoted artists, but you worked for companies who had the budget to create enough product for you to use as promotional giveaways. What about artists today who don't have the budget or the extra products to give away for promotion?

Michael Nixon:
I don't even know how they do it, especially for a brand new artist. It's such a crap shoot. There is an artist named Slauson Boy. He's been around for over ten years easy. He's blowing up now, but he's been grinding the streets. He's like a Snoop Dogg clone. He's broken out of that now, but that's what put him on the map, and he's finally selling lots of records. He's been doing some schemes that you do with Internet and Facebook, and doing some pop up shops. By that I mean he talks to his audience on Twitter or to his Facebook universe only, and he tells his

fans where he's going to be for a short time, and he pops up and sells product that way.

People just love that type of thing. He's got a bunch of Twitter and Facebook followers and people show up and it becomes this whole little event with that type of interaction with their own personal universe. What is happening in lieu of that is that my lifestyle marketing and street team promotion business has hit the crap about 90 percent because of all of this. So if you're not doing Facebook or Instagram or Twitter, then you're not with it. In lieu of all of that, new artists and whoever is in the business, you really have to build up your own universe.

When you're out in the streets or performing in clubs, you have to get your fans' information and pass out your information or have your people giving out your card, or passing out a piece of music on a jump drive and they'll start to like you on Facebook or follow you on Twitter. This type of advertising, or connection, or universal appeal is the most direct connection because it's not really happening on radio unless you're a Jay Z or a Beyoncé or an artist like Eminem. It's not equating any more on radio. It doesn't matter what station that you listen to now. They are not playing anything unless it's a big proven hit. For anything that's new, there is still room for it. There is only a certain amount of time in the day. For most major stations it's not the way it was, it's just all consultant driven now (meaning they play what consultants approve of as hits). The last thing you want to do is newspaper advertising because they hardly exit any more. The whole model is just so different. The only time now I can get a call on something for street promotions is for something that is not music related. Anything music related is straight digital, it's straight mobile and that is what it is.

How do you plan to archive all of your Rap and Hip Hop publications?

Michael Nixon:
Per Logan, I have been in touch with Portia Maultsby at Indiana University, which has one of the biggest Black music archives in the world. They want to create a Michael Nixon collection. There is nothing on the information superhighway about these publications, so I am in the process of creating some type of exhibit or communications program.

Contact:
www.N5Marketing.com

Dr. Westbrooks:

Early street promotion required a creative mind, a certain kind of gravitas, and a flair for the dramatic. Michael Nixon possessed all three of these, and that's why he was so successful. Technology and changing times decreased his business and bottom line because artists were now able to do a lot of grassroots promotion for themselves. Today Internet radio has shown to be an easier path to airplay for Indie artists with many of them bypassing terrestrial radio altogether. There are now many free and/or affordable powerhouses of promotion that are popular among Indie artists, among them Bandcamp, Reverbnation, Facebook, Twitter, Instagram, and several other social media outlets. This ability to self-promote by Indie artists has decreased and even eliminated work that was once outsourced to independent promoters.

*Vernon Slaughter passed away on April 22, 2014.

THE DIGITAL MUSIC & MEDIA EXPERTS

INFORMED SOURCES

Marc Brogdon
Greg Coakley
Gregory Savage, Jr.

CHAPTER TWENTY-TWO

MARC BROGDON

CEO of N2U Creative Marketing Group

"It's crucial for fan engagement that you touch me and we have some degree of a social relationship beyond just a static image on a magazine or a billboard or traditional media that we used to share."

Marc Brogdon attended Michigan State University before going on to the prestigious University of Stockholm in Stockholm, Sweden, to study International and Global Marketing. Marc has served as a Chief Marketing Officer, Senior V. P. of Marketing, and marketing executive for brands such as Saturn, The Disney Channel, Disney ABC Cable Networks, VH1, The Walt Disney Company, Motorola and Hyundai.

It seems like in today's world, it is an absolute necessity for musicians to be tech savvy. Why is this so important?

Marc Brogdon:
The channels of distribution of music has certainly changed over the past 15 years. Although music is still a profitable tool, the revenue streams have changed. Labels and artists are, in some instances, giving away the product with hopes that they can aggregate a large audience of people who would want to participate in seeing them perform live. Or, to do what we look at as crowd promotion, which can be done through social media technology like Facebook, Twitter and all the different platforms that allow for people to become ambassadors of your music. The end goal is to drive traffic to hopefully purchase a download, encourage purchase of a ticket to a live performance, or to create a licensing opportunity for film and/or television.

How important is it for artists today to be more versatile in their thinking when it comes to marketing? You also talked about artist fan engagement and the importance of engaging both your digital audience and your terrestrial audience as well. Can you elaborate on this?

Marc Brogdon:
I think that any artist today that does not participate in digital marketing will probably have a hard time really selling any product or communicating to a fan base, because right now our attention spans are limited. We look for quick hits, we look to be connected to everything from that artist, and that artist has to communicate to us electronically. Back in the day we had devices that were for a specific service. That device may have been a cell phone that you talk on or a camera that took pictures. You had a pager that took texts. We are now the Internet of everything, which means I can have one device (that being my smart phone, or my tablet or my laptop) that does all those things engaged in one location. So as an artist, I have the potential to communicate with you everywhere you go through devices. If I don't talk to you via all the opportunities I have available to me, then I've become less relevant than an artist who has touched me on Twitter, or my cell phone, or who has sent me a viral video through YouTube that I watched on my tablet. It's crucial for fan engagement that you touch me and we have some degree of a social relationship beyond just a static image in a magazine or a billboard or traditional media that we used to share. Digital is really becoming the number one form of communication and engagement with the fans.

How did you get into the industry and what inspires you most about it?

Marc Brogdon:
I am a kid from Detroit, Michigan, which you know is (as of 2013) in bankruptcy, and the reason that's important is because we have resilience, we bounce back. We fight hard and if we need to press restart, we do whatever we need to do to come out on top. I'm taking that same attitude with my professional life as well.

I left Michigan in 1987 after graduating from Michigan State University and went to the prestigious University of Stockholm in Stockholm, Sweden, to study International and Global Marketing. On my return to the states, I began working for Carlson Resource Group, which had just launched Saturn, a new car company. I came out here as the first Product Specialist and Marketing Specialist for Saturn Automotive. What an amazing experience it was for the first new all American car company in 65 years. To be a part of that launch set the groundwork for my understanding of how to launch products.

Launching products became the hallmark of my career because when I left Saturn, I went to Disney. I left Saturn to work as the Senior Executive at the Disney Channel—Disney ABC Cable Networks as it's referred to now. With Disney, I was a Senior Marketing Executive, and I worked on the distribution strategies and repositioning for Disney Channel, Soap Net, Toon Disney, and the eventual acquisition of and retransmission of ABC Networks. For almost ten years, I worked almost every aspect of marketing with the Disney Channel.

Leaving the Disney Channel, I went to work in eCommerce for Dunk.Net, a business owned by NBA superstar Shaquille O'Neal. As Senior Vice President of Dunk.Net, which some might remember, we were early adopters of eCommerce and Shaq's answer to creating his own branded line of apparel and footwear that was sold exclusively online. When he left his deal with Rebook, he wanted to figure out a way to use technology to benefit sales of his brand of merchandise, which he referred to as Dunk.net.

I learned a lot during that time of eCommerce and the Internet, and it was an amazing experience. With all that I had learned from consumer marketing, to automotive marketing, to entertainment and now eCommerce and the Internet, I felt it was the perfect time to hang my own shingle and start my own company, which is the letter "N2U Creative Marketing Group." We are a full service marketing agency. Our goal was to create amazing experiential programs to touch consumers in a 360° fashion.

We did product integration for VH1 while we produced. We created the first Motorola Phat Farm and Baby Phat Cell Phone. It was among the first ever targeted urban community phone, and it was the highest grossing product to that date for co-branded phones under Motorola and Nextel. We launched a fully televised music series for Entertainment Tonight "Live from The Grove" (a Los Angeles open court mall in the popular Fairfax district). We helped build what we now know as The Grove Live Music Series, which was the launching pad for what Mario Lopez is doing with Access Hollywood now. We really had an amazing run with clients such as Disney, Walt Disney Corporation, Walt Disney Imagineering, Hyundai, Kraft Foods, General Motors, Clorox and other consumer brands utilizing our rich history in marketing to help brand and market their products. That was my foundation.

Moving to the tech side, it was inevitable that with new media we have to really be conscious of what new media represented. I sit on the Board of the Duke Media Foundation, founded by Bill Duke. Our goal is to educate youth in underserved communities about what new media really means. It is our thought that if the student is learning film production and getting a loan to study film production, by the time that student graduates from college, he will still be paying on his loan. But, the information may already be outdated because of the rapid expansion of new media.

We want to make sure that we educate young adults in all facets of media, including digital technology, web series, webisodes, and shooting for content on all platforms including the phone, the tablet, the desktop, and the television so that they won't be limited in scope for potential careers in the future. I had to use all of my background and experience to lead me to this point in the tech world, and it's been an amazing ride.

I'm excited to educate and hopefully inspire and motivate other people who believe that there is room and growth in their lives in technology and even outside of technology in just new media in general.

Contact:
N2UCMG@gmail.com
Facebook.com/MarcBrogdon

Dr. Westbrooks:

Marc Brogdon discusses how entertainment has become so specialized that there is an app for just about everything. In addition to being creative, it's mandatory that artists and everyone else must now be tech savvy in order to stay in the loop. Today's technology changes in warp speed, so you have to stay informed and be knowledgeable about current trends and what's being phased out. But, for every road that ends, another avenue opens up. Sometimes you might have to pave a road to make your own way. That's called having a pioneering spirit, and that's what it takes sometimes, especially in today's music industry climate.

CHAPTER TWENTY-THREE

GREG COAKLEY

CEO & Founder of Music Triage, LLC
Music Analyst/Consultant

"Your fans are your customers; they're your clients. You have to go through all that noise and figure out who your clients are, and nurture those clients and grow them."

Greg Coakley has 30 years of music industry experience. He has worked as a production assistant, a floor manager and an artist manager whose clientele includes Maurice White and Verdine White (of Earth Wind & Fire), whom he assisted for over fifteen years, along with many other R&B acts. Greg kicks off his dialogue with us by telling us about his relationship with Earth, Wind & Fire.

Greg Coakley:
Earth Wind & Fire became my family, actually. I love them even though I don't tour with them anymore. They don't tour very much anymore either, but we're still like family.

Your website says that you show artists how to create an immediate actionable plan to grow their business and profits. So let's just assume that we are all potential clients of yours. Where would we start first? Let's just speak to the artist. If someone were coming to you to say, "Hey, I've got the talent, but you said the talent alone is not going to cut it. Then where do I go from there?"

Greg Coakley:
It's kind of funny, because I got an email this morning from a young man. He asked me exactly the same question. He told me that he had been playing the guitar for seven years. He has a band that's pretty decent, and he needs to know what's next. My answer to him is, "Now we know where you are, let's get you to where you need to go." I start with this. I focus on the business end of music. I personally believe that I have no musical talent whatsoever. I'm not trying to be an A&R person.
146

I'm not trying to tell you how to be creative. I assume that when you come to me, you have that under control. I'm just going to introduce you to the business end of it. My goal and the reason why I say "No B.S." is because throughout my career I've worked with numerous very well-known and successful artists. What I've seen happen with their careers is that with a large percentage of them, no one teaches them the business. So I've had some that are my friends that ended up kind of sitting around—especially now that the music industry has imploded on itself—trying to figure out what's next. Because they never took control of that business side, they're very much lost. In fact, a lot of my clients that I've worked with in the past are now calling me for consultation. I call it my "On boarding for 21st Century music."

So what do I do? To answer your question, I'll take that client and teach them what they need to do to develop a business. I'm talking about a business entity. I'm talking about knowing what it takes to be a business. Of course, they'll have to start with a budget, so we start with a budget and figure out how much money they need. If it's an artist (who in most cases doesn't have financing), I start them from where they are, and we kind of develop from there. I spent the last five years in Silicon Valley. What I'm doing is researching the startups in Silicon Valley and applying those principals to the music industry. In my opinion, musicians—especially with emerging musicians—their startup is not that much different from a tech company when it comes to business structure.

That's interesting. It's the first time we've heard that particular analogy. We often hear people say, "Well, you know there ain't no show without the business, that's why they call it show business." However, creative people tend to spend their time developing the creative entity. What used to happen when there were more music companies that were appealing to a wider range of talent from all ages, the companies provided a business structure for artists, and in between was something called a contract that even fewer artists understood. But nowadays, there's a wide gap between the artists and this perceived business entity that's going to take them and develop their brand into a profitable product. It can be overwhelming. So please break it down to the elementary level.

Back in the day, one could be talented and have an expectation of being what we called 'discovered.' After that, during the earlier stages of the Internet, there was an expectation that you could just throw something out there, and it would land upon this audience and just catch on wild fire, or go 'viral' as the saying goes. However, in reality there's such an influx of music and media today that it takes a whole lot more to stimulate that potential customer and potential fan. So please elaborate because our focus of the book is for every individual who has a talent or a service to share the good news of what they do and how they can help. What is it that makes your services different and special to the people who need you the most?

Greg Coakley:
First and foremost, let me address what you just said that's very true. There was a time when if you had talent and you were graced to get a record deal or find a great manager or something like that, they pretty much let you focus on your talent, and they did everything else for you. Those days are long gone. You are truly a very lucky individual if you can find that. The analogy that I use is the Internet startup or the tech startup.

Another analogy is that of a professional lawyer. My brother is an attorney. Let's say you have a very, very talented attorney, but he doesn't finish law school. He then goes and hangs out in the court and says, "Hey, can I get a gig? You know you want to hook a brother up. You know I can do that case for you. I can win it!" He has a business structure to go out and become a successful attorney. Unfortunately, because of the way the music industry has been developed, no one has developed that structure for artists. That's where I come in. I give them that structure. I show you the steps you need to take to avoid a long drawn out scenario. What I do with an artist is teach them what the priorities are. You have to get in front of an audience. In this day and age because there is such an influx of music out there, you have to get beyond the crowd. You have to figure out how to do that with your talent.

One of the things that I get artists to do is the most important thing that an artist has. It's hard for a lot of artists to understand it, but that's your fans. Your fans are your customers; they're your clients. You have to go through all that noise and figure out who your clients are and nurture those clients and grow them. We saw that back in the days of Earth Wind & Fire, the Rolling Stones, Stevie Wonder, and on and on. Those people, even though the record labels gave them that support, they connected with that audience. When they connected with that audience, they developed a relationship with that audience that took them to the top and actually have them where they are now. I was amazed when I was on the road, and I went outside in front of the building with Earth Wind & Fire and the Rolling Stones. We had guys out there that were in their fifties smoking a joint and acting like they were back in college. When you talked to them, they were telling you that they were reliving

148

those days. So that connection was made 30 something years ago, and these people are still connected to that band.

In my opinion, when it comes to an emerging artist right now, you've got to make that connection. The wonderful thing about today is, technology gives you a lot of things that those bands didn't have. If you deal with social media, develop a website, if you can get online, you can actually touch your audience and find out who they are. The unfortunate thing with a lot of artists that I work with is when I ask them who their target audience is, the number one answer all the time is, "Everybody." They truly believe that their audience is that wide. It may someday grow that big, but right now you have to find out who your music appeals to, and technology gives you that ability. There's all kinds of analytics out there and there's all kinds of matrixes out there to help you measure that audience. Facebook can give you an analytic. If you're on Facebook, Facebook will tell you who is liking you and who is not liking you.

So musicians need to think of themselves nowadays as market-ers, and you have to at least know something about marketing to even recognize the terminology such as target audience, demographics, and analytics.

Greg Coakley:
What's funny is you're absolutely right about that, but marketing nowadays is based on metrics and analytics. It's not that complicated, and understand I'm talking about people that I deal with—who I bring in as my clients. I'll give you another example. I had someone call me up about a month ago. He's a very well-known artist and he basically said, "Greg, I just dropped an album and I have no idea what happens." The first thing I do when I get an artist like that is to actually run analytics on him. I pull up a report, sit with him, and I say here's your analytics. This is what happened. As a marketer, I educate him on what these things mean, because he has to know it. He has to understand that there was a time when you dropped an album, it hit Billboard, the record label pushed it, and it went wherever it was going. But nowadays, you have to see where you missed the mark, because when you drop a project these days and you miss that mark, it doesn't mean that it's over.

I do understand that in the past when you dropped an album and if it didn't go anywhere, you pretty much walked away from it. Just like that it was another flop. But today, you can take a flop and breathe life into it, because you can look at these analytics that I'm talking about and you can see, "Oh, my core audience that usually buys my music, it didn't hit too well. But, there's a bunch of 25-35 year old girls, and they bought a bunch of my music. So obviously this new album is geared towards them. So let me tweak my marketing towards those 25–35 year old girls and grow that audience, because this particular product is geared towards them."

Are you saying that today's artist must be the President, the CEO, the accountant, the Chief of Business Development, Marketing & Promotions Director and Publishing Administrator for their musical entity?

Greg Coakley:
For their brand, yes, they have got to be these days, and I don't care who you are. The difference is—and I'll go back to my tech startup scenario—the difference is, when you are all of those entities, if you have the income, you can outsource those things. Let's say I really want to focus on my music, I made a little bit of money, but I don't want to be a marketer, then you can hire someone to do your marketing. But, I do not advise that you just give them your marketing and let them go on their way. In this day and time, you have to have an active role in your career.

I've actually had a few experiences where I sat with a guy (and it was really funny to me because he was a very educated guy), and we were talking about music. We went through this whole thing and he said, "Greg, I have no idea what you're talking about. You're talking way over my head because I don't understand all of these things." Specifically, his knowledge was pretty much focused on what he did for a living, and he didn't get anything else out of that scope. But it brought me around to understand that people—especially musicians—don't get all this. So I sit down with them and break it down in a very simple form. When it comes to analytics and things like that, I show it to them and explain what it means and what we have to do. Basically, that's all you need to understand. When you look at a chart, it says the people that bought the most of your music are women between the ages of 25-35. That's your target audience, so let's forget all the other people for right now, let's grow that audience. That's what he has to understand. Now if he wants to hire someone and outsource it, someone comes in and runs his social media and his website for him, all that is fantastic. But they need to report back to the artist and explain what's working and what's not working.

These are the things that I've learned in Silicon Valley, because when you take some of these companies that have gone in seven years from someone's garage to multi-billion dollar companies, those didn't start off with a record label behind them. They didn't start off with all these things. Basically they started off in their garage with their buddies and maybe some other friends from school. They built up a brand, which is what must be done for your music.

You develop your music. From there you find that core audience that likes your music, and you focus on them. They'll tell their friends, who'll tell their friends, who'll tell their friends. And the one thing you have to understand is that they all have something in common. They all have friends who like what they like. So that's where you get this viral marketing thing coming from.

Are you developing books, seminars, teaching materials or coaching products so that people who desire the information can get it?

Greg Coakley:
So far, I have worked one on one with a number of artists. I've drilled that down, and trust me, I have not been extremely successful because a lot of the people that I work with resent it (the current status of the industry). They want it to be the way it used to be. I've worked with them, and I have a number of independent artists that are doing very well. What I always say is when you can stop working at Starbucks and make a living off of your music, then you're a musician. And I can proudly say that I have a number of artists that I've taken from working at Starbucks, to feeding their family strictly from their music.

Are there any names that you can share with us?

Greg Coakley:
I always keep my clients close to my bosom because they don't want the world out there to know that they didn't do it themselves and that they didn't do it on their own merit. So I don't share my clients with most people.

What is your preferred title, consultant, or marketer, or artist developer?

Greg Coakley:
I call myself an Analyst/Consultant. The reason I use that title is because I spent the last five years in Silicon Valley. I literally walked away from working with Stevie Wonder to go there and study just how Silicon Valley worked and to see where it applies to the music industry. For the last five years, I've literally been an Analyst. It's been a great

experience because a number of my clients are tech people who wanted to have careers in music. They were somewhat successful tech people, but they wanted to be musicians. So, I have a few clients that are technology people that are doing very well in the Silicon Valley area. They are local musicians using what they've learned with technology, applied it to their music career, and they're taking their careers where they want it to go. I've taken what I've learned from them and taught it to other musicians that are musicians and not technology people. So the title I give myself is Analyst/Consultant.

In years past, music has been very definitive in terms of age and styles of music such as Pop, Blues, Jazz, Urban, Country or R&B. With the influx of technology and the age of the independent artists, do you think that those lines of distinction are softened, or are those lines of distinction more stringent than ever?

Greg Coakley:
No, there are fewer lines. I really think that the lines have been blurred. I've met 16-year-old kids that knew about artists that I'd worked with. I mean that completely shocked me because they knew about artists that I thought were way out of their spectrum. But they were like, "No, he's my favorite artist." I mean they even knew about Maurice White. I had a 16-year-old kid talk to me about Maurice White like he grew up with Earth Wind & Fire. When it comes to Blues, I meet a number of people across this country and throughout Europe that are heavy into Blues. And what they do is, they take that Blues influence and they kind of mix it with their folk influence that they have and they get some kind of mesh that is very funky and really nice. But you can't really categorize it as Blues or Folk. It's like some kind of hybrid. It's the same thing with Rock & Roll. I meet some rock guys that are rockers and they look like 100 percent rockers, but when they really get down and start jamming, they can compete with a lot of the R&B artists that I know of.

What do you find most distressing about the anatomy of today's industry?

Greg Coakley:
What I find most distressing about today's industry is that you have a large number of industry people that are fighting tooth and nail to keep the industry where it used to be. I find that very distressing because when you look around us, the world has been disruptive. Everything has

changed, the publishing industry has changed, the movie industry has changed, and a lot of them are making adaptations and becoming very successful. Let's look at Amazon music and books. They have turned publishing upside down. And what the publishing houses have done is they've adapted to it. I find in music, people my age are fighting tooth and nail not to change. They want it to be the same. I always tell them, you're trying to play an 8 track on an mp3 player.

And what do you find most invigorating?

Greg Coakley:

What's most invigorating is the youth—the kids. I'm meeting kids now that have no fear. They don't live in the box that we lived in, so they have no fear. They'll try almost anything. I meet these kids that are doing shows anywhere they can get electricity. They are performing! Actually, there's a group out of San Diego that I'd like to mention. They'll even perform in the park. If you look at their itinerary, you'll see that they work all the time. But the reason they work all the time is because they don't set limits on themselves. They'll be at a grungy bar tonight, and then tomorrow they'll be at the LPAC (Lancaster Performing Arts Center). They'll go from there to playing at someone's house the next week. That's what's invigorating to me today.

This is around the world. I worked with a group of Japanese guys that are (these guys went to Japan's version of MIT) very, very geek, but they are phenomenal musicians. I brought them here to America and we did a tour of America back in 2009. They were absolutely phenomenal musicians; it was amazing. The American audience loved them. Only one of them spoke English, everybody else only spoke Japanese. But, their music spoke for them throughout the audiences they played for while they were in America.

Contact:
greg@musictriage.com
www.musictriage.com
www.gregcoakley.com

Dr. Westbrooks:

Greg Coakley encourages artists—all of them—to learn the business, and then fine tune that knowledge specifically around how it affects them personally. He stresses the knowledge of analytics, which can pinpoint specifically where you should focus your marketing effort.

Dr. Logan H. Westbrooks

As a consultant, he advises his clients to embrace the changes in today's industry, because those changes are here to stay. In fact, things are changing even as you are reading this.

CHAPTER TWENTY-FOUR

GREGORY SAVAGE, JR.

Freelance Composer/Sound Designer
Owner of Do It Yourself Music Biz

"When a lot of people hear music industry they think of records, touring, bands and things like that. The music industry actually goes a lot further than that. It goes into music licensing, it goes into film scoring, it goes into game audio."

Gregory Savage, Jr., took the route of video games and merged it into creating his own business as a music producer and sound designer. Through his company Do It Yourself Music Biz, he consults artists, and composers, and urban Hip Hop producers about the vast opportunities for making money in the current industry.

Greg Savage, Jr.
I'm a nerd, just a huge nerd. Technology has been my life since I can remember. Actually, it was more so martial arts, then technology. When I was younger, everything started off with video games. When I got to be about 15 or 16 years old, I was a semi-professional gamer. I was sponsored in a game called "Medal of Honor" and much later I went to the "Call of Duty" series. I fell off of the professional gaming after "Call of Duty II." At that time I was doing a little music production; at least I was dabbling around in it. Once the sponsorship ended with "Call of Duty II," I was kind of freelancing and got a few placements in video games here and there. One of them was called "Söldner." It was made by JoWooD. That was my first taste of music in the video game industry.

Exactly how did your experience with gaming lead you into your experience in music?

Greg Savage, Jr.
When a lot of people hear music industry they think of records, touring, bands and things like that. The music industry actually goes a lot further than that. It goes into music licensing, it goes into film scoring,

155

it goes into game audio (which is like a slang term). So the music side of it actually progressed me into sound design and into the game audio world. Does that make sense?

Can you explain the pathway from being just a tech and gaming junkie into someone who can discover a career in designing audio for video games?

Greg Savage, Jr.

Basically, while you're sitting there playing video games, the easiest way to get a taste of the video game industry is to actually start looking up gaming engines. There's a bunch of gaming engines. Just Google gaming engines. One of them is Android iOS for the cell phones and Smart phones. Those are the platforms. The easiest way to jump into this industry is to actually search on forums and look for people that have free flash games. A lot of these guys are coming out of school, and they only have budgets for just their gaming engines. Maybe some graphic designers or some other programmers, but they don't think about the audio. When they do think about the audio, they're trying to do it themselves to save a couple of dollars. What musicians can do, they can actually embark on that market. The reason why it's really lucrative is because they don't have a lot of money. That opens the door for an independent, like someone that plays games on the side, but they also are dabbling into music.

One thing that is a little different from somebody that produces records from someone that's trying to get into the game industry or even the film industry is that people who make records are used to linear compositions. Which is all the same across the board. But when you do it for a record, you're thinking of three to four minutes in time, which is the same across the length of the song. When you're making music for a game, it's not just three or four minutes. You're trying to create a loop that doesn't really sound like a loop. It is a loop, but you want it to mesh with the game. When the gamer is playing the game, they don't realize that the music is enhancing the visual graphics. For example, a Hip Hop producer just might do four bars or eight bars of drums and maybe a couple of lines, but after a minute or two that repetition will start to get boring. The hard part is, making the audio cohesive enough with the video game to where it doesn't get boring.

Another kind of difficult aspect and one thing that should be learned is the importance of file sizes. Anybody that has worked with audio knows that there are different compression sizes or formats, WAVs, your MP3s and things like that. When you get into the gaming

156

world, the last thing that the company is thinking about is the audio. You have to be good enough to understand the compression sizes well enough and the frequencies of the audio to know how to produce quality music on a compressed level. I say that because a lot of times when they hand you the project, they will say we only have 400mb of space. If you're working on a record, 400mb of audio is nothing. You can record one minute at 24bit 96k hertz and that can be a couple hundred mbs right there, and your whole session can be four gigs for a full song. It has the quality, but when you get to the gaming side you have to compress that and still keep the quality in some respects. If you're going into the iOS phase, it's a little harder because a lot of the cell phones don't reproduce low tones very well. You then have to take your lows and boost them up and things like that. The true transition is more so educating yourself in the gaming engine, because what's happening now is that a lot of these kids are coming out of school. These gaming developers understand their engine, but they don't always understand just how to implement the audio into the gaming engine and keep it quality, so they need someone that understands the audio and that can be a sound designer or composer.

You are speaking on the evolution of music from the traditional idea of opportunities in the music industry and to bridging the gap into today's digital industry and the new types of interesting positions that are now available. What is it that you do with DIY Music Biz?

Greg Savage, Jr.

With DIY Music Biz I teach people how to make a living with their craft, whether they're artists, composers or urban Hip Hop producers. I teach them how to make a living in music without the need of the A&R, the record label or publishers. I just basically teach everyone how to do it on their own.

You offer a diverse platform, and because of digital media, the tapestry for music these days is more diverse than ever. We have had plenty of perspectives from the artists, artist developers and traditional marketers. Can you hone in on just the digital music industry? Let's talk about some more of those eclectic positions from audio design to gaming. What are the starting points for completely embellishing your brand digitally? How many sites are there that are similar to yours?

Greg Savage, Jr.

To be honest, there are a lot of sites out there like mine. Actually, I wouldn't say just like mine, but there are a lot of sites that say that they're trying to teach people how to make a living in the industry. You kind of have to be careful about some of the sites because you land on the page and the first thing that happens is a pop up claiming that they can sell you a secret for $97 or for $100 or whatever dollars. My advice would be to do your research. Most of the sites that are promoting these products don't even own the products but are affiliates of somebody else's product. They have actually never used the information on that product. They are only trying to make a quick dollar for themselves.

There is a culture of musicians who are now beginning their compositions in Garage Band, or downloading beats on their iPhones, voicing it on their computers and posting directly to Sound Cloud. These are new conventions. For those who aspire to create and market their product that way, what is the best way for them to make money?

Greg Savage, Jr.

Let me start by saying that I honestly think from my perspective that when people look at the music industry today—even though there are a bunch of people that are new and upcoming—they are using the digital platforms and all the high tech software. Years ago, you needed 15 to 20,000 dollars to run a studio. To even make bad music, you needed that. These days you can go and get a laptop for $1,000—and I'm not an advocate of Piracy—but there are kids that are pirating software and are making tracks that are just as good as the pros that are coming out of the studios. There are so many tutorials on YouTube teaching you how to make music. You don't even need music theory these days. You can download and buy a program like Harmony Navigator, or you can get chord software—that's free—and it tells you about the many cycles of fifths. You can download many files to your favorite songs. It'll let you know the chord structure. It'll show you the note, and the only thing you'd have to do is replace the instruments. If you have a decent ear to mix—even if you can't mix—there are tutorials online. Everything is online for today's music producer.

The disconnect is in the marketing and money making aspect. What people are still thinking in this digital age is that you need a record label. So Johnny, who buys the beat machine or buys his first piano or Logic Pro, starts making tracks. The first thing they start looking for is a manager or a publisher or someone that can sign them and give them that big break. What they don't understand is that the business has shifted and the record industry is no longer in its artist development stage. They don't develop artists unless there is a potential back end profit for them, because you are a product. I know some people don't like to hear that, but you are a product. They go around and they're making the music. They start looking for the record label, and they get frustrated because no one will listen to their music. But the best way to actually get the attention of a manager or a label is to build your own following.

There are so many platforms that you can do this on. You can do this on SoundCloud. You can do this on YouTube. You can do this on Twitter. You can do this on Instagram or Pinterest. I know all of these things sound really odd and Instagram is all pictures, but they do have their 15 second video features, which I will explain how it's beneficial in a minute. You want to utilize these platforms to build a following. A perfect example is YouTube. People are getting on YouTube, and they're showing how they composed or how they remade a track, or how they're making their own music. The labels don't care how good their music is. What they're looking at is their following and how many views they have. If you have the views and the fan base, they can tell you yes or no.

At the point where you have 30,000 members, that's like your own cult or your own religion. At that point, you don't even need the label and they know that. So once you build your own brand, you more so have the power. You can either walk into a label or say this is my product, this is my brand, and this is how many people are following me. You can either go with it or I'll do it myself. At that time, it really doesn't matter because you have a big enough fan base to live off of. Now when I say "live off of because it's big enough," I don't just mean by selling music. I mean by endorsements, because when you do have a following—whatever the magic number is. Sometimes it's 20,000 or sometimes it's 30,000.

My YouTube following is not that big, I have less than a 1,000 and I'm endorsed by Arturia. Arturia is a company that makes music gear for composers. They specialize in making the old gear—making the old analog Oberheim SEM. They recreate this in digital space. Since I helped design the Oberheim SEM I, which Herbert Hancock is a big fan of, I get a lot of projects through them, and I get a lot of gear through them. When you start to have followings that are huge, you don't need to contact the record label. You can go to the company directly, and they will sponsor you and hook you up with good discounts and with gear and have you speaking on panels to promote their gear.

Through YouTube you can also help with a partnership program in which they give you a percentage on the ads that show up on your videos. Some people who are like 14 to 20 years old, those young guys they're not even doing music. They're just doing product reviews, and

Apple is giving them everything for free, everything! They're getting the gear free. They're getting the views and they're getting the percentage on the ads that are showing up before and after their videos, in the middle of their videos. The digital age of marketing is all about building your own brand. If you want to go back to the music side of that, the managers and A&R people have gotten lazy. They're now doing their own market research, and they only go after people that have a following because when you go after someone who has a following, that's less work that you have to do as an A&R or as a manager. It's a lot easier to pick up a 14-year-old kid who has 500,000 followers and give him a one-song deal or something in a commercial where you're taking part of his publishing than it is to pick up someone who has talent, but has no fan base.

So your website is not designed as an artist driven fast track to fame approach to the music business. Can you share a specific call to action for young people about the importance of investigating all their options and the importance of having good business sense?

Greg Savage, Jr.

I believe everyone getting into music needs to be aware of what options are out there. Even if you don't understand every little nuance about the business, because it can be frustrating. There's a lot of technical jargon that can be intimidating. When I first started out, I didn't pay much attention to copyright. I actually started sound designing. When I was making beats, I was sound designing without even knowing it.

I was actually hired by a recording studio to do nothing but knock off (or emulate) tracks. They put me in a studio and said, "Here are the tracks. We need you to do those drums, we need these synths (short for synthesizers), and we need these pianos. I didn't know music theory, but I did know how to replicate stuff through the MIDI editor and the sequencer. I would get like $300 to $400 every time I would knock something off. What I did not understand was copyright, and I ended up getting subpoenaed for court because I was basically remaking somebody's stuff. I didn't know it would come back to haunt me. I had no idea, and I was led to believe that the material that I was making was of their own, but it wasn't what they wanted. Had I known a little bit more about the business, I would have had a contract that stated they were responsible for clearing any rights that are unclear. If you are creating music that doesn't sound like anything previously published, or if you use a sample, sometimes you do not have to worry about it. But, it is always good to have a safety net, or something that disconnects you from the product. This is especially true if you're working in a shady position, or a position where you're not too familiar with or if you're dealing with samples.

One of the false beliefs—especially with young producers (male or female), it doesn't matter what genre—is if you use a sample and you're not making any money with it or if you never sell it, then you can't get sued. That is false. If you use a sample and it's not yours, you have no rights. It doesn't matter if you made money. It matters what the rights holder want to do. If they sold it to you and it infringes on their intellectual property, then you devalued it anyway and they can sue you. So if you're a producer or composer who's using a sample, it's always wise to have a contract that frees you from that sample, especially if you're going to give it off to another person.

Here's a word of advice to anyone entering the music business. Don't enter the business with a one-track mind. Don't put all of your eggs into one basket. If you are a singer, you can also make a living as a voiceover artist. You can also make a living in the video game world, in the commercial world doing commercial ads. The lady who does the voice of Siri on Apple is actually a voiceover artist. She does voiceovers for Apple, Target and a bunch of other companies. If you're an artist, you can do voiceovers for movies. You can do them for commercials, you can do them for games or for GPS systems. You can do them for toys. If you're a singer, don't limit yourself to that one path.

If you're a mixing engineer or you're trying to become a mixing engineer, you aren't just a mixing engineer. You're an audio book editor, you're a mixing engineer as well as a sound designer. You could also be classified as a "recordist," because you know how to use a microphone. You could also be a field recording specialist, or a Foley artist because you understand how the connections work in a studio. You understand the acoustics and you understand game staging. There are a lot of things that you can do besides just being an engineer. If you are a composer, there's a chance that you can also be a sound designer like myself. And I say this because not only are you making the music, but you're molding the sound to fit your vision. Anytime you take a sound and you press it and tweak it when you turn the knob, you are essentially crafting and designing the sound.

What you are bringing to this is so incredibly viable and even in breaking down the specifics. Please venture onto this particular note. What is the importance of reading? Many creative people are so imbued in the creative process, but how important is it to slow down and read? Read the fine print; read to get an understanding of your contracts and your agreements from sites you are visiting?

Greg Savage, Jr.

You want to read everything. Everything! Let me give you an example why you would want to read everything. Earlier this year on my site I have a few members who joined my membership program, and they were getting into music licensing. I actually went over the importance of going over the contract. The reason why this is important is because one of my members signed a contract with a music library. Music libraries are non-exclusive, meaning that you can put your music in their library and you can do other stuff with your music. This is very beneficial as it's always beneficial to work in a non-exclusive field. It gives you freedom because it gives you the possibility to make more on your tracks or whatever it is that you're giving up to the company.

What my student did not realize is that he joined several non-exclusive libraries, which is fine. But on one of these music libraries it had written in the fine print that if you are associated with XYZ library, you are in breach of their contract and your music will be taken out of their library. At the time that they took his music out of the library, it was also picked up by a company that was supposed to be working on a show "Scrubbing In." By him being rejected from or kicked out of the library, they also took the song out of rotation, and it wasn't even up for grabs anymore. So he missed out on a music placement.

There's another incident that happened to me earlier on in my career where I didn't read the fine print of a music library. In the fine print, which I did read the first time, it told me that I could cancel or basically pull my songs from the library if I informed them in writing and it would take six months to get everything out of the library. Well, when I went back this year to look at it because I was doing a tutorial on it, they had made an update—an addendum to their contract. It said that if you joined within a specific time frame, then you could no longer take your music out. I had no idea about that (referring to certain statues and limitations).

It's important to read your contracts, but especially if you're dealing with a business that's online. It's always good to go over the contracts multiple times throughout the year, because they can change at any time. That is actually a term that you should get accustomed to *"that things can change at any time."* They always tell you that the terms can change whenever they want. Once you agree to that, they CAN change your contract at any time. And there is no such thing as "I didn't know you changed it." You have to check up on that. Hard copies are different. But when it's digital, they can change it at any time. It's just like when you sign up for Comcast Cable, they have the right to terminate, and they have the right to change their terms. It's your responsibility to seek those terms out.

Contact:
www.diymusicbiz.com

Dr. Westbrooks:
The online gaming industry is huge, almost paralleling the movie industry. And just like the movie industry needs music for their soundtracks, so does the online gaming industry. One of the new games called "Just Dance Now" got six million downloads in a little over a month. Just like the name of the game, it is music for people to dance to, and it is very popular.

Gregory Savage, Jr. has used his talent as a composer and sound engineer to establish his own company to create music for the games. It requires the skill to know when and where to place musically dramatic sounds and effects just like in the movies. He considers himself as much of a tech nerd as he does a musician, so this aspect is the perfect fit for him. But, he also stresses that everyone understand the business aspect and to clearly understand the contracts that you sign, especially digital contracts.

And here's a perfect example of what Gregory Savage, Jr., was speaking on about the possibilities of success through social media. One of the biggest hits in the summer of 2015 was the dance song "Watch Me (Whip/Nae Nae)" by Silentó, a 17-year-old high school student from Atlanta. One day at school he was having fun rapping and singing, and his catchy hook line caught on with the other students. He recorded it, uploaded it to SoundCloud and Instagram, and it went viral. He caught the attention of Capitol Records, who quickly signed him. "Watch Me (Whip/Nae Nae)" was on several Billboard charts and was nominated for the 2015 Song of the Summer at the MTV Video Music Awards. As of this publication, the song has had almost 215 million streams and, more importantly, 100 million downloads.

THE PUBLIC RELATIONS PROFESSIONALS

INFORMED SOURCES

Angelo Ellerbee
Eunice Mosley
Gil Robertson
Rick Scott

CHAPTER TWENTY-FIVE

ANGELO ELLERBEE

President and CEO of Double XXposure Media Relations

"You've got to be punctual. You've got to be clean. You've got to be presentable. You've got to understand that first impressions are lasting impressions."

Angelo Ellerbee has spent the past 40 years in artist development, marketing, promotions and media relations. His roster of artists has included James Mtume, Michael Jackson, Vincent Herbert, Patra, Ginuwine, DMX, Ziggy Marley, Jocelyn Brown, Mary J. Blige, Alicia Keys, Ray Chew and more. He explains how his path led from fashion design to being a business owner in the music industry.

What is the history of your company, and what inspired you to get started?

Angelo Ellerbee:
I started my company in the corner of my mother's basement in Newark, New Jersey, with a very humble beginning. I began because my mother said, "You could either go to college or get a job." She said, "I don't care what you do, but you're gonna do one thing!" Because she wanted to make sure that she was going to be given her monthly rent.

My degree is in Fashion Design, I used to do a lot of fashion shows in my community. I was born and raised in Newark, New Jersey, and I did fashion shows. I attended the Fashion Institute of Technology. When I started my degree, none of the stores like Bloomingdales had a section for "one of a kind" designs. So I began to do that, and I did that for a span of four or five years. I went to Paris, and I lived there for about two and a half years. I came back when I turned 16 years old, and I was a little lost as to what I wanted to do.

I went to work for an artist by the name of James Mtume. I think your readers would understand or know his history. Mtume is a two-time Grammy Award winner. Rapper Biggie Smalls re-made Mtume's record titled "Juicy Fruit." With this record, he attended the fashion show each and every single year, and two or three thousand people would attend. We did not know who was in the audience, but Mtume's wife—who also has a degree in Fashion Design—loved to come to my shows because they were very theatrical. I had animals in the show and each and every single year, people would come in the thousands. I would use the Alvin Ailey Dancers, Geoffrey Holder and Carmen de Lavallade; it was an extravaganza. Mtume's wife came one year and came backstage and she said to me, "Hi, my name is Emily Mtume. I know what you do for the community, and my husband is James Mtume." I did not know who or what an Mtume was, but anyway she said, "We're doing a song and we're doing an album cover called "You, Me and He." We want to know if you'd work with me on creating the album cover concepts and styling it?" I said, "Okay." So I did that. Mtume came to me and said, "Man, if you're doing all these things for and with my wife, I think that maybe you should manage me." I said, "Manage you? You're a recording artist, man. I do models and that kind of thing." He said, "If you do models, then you can work in the music industry." So I went to work with James Mtume. I think that's where I earned my degree in music because I learned for five years the who, the what, the when, the where and the why of the music industry, and I began to represent him.

I would go back and forth with his record company every day and I would feel dumber and dumber, because I knew nothing about the music industry. Each and every single day would be an Epic back and forth. Epic is the label that was a subsidiary of the CBS family. They would call Mtume and say, "Are you sure this is the guy you want to manage you?" He would educate me about diplomacy; about getting your point across; about reading and understanding the fundamentals.

That's actually when Double XXposure was born. That was about 1983 or 1984. I started it in the corner of my mother's basement with absolutely no money. All of the money that I wanted to reach out and get from lending sources were not open to lending to a person of my age, with no credibility and no credit established. So I did what my mother taught me to do. I used my survival skills and my relationships.

I began to build the company and started out doing club music where people like Jocelyn Brown (who recorded the hit "Somebody Else's Guy"), Sybil, Jomanda, Adeva and there was a group called Phase II. Phase II was very special. The lead singer in Phase II is now the music mogul Vincent Herbert. And, of course, we know he discovered Lady Gaga. Now he's working with his wife, and he's on the reality show "The Braxtons." Vincent and I worked together for 15 years and I developed his career. As time went on, I began to get Double XXposure the kind of props that it needed to have so that I could be a publicity firm.

The most important thing for me is that I found in my research by working with various people, that my people (who looked like me) didn't have the knowledge or the education about the music industry. So I researched it and I found a very successful African American man by the name of Berry Gordy. Berry Gordy was the founder of Motown, and he was, to me, very brilliant. I had the pleasure of meeting him, along with Dionne Warwick a couple weeks ago. Berry Gordy understood the philosophy of the people of White America and the music of White America back in that day and time. It was the 1950s and '60s, and our music was looked at very strongly, very misunderstood. They called our music "beach music." When I say beach music, I mean R&B music because when they played our music, it went along with them to the beaches. It was never on the airways, or if it was, it was put into the urban market. What we would find is that they would take songs that our people had recorded and give it to someone White who would re-record it and put someone White on the album covers. They would go out and they would do their national line of promotions.

So I created a 24-week artist development program based on that. It was to teach diction and speech mannerisms. It also included travel, finances, business management, and how to set up a manager. Those were the core things that Berry Gordy had to do. He had to train his people to be non-threatening in White America as it related to the kind of music that they were going to do. My mother said, "When in Rome, do as the Romans do." And in America, believe it or not—the gangster society that it is—it is a country that wants you to follow the yellow brick road. That's what Berry Gordy did. He took Diana Ross and the Temptations, and he taught them manners, diction and speech, image and style. All those things became very important.

I later worked for Mary J. Blige in the '80s and early '90s. I was approached by Jacqueline Rhinehart and the people at Uptown Records to come and sit and have a conversation with them about what they were doing. There were a lot of people there at that time. There was Hip Hop, which was one of the most misunderstood music genres. It was music that would not be accepted by the mainstream at that time. Mary J. Blige was one of my first clients under my new artist development program.

We immediately got into reading, writing, and understanding the importance of business. We talked about the importance of having a manager, knowing what it is to have a manager, and what the manager's job is. We spoke about how to diversify as an artist, not just for entertaining but the marketing and the branding of an artist. We dealt with how to sit in a chair, how to conduct yourself in an interview and turn it into a conversation. A lot grew from that. *The New York Times*, *The Daily News*, every newspaper in the country bit into the fact that we had a company. *The New York Times* called my company "The charm school for rappers."

We were really on a springboard by expanding and branding Double XXposure as a media relations and artist development company. The doors were now open. We took on Alicia Keys and Ginuwine, and we took on a number of other artists. I had to understand in my mind the difference in how our artists were being presented when they got into trouble. How they were being denied the right to speak and to understand what it was that they did wrong. So a lot of people started coming to me to solve problems—damage control.

Back in the early '90s, Bob Jones was Michael Jackson's V. P. of PR. I began to work with Michael Jackson and a number of other people on damage control, and understanding the importance of how we need not run from the scene of the accident, but how we need to go back to the scene of the accident and how we needed to be truthful with this. From that, I began to work with a gentleman by the name of DMX (Earl Simons). I managed DMX for five years. I was his publicist for two years, and the list goes on.

We've celebrated 40 years at Double XXposure, and it's not just a media company. I look at Double XXposure as a one-stop kind of shop. It is very important that we educate, stimulate, and motivate our young people and make them aware about this industry. This can be a gangster industry, and if you are not prepared to deal with the gangsters then you need not be a part of this industry. You must come in a suit and be intelligent. You must research and understand the who, what, when, where and why of the industry. Understand that your commitment cannot be a part-time commitment. It has to be a full-time commitment. You cannot just want to record, but don't want to do performances or press. You've got to be punctual. You've got to be clean. You've got to be presentable. You've got to understand that first impressions are lasting impressions. That's what my company does. It still serves as a vehicle to create awareness and educate young people about the music industry.

What are things that an artist must do to remain relevant or what must be done for new artists who are just getting started?

Angelo Ellerbee:
I believe wholeheartedly in the education of the music, before I believe wholeheartedly in the performance, the image, and the salaries of an artist. I believe that an artist has to take on the right to manage himself internally and needs to know what management is about. The next thing you need to know—if we look at African American success

stories in the music industry from the '30s, '40s, '50s, '60s, '70s, '80s, '90s—we've been ripped off of our cultures in music and our communities because we have not had that kind of education to understand how it all goes down and how it all works.

So the first step, as to terms of success, is to understand that an education is the first course you have to take. That means you have to be able to read and write. I don't say that to downgrade anyone. If you are unable and your confidence level is not up, you need to be straight up and honest with your lawyer and say, "Can you do me a favor? Break this down to a third-grade level so I can get an understanding as to what I'm about to sign?" Don't go signing stuff because you're 'amBITCHus' as opposed to being ambitious. Being amBITCHus is when you're all over everywhere, excited about being an artist and not about reading and writing and understanding what you have signed your name on.

You can't be all over the map. You have got to be focused so you can understand what the commitment is all about. I say these things and then I say that in this day and time we're selling not music anymore; we're selling images of stylization. We're selling the diversity of our artist. Our artists just can't sing today. They've got to dance, they've got to act, and they've got to be able to diversify themselves. You know most of the deals that they're giving out now are 360.

That means that a manager is given a percentage of everything that you are going to do. You need to understand that in order for you to make your percentage. You don't want to go to work and only make six percent of your money because you've got managers and accountants. And they're taking percentages for merchandising, and your acting, not related things that have to do with music. You really need to understand what it is that you're getting yourself involved in. Understand what your publishing rights are. Understand the royalty statements because that is your social security benefits—your 401k plan.

If you aren't being a student, you're being excitable about the fact that you're an artist and people know who you are and not protecting all of the properties around you. You're going to be a sad soul when you get to be 30, and when you get to be 40. Be clear to understand when you go to sign any kind of agreement. You should not sign over a two-year period. I believe that any management or record deal should start off as a courtship. From a courtship, it can go into an engagement. After you've grown and understand from the courtship to the engagement, then you want to go get married. Don't go signing something and longevity is not there for you. If someone's signing you away for five or six years, that's your career! So those are the things that I say to young people.

What are your greatest joys?

Angelo Ellerbee:

I'd say my greatest joy is that I'm still in this business 40 years later. And my greatest story is that I hope my contribution to the music industry will go on for the next 40 years. I want people to understand the importance of 1) paying your taxes as a recording artist, and 2) understanding your obligations and your support. Some of my greatest successes for me are to educate, motivate, stimulate. Yes, I've worked with Shabba Ranks, Ray Chew, Patra, Ziggy Marley and a bunch of people, but those things don't mean anything without encouraging others.

What are your contributions going to be? What is your goal, and what is your plan on how you are going to grow? Are you going to water yourself and make sure you get the nourishment and the education to continue doing what it is that you want to do? And if you're into anything, you must be into the man above which guides you. You have to have faith in Him. Don't have faith in any man, woman, or child walking in the universe like you. If you take the word friend and you split the letters, you've got "end" E-N-D. That's what a friend in this business will do to you, they begin and they end. Have a friend in Christ.

Contact:
theellerbeegroup@aol.com
www.DXXNYC.com

Dr. Westbrooks:

Angelo Ellerbee is an example of a person who was 'called' into his profession. He saw a need, recognized the problem, and stepped in the fill the void. He took this role seriously and learned the business as he went along. He has a nurturing spirit and a natural inclination to take care of people and to teach them to take care of themselves. Double XXposure has lasted 40 years because he kept the best of the old business model and incorporated the necessities of the new model. This merging of the two has been his secret weapon of success, because everything from the old model was not bad, especially artist development, which is almost non-existent in today's music industry.

CHAPTER TWENTY-SIX

EUNICE MOSELEY

President of Freelance Associates
Public Relations, Business Management & Consulting

"I think we are at a point now that the power could be taken over by marketing, PR and management companies because the artist themselves don't know the business. So if they want to keep the power, they need to learn the business of entertainment."

In addition to presiding over Freelance Associates Public Relations, Business Management & Consulting Firm, Eunice Moseley is the syndicated entertainment columnist of The Pulse of Entertainment. She is bi-costal and serves as the Promotions Director at Large for the Baltimore Times newspaper. Fifteen years ago she began producing the Uplifting Minds II Talent Conference, which has continued as an annual event that is both a talent show and workshop for aspiring artists.

Can you give us a synopsis of your career in the music industry?

Eunice Moseley:
My life has been music from the beginning because I'm a singer/dancer. I attended a high school of the arts. I got back into music as an employee of the Baltimore Times. As a reporter, my focus was the music industry. Later on I became an Entertainment Editor. Now I'm a syndicated columnist where I interview and cover entertainment, music, events, and people in the industry. Also in 1999, I founded the Uplifting Minds II Entertainment Conference. It's 15 years old now. I took it to Los Angeles and Atlanta. Now I'm in Baltimore and Los Angeles annually with the conference. In the conference we educate young artists about the music business by bringing some of the people I interviewed via my columns to talk to them. Then we have the talent showcase where they judge the performances, as well as provide constructive comments. We also give awards and prizes to help them on their way.

Who are some of the artists that have directly benefitted in their careers because of your talent showcases or conferences?

Eunice Moseley:

I don't know, because I learned years later the affects that the conference has had on some of the artists. Many have come through. The only thing that comes to mind is a young group of brothers called the Featherstones (songwriters/producers). They competed in my conference. They didn't win, but Sisqó from Dru Hill was there that day, and he liked their song. It was included on one of the albums for Dru Hill. I think it's the one called "I Should Be." What the Featherstone Brothers told me is that particular single went Platinum or Gold. That's the only one that comes to mind, but there are so many instances like the young lady who was at a competition and was asked to go on Broadway. There are many more stories like these.

Are contests and talent showcases still relevant? And are you saying that an artist can still hope to be discovered?

Eunice Moseley:

I believe they are relevant, but what I see happening is people (as in the promoters) are using the opportunity to try to make a living off of it. Maybe it's just me personally, but I believe that things like that are more of a community outreach type event. Something that you give back to the community. You're not supposed to try to make money from it. I try to warn those that I consult in public relations and business management to just be leery of them. Use them carefully because they charge for their stages. Some of them will take the money and run. Some are stable, and some promise that certain people in the industry will come to the show scouting for talent, and those people are just not there.

The artist needs the opportunity to perform. They need the stages, so it's still relevant. You just have to be very careful about that. I tell the young artists that the showcase at my event is not about whether you win the competition. It's about showcasing your talent. Not only practicing your art, but being visible to people who can help you. I think showcases are still relevant, you just have to be leery of the ones you participate in.

Explain what makes the Uplifting Minds Talent Showcase and Conference different from the rest?

Eunice Moseley:

Initially the whole conference was free. It's still free in a sense, but there is a registration fee for the talent. I did that because the panelists that I usually get are high profile people, and their time is money. They also understand my financial struggle. One of them said to me at an event, "Well, Eunice, if you don't charge some type of fee to help you financially, we're not coming back." Basically, I charge a fee of about $25, but that money is soaked up on printing materials, purchasing the trophies, renting the venues, banners, posters, flyers, and any needed staff. So the registration fee I collect is really spent up, and I still have to come out of pocket. But my point is, the event is supposed to give back to the community as far as I'm concerned. And I do try to keep in touch, especially with the winners.

I bring the winners back to the next event so that those who are just coming in can see the progression. A lot of the talent in Uplifting Minds come back year after year after year. I have a young man who called me yesterday, and he has won six times! He has been competing for as long as the event has been going on. Right now he has grown into a very successful producer and label owner. He's very successful now as far as his income that he brings home. There are a lot of stories like that of young artists that keep coming back to the conference to learn.

The managers and producers of the artist tell me every time: "Eunice, every time I come here I learn something different." So that is what they get from the conference. Not only is it free education, they also get material. I give out a music business handbook. I got authorization from the authors of two books to put certain parts of their book in the handbook. The winners get prizes donated. It could be legal consultations, free music tracks, free studio time, you name it. They get a lot from that. Networking and hooking up with like-minded people is very important as well.

When did it click for you that you had to be an artist and a business person? And why is it important for other artists to do the same?

Eunice Moseley:
The music business is a business. Basically, it's about making money, and I honestly feel I'm an entrepreneur by heritage. My family always started businesses. I'm always thinking about entrepreneurship. I think that we all should be knowledgeable about the business, not only because of the product, but because the product has to be marketed. It has to be managed. In the 20 something years I've been in the industry as a journalist, I've seen the tables turn from power in the music industry being in the hand of major labels, to the power being in the hands of the independent labels. What I'm finding now is that the independent label or artist doesn't know the business.

I think we are at a point now that the power could be taken over by marketing, PR and management companies because the artist themselves don't know the business. If they want to keep the power, they need to learn the business of entertainment. That's very important, because they need to know the business in order to run it. If you don't know the business, then someone else is going to run the business for you, and they can take that power from you. I think that is very important. I knew that from the beginning as an artist a long time ago—which is another reason why I started Uplifting Minds—because I saw the transition. I just wanted to teach young people about the business so they can take the power back. It makes no since to me that you're the product and you're the reason why they're making money, but you only get between three to ten percent of that money you're bringing in.

How can the artist better understand the components of the deal?

Eunice Moseley:
You have to take one step at a time. As an independent artist, the need to have it all immediately is unrealistic. If you want that, you have to give up the power. Again, I am into entrepreneurship. I'm a do-it-yourself type person. I've proven with some of my clients that you can do it yourself, but a little bit at a time until you make enough noise that those people with the big budgets will come to you. When they come to you, it's a different deal on the table as opposed to you going to them and saying, "I need your help." If you go to them and say, "I need your help," the ball is in their court. But if you make enough noise independently, they come to you, and then the ball is in your court.

I sometimes talk about an interview I had with Master P at a seminar about how he sold his records out of the trunk of his car, and then he opened up a record store to sell his own products. He made enough noise that the majors came to him, and he said that his family was so broke at the time. The major label offered, say a million dollars, but he had to give up too much power, and he turned it down. His family said, "Why? Why? Why? We need the money!" He didn't want to give up the power, so he kept it independent. He struggled a little bit longer, but about two or three years later he made even more noise. When they came to him, they came to him with more than a million dollars, and they allowed him to keep his name and his power.

What do you say collectively to parents of talented children who want their kids to be successful in the industry?

Eunice Moseley:
First, as gently and as easily as I can, I try to be honest with them about their child's talent. They come to me and say, "My daughter wants to be a singer." If I really don't see that the talent is there, I ask them what other talents their children have because in the industry whatever door of opportunity comes to you, you should walk through it. So if your daughter wants to be a singer and the door opens for her to be an actress, walk through it. If your son wants to be a rapper and the opportunity comes that he's talented enough to be a comedian and that's the door that opens, then walk through it. What that does is to allow the manager and the parent to take another look at the talent of their children.

Again I'm a singer; I'm an artist. I believe when you're an artist, you're talented in all of the arts. It's just that a certain area of the arts is more prominent than the other. I'm a singer, but I can also draw, I can paint, I can dance. All of those arts come naturally to me, but the one that I love the most, the one I think I'm the best at is singing. So when I present that to them over time, then they start to see, "Oh! She's more talented in this. She's more talented as an artist or as a painter." We start tapping into that talent. Eventually they start to lose interest in the singing part, because the drawing part is the one that's blossoming. It's the one that's growing the fastest.

With my event over time, the more they come the more I start to tap into the other talent. They start to change their goals and change their plans. I've had young guys, and I'm thinking of one in particular, who came in to be a rapper. By the time he saw the flow and the style and delivery of the more talented rappers, he decided that he was a better producer, which he was. He started producing tracks, which was really awesome. Now he's a producer and label owner and making good money, as opposed to being a rapper. A lot of times you are so into the bubble that you can't see the whole picture. That's what I try to do. I try to show them the whole picture so they can clearly see where they can tap in to get that money. It's very hard because grown people have their own way of doing things, and it's hard to change a grown person's thought process. I remember, back in the day, some of the panelists were A&R reps at major labels.

When I was trying to get guidelines, we used to have like 20-30 acts competing and the panel said it was too long—too many people. So I had to cut it down. I had to come up with guidelines. I talked with them about the age, should there be an age requirement? They said yes. They said the younger, the better because with young people, we can mold

175

them, they're more willing to be molded into what we feel is more marketable. I find that with mom managers, dad managers, and young managers, they have their own thought process on how to get to the goal. As a consultant, I try to show them the bigger picture.

Contact:
Eunice Moseley (562) 424-3836
freeassocinc3@aol.com
freelanceassociatesinc.com
Column website: www.thepulseofentertainment.com
Conference: www.Upliftingminds2.com

Dr. Westbrooks:
Eunice Moseley started her organization out of a love for artists and community. Through her music conferences, emerging artists get a chance to showcase their talent and get feedback in real time from a panel of professionals. This could be considered something like the frontline to exposure for an artist. She also provides an honest assessment of a person's talent, which could be helpful in steering them in the direction that might be better suited for them. Eunice encourages the artists and everyone to learn the business, if this is the business that they intend to make their living from. She stresses that understanding the mechanics of this business is a necessity because you relinquish a little bit of your power whenever you need to bring in others for help.

Eunice mentioned the Featherstone Brothers attending her conference. Even though they didn't win, they came to the attention of Sisqó of Dru Hill, who used their song "I Should Be." That song went on to reach No. 5 on the Billboard charts." Since then the Featherstones have become quite successful and have produced for Trey Songz, Wiz Khalifa feat. Izzy Azalea, August Alsina feat. Young Jeezy and 2 Chainz, Kid Ink feat. Chris Brown, B.O.B. and more.

CHAPTER TWENTY-SEVEN

GIL ROBERTSON

Journalist, Media Executive &
Owner of The Robertson Treatment, LLC

"It's important to create value with your work. People don't get rid of people they need."

Gil Robertson is a public relations expert and entertainment journalist. Gil's work has appeared in the music trade publication *Cash Box*, *The Music Connection*, the *Los Angeles Times*, the *Atlanta Journal Constitution*, *Black Enterprise,* and *Essence*. He's the visionary behind "The Robertson Treatment" syndicated column, a popular urban lifestyle column. He is also the editor of *Not in My Family: AIDS in the African American Community*, for which he received an NAACP Image Award nomination for Literature in 2006, among other awards and distinctions. Gil is a member of the National Press Club and the founder and president of the African American Film Critics Association.

When did you get into the business?

Gil Robertson:
I began my career in A&E journalism in 1992. Back then the entry way for most African-American journalists entering the field was through music. My first byline came through the *Tri-State Defender*. I then began working as a freelance journalist for fanzines like *Rap Pages*, *Word Up* and *Right On*. I quickly advanced my résumé writing for higher end publications like *Essence*, *Vibe* and *Black Enterprise*. When *Cash Box* put out the word that they were looking for an R&B Music Editor, I applied and got the job.

What are your greatest success stories in the music business?

177

Gil Robertson:

My greatest success was in seeing the artists and executives whose careers gained an added value through my work as a journalist and media professional. Professionally, I've interacted with all of the majors, and I provided valuable support to countless Indie labels as well. Overall the thing that I am most proud of is my body of work. I've amassed over 50 national magazine covers, bylines in the *L.A. Times* and the *Atlanta Journal Constitution*, as well as my syndicated column, which has been delivering lifestyle news for over 16 years in 30 markets.

How have you seen the industry change?

Gil Robertson:

The advent of technology has probably brought the biggest change to the industry. The Internet completely transformed the industry. If you weren't ready for it, you were in trouble.

What was good about this change?

Gil Robertson:

It forced artists to become more entrepreneurial.

What was the downside of this change?

Gil Robertson:

That so many people lost their jobs and careers.

Would you like to share any horror stories?

Gil Robertson:

It was when I saw people who weren't prepared for change. I witnessed countless executives who had settled into their jobs, only to be left without a clue when they were fired or their jobs were discontinued. You must stay connected to the trends and issues affecting the industry you're in and know how to position yourself for longevity. It's also important to create value with your work. People don't get rid of people they need.

What must any artist, music executive, producer or lawyer know about selling, marketing, and/or collecting royalties on digital music?

Gil Robertson:

As far as marketing goes, what's key is staying the course. Keep on message and don't lose your focus on your bottom line, which should be building a sustainable career. That's a career that generates enough capital to support you and your family over a life time.

Where do you think the future of the music industry will take us?

Gil Robertson:

Technology is certainly leading the way, so it's important to stay on top of what the new technology is and understanding how you fit in.

What cautions would you provide to others about staying relevant (or current) in the music business?

Gil Robertson:

Follow your passions. The thing about my career that I enjoy most is that my career has developed in stages that have matched my goals at the time.

What is the best way to make money in the industry today?

Gil Robertson:

Work on your talent and add value to it. Own and control your own product. Also, it's essential to follow your passions and figure out methods to monetize your core interests.

Here is the standard question we've all heard a million times. What advice would you give anyone who wanted to be successful in the music business?

Gil Robertson:

Research, be proactive and build relationships. Have a clear understanding of what you want out of a career in music. What's essential is building strong alliances with other professionals throughout the industry. It's also important to stay true to your word. If you say you're going to do something, then make your best effort to do it.

Contact:
www.robertsontreatment.com
info@robertsontreatment.com

Dr. Westbrooks:
Gil Robertson speaks on the importance of relationships in this business. It has been said that it's not what you know, but who you know. That is a key element in keeping open the doors of opportunity. As a reporter, a good reputation can get you an important interview or celebrity access. That is still true in this industry, so it's ideal to nurture relationships, have integrity, and maintain a good reputation.

CHAPTER TWENTY-EIGHT

RICK SCOTT

Great Scott P.R.oductions
Public Relations, Marketing, Management

"I think the most important thing is to get a U-S-P, a Unique Selling Point."

Rick Scott began working for a publicist in a boutique PR agency before branching out on his own. He started with one client, and now 22 years later Great Scott PR has provided publicity for a range of artists in Gospel, Jazz, Rock and alternative music. His talent pool has consisted of Jonathan Butler, Peter White, Earth Wind & Fire, Richard Elliott, Erasure, Martin Page, Jennifer Paige, the late Rick James and Brian Culbertson.

Who are some of your stellar clients?

Rick Scott:
My roster is diverse and has included some Rock & Roll Hall of Fame members. I've been in the urban world, the teen world, the Jazz world, the Gospel world and alternative Rock. My longest associations were with Earth, Wind & Fire. I was with them for about nine years, and I continue to get calls about several members and their solo projects. The other long term artist is Richard Elliott, and we've worked on several albums since 1994. So those are long term relationships.

Other clients include the major Pop act Erasure, the alternative Rock band Spoon. Martin Page had a number one Adult Contemporary single the year I represented him. Jennifer Paige also went to number two on the Pop charts. Rick James I'm proud to have represented, but that was unfortunately after he left the body. I handled the final album that he ever recorded, and also his autobiography that he put out in conjunction with the album release. So that's another legend, but I had other long term associations with many contemporary Jazz stars like Jonathan Butler. I've been working with him on and off since 1997, and we're working together again now.

Peter White, I've done three albums with him. I just came back recently from Napa Valley where I worked with Brian Culbertson on his Apple Valley Jazz Getaway. I represent the Smooth Jazz Cruise and also Entertainment Cruise Productions, the company that produces it. They now produce the Soul Train Cruise as well. I've had a finger in that as well. It's diverse. There's a music side of it, and I also have a sports side.

I've been an athlete as long as I've been passionate about music. About ten years ago I started working with athletes in my chosen passion, which is pro-cycling and triathlon. My athletes came home with silver medals from the London Olympic Games in 2012. I've worked with the Amgen Tour of California, which is the biggest pro bike race in the U.S. I work for a bunch of different health and fitness sports products. One is Bonk Breaker, which is the official energy bar of the Ironman Triathlon. We have a partnership with Wes Welker, the pro ball wide receiver. Wes is one of the partners of Bonk Breaker and is the owner of the Milwaukee Brewers. The Milwaukee Brewers are actually now selling Bonk Breakers at their stadium. Bonk Breakers are energy bars and protein bars which are dairy free, soy free, gluten free and all natural.

Are there any specific guidelines you can give to up and coming artists, or up and coming labels in terms of what to look for in their PR and marketing campaign, or the person they're hiring to perform such duties?

Rick Scott:
Those are two very different questions. About whom to hire, I think the idea is to look for someone who is passionate about you and your music, and, of course, is going to give you priority attention. If you're hiring an independent publicist, if you're with a record label and you are afforded the use of the publicist from the record label, then fine. But, if you are hiring an independent, then hopefully you are hiring someone that is passionate about you and understands you, your vision, and where you want to go, and is going to make you a priority, and is going to devote their time and attention to help you achieve your public relations goals.

As far as advice overall, I think the most important thing is get a 'USP.' This is an advertising concept that I just always adopted. I think every time before I sit down to write a press release, an autobiography, or a pitch letter to the media, I always try to think u-s-p. What is a 'unique selling point'? What is a unique selling point about this artist? Why should anybody care? From what I understand, journalists receive about 150 to 200 music submissions per week. And they receive about that many press releases per day. How do you cut through the clutter of that? You have to be able to tell a compelling story, and that is what is unique about this artist.

What are some other things you would say to the new artist to look out for?

Rick Scott:

I'm a passionate guy. I work on a handful of projects at a time, and I have to be passionate about each one. It's my greatest strength and it's my greatest weakness. I can't do anything if I'm not passionate about it. It's plain and simple. I need to fall in love with my client. I'm going to take this in a different direction and elaborate on that for a second. I think that maybe a Rick James anecdote might fit in nicely.

Because of my spiritual beliefs and wanting to promote clean things, as much as I might enjoy Rick James's music, when I got the call about representing him, I had to pause because he's also known for promoting a little bit of raunchiness. I mean there's the sex appeal, but there's some themes that go over the line a little bit. I had to sit down and think about whether I was comfortable promoting Rick James.

When I got into working with Earth, Wind & Fire, like a lot of contemporary Jazz stars, it happened to come at a point in my life where I had to look into what I'm doing and think about the messages that I am promoting. So I don't represent rappers, for instance, that are rapping derogatory things about women and promoting drug culture or violence, things like that. An answer to a prayer was when Earth Wind & Fire starting singing about universal love and peace and joy, and working with a lot of contemporary Jazz artists where there aren't any lyrics, so I don't have to worry about it.

When it came to Rick James, I got a phone call saying, "Are you interested in representing Rick James and the one album he's working on?" This was before he passed. Instantly, you want to say yes, but think, *"Well, what is his message?"* The interesting thing about Rick was that Rick was an extremely gifted singer/songwriter, but most people didn't really know that because he had the sex and drug culture. But, on his final album he basically wanted to leave a legacy of his gift as a singer/songwriter. When I looked at the lyrics, yes, there were a few terms on that record that were traditional Rick James and very sexually oriented, but most of it was about love. It was about searching for love. It was about love. It was about the desire for love and wants; the need of love. I went and read his autobiography. The autobiography was unedited. It was what he wrote when he was in jail ten years before it was released. It was raw and raunchy, and it talked about everything that he had gotten into in all his glory days with all the excesses and everything. But the message behind it all was his search for love. Once I connected with that, it was easy to represent Rick James.

What would you say to an artist or a client who expects to be the best in the world and believes many of things will come overnight?

Rick Scott:

For new artists coming through, again, why are you unique? What is unique about you? For one, as an artist, creatively, you should be at the top of your game and you should be doing something every day to further your skills and develop your craft. Whether it's producing, writing, performing, working on your instrument or whatever, you should be working on your craft every day.

I think one of the biggest things in the industry that's changed over the years since all those years ago is that everybody is independent now. The stars are now releasing their albums independently. They can hire the same publicist, the same radio promoter, the same marketer and everything that you would if you were with a record label. So the game has changed. That's good and also bad because the field is cluttered now with new releases, and new artists, and everything.

Again, how do you cut through the clutter? Number one, you must be at the top of your game, having the best product that you possibly can. Number two, have a compelling story and what makes you unique. Focus on what makes you unique because there's a lot. There are so many talented people out there. But what is unique about this artist? Why should I pay attention when I got a stack of a hundred CDs or new digital submissions that just arrived this week? Why should I listen to that one? So it goes, and say that out of those hundred, 30 of them are actually really well produced and at the highest level. After that, now you've narrowed it down to 30, how are you going to get through that? That's when the unique personality or the unique aspects come into play.

What would your advice be to veteran artists or those who are trying to stay in the game?

Rick Scott:

Again, the media has changed as well. There's a lot less space in newspapers. There are less magazines, and there is less space in those magazines to get covered. There's one major area where you can get published, where you can publish daily or several times daily if you like, and that is social media. You need to be in touch with your fans on a daily basis, a minimum of once a day. I wouldn't recommend more than three times a day. But if you have things going on, you need to touch base and communicate with the fans directly. That's through Facebook, Twitter, YouTube, and Instagram. Be aware of where the fans are. Be in touch with them, nurture, keep them involved, and engage them on a daily basis. People's attention span is short—shorter than ever—so if you can nurture that fan base, cultivate that fan base, then that's the way you'll be able to release records and sell concert tickets and things like that.

What's the greatest part of being in this business, and why should anyone have a great deal of faith, hope, and excitement about today's music industry and the future music industry?

Rick Scott:
That's a great question. Honestly, you have to be doing it for love. Anybody can look at it and say, "Wow, that's so glamorous!" And anybody can look at it and say, "Wow, you live such a glamorous life!" But what I tell people is, "You're seeing those two hours when my artist is on stage. You're not seeing these 200 other hours where I'm slaving away. It's not glamorous when it's three o'clock in the morning and you're trying to finish a press release, or pitching the media by email or anything like that. It's not glamorous. You've got to be doing it for love. When I am at a concert looking at one of my artists up on stage, I'm just sitting in the audience or on the side of the stage just proudly beaming. It just reawakens my creativity and my passion, and that's what it's about. It's a passion thing. It's a love thing. Otherwise, it ain't all glamour and glitter. It's not that at all. You've got to be doing it for love, and hopefully the money will come as well.

Contact:
Great Scott P.R.oductions
www.greatscottpr.com
www.twitter.com/greatscottpr
www.facebook.com/rick.scott

Dr. Westbrooks:
Rick Scott focuses on an artist's unique selling point. Exactly what qualities does an artist possess that sets them apart from everyone else? Understanding that the game has changed, many artists and even

well established artists are now releasing their own music. They must go up against the major labels who still have large budgets, and they're also competing with a new flock of Indie artists who are trying to get a foothold in the industry. Rick stresses that it is imperative to have something about you that is compelling enough to distinguish you from the rest—be it a style, a different voice, a look, or, hopefully, beautiful music that cannot be denied.

THE MUSIC INDUSTRY EXECUTIVES

INFORMED SOURCES

Michael Brae
David Wasserman

CHAPTER TWENTY-NINE

MICHAEL BRAE

CEO/Record Executive at Hit Man Records, Inc.

"You must be able to identify the paradigm shifts that are going on around you and position your brand accordingly."

Michael Brae came out of the financial side of things on Wall Street in New York and headed out to California where he started Hit Man Records in 1991. He moved on to solidify a joint venture with Solar (Sounds of Los Angeles Records), a division of RCA Records in 1995. His company was able to expand its distribution while adding manufacturing and promotional support. Since then, Hit Man Records has established itself as a one-stop music industry leader with a multitude of capabilities. Hit Man is currently distributed by MVD Entertainment Group and Planet Works, with a network of partners and distributors that include Universal Music Canada, Barnes & Noble, Best Buy, Baker & Taylor, Fry's and several other key distributors that factor into Hit Man's global distribution. Michael Brae explains his core business model.

Michael Brae:
The Hit Man Records business model is loosely based on the Japanese keiretsu system—a form of organization based on networks rather than hierarchy, which, in effect, achieves the scale economies of vertical integration with a network of affiliated companies working in conjunction with all the capabilities of a major label and flexibility of an independent.

What are your greatest success stories in the music business?

Michael Brae:
A few success stories are that I have been fortunate to represent well-known and established artists, such as Samuelle (double-platinum and Grammy Award-winning singer from R&B group Club Nouveau); Mac Dash Mone (former member of the double-platinum group Digital

188

Underground); and Johnny Paycheck who produced six Gold albums, one platinum album, one double platinum, and 33 hits. Additionally, I had my first joint-venture deal with Solar Records, which was a division of RCA Records. This gave my company Hit Man Records its first major distribution platform. I learned the nuts and bolts of the distribution business through CEO Dick Griffey and General Counsel Virgil Roberts. Moving forward, I closed several major partnerships and distribution deals, which, in the end, positions Hit Man's music (both physically and digitally) in major retailers worldwide.

How have you seen the industry change?

Michael Brae:
   The product platform, and delivery of music, and the distribution platform have all changed.

What was good about this change?

Michael Brae:
   With all the changes in the music industry, the goal for any artist or Indie label is to make their mark in history. It's all about mastering 'paradigm.' The most critical point to understand about paradigm is that in a paradigm shift, everything goes back to zero. What does that mean? It means that whatever made you successful in the old paradigm may not even exist or be necessary in the new paradigm. Sound familiar? Sure, it's the old music industry platform and the old brick and mortar retail systems versus the new digital world of music with hundreds of online digital retailers, online radio and social media support. To master paradigm, you must be able to identify the paradigm shifts that are going on around you and position your brand accordingly. Position yourself for the future, which is now. Take advantage of corporate sponsorship partnerships, develop artists, build and expand your label's brand by finding the choice music aggregator in expanding your music worldwide while marketing your brand.

What do you see as the downside of the major changes in the industry?

Michael Brae:

The downside is that with the shift towards digital, there are more and more retail store closures, and this cuts into your price points in your overall sales. The royalty payouts do not balance out between the two platforms. In regards to the two platforms digital versus physical, you are paid much lower percentages on your digital album or single sales versus a higher percentage on the full-length CD. However, the immediate solution is to leverage both platforms along with positioning your music and associating yourself with licensing and publishing companies. It's also beneficial to examine alternative distribution solutions in maximizing your overall opportunity, your growth and sales potential.

Would you like to share any horror stories?

Michael Brae:

The closure of Tower Records started a ripple effect on other brick and mortar stores in which hundreds of major chains closed. The bankruptcy of Tower Records effected our label in which we had a large sum of inventory in their distribution center with several of our titles as well as a balance of payouts still owed, which was never realized due to the bankruptcy. In most bankruptcies you're lucky if you even receive 12 percent or even a dime of any balance owed during the bankruptcy. However, the bigger picture was the relationship and distribution we had through Tower Records. We dealt with a great team over at Bayside Distribution, which was really another entity of Tower. Their distribution center was responsible for fulfilling Tower.

The real horror story is the loss of opportunity and positioning, meaning our company Hit Man Records had an exclusive deal for U.S. national distribution in all of Tower Record stores. This gave us great product placement, positioning along with great servicing from product managers and sales reps, and in the blink of an eye it was all gone—everything down the drain due to the closure of Tower. At one point, Hit Man was one of Bayside's top independent labels, in which we even had our own catalog section of titles in an exclusive catalog distributed to retail buyers throughout the U.S. Imagine that, having all your titles with five to ten CDs in every Tower Records store throughout the U.S. (close to 450 Tower Records) all gone, vanished along with all the Tower stores, closed. That in itself was a wake-up call in adjusting to the times.

What cautions would you provide to others about staying relevant in the music business?

Michael Brae:

Not changing with the times. This is a huge problem with labels as they are stuck in the traditional model of selling music. Understand the new channels of marketing and adapt as needed. Music is always evolving, so should all facets of the business. Learn and understand every new channel of marketing, promotion, distribution, and adapt as needed. Artists should always be growing, evolving, and experimenting.

Not having multiple streams of music business income. Most musicians go into the music business looking to find a 'job' and plan to primarily make money with a single source of income, such as through performing or recording music. There is nothing wrong with making money in this way, but it may be challenging (particularly in the early stages of your music career) to consistently generate a high enough level of income through any single activity in the music industry.

That being said, it's very realistic to build a range of independent income streams that will add up to provide a very stable and secure way to make a living in music. This means that regardless of what your primary goal is in your music career—be it as a performing artist, a songwriter, a studio musician, a record producer, an author or anything else—you must have a variety of ongoing projects that you earn money from in both active and passive ways. In addition to the obvious benefit of helping you make more money from multiple sources, having several streams of income makes your music career much more secure overall because you protect yourself from becoming dependent on only one source of income.

What must any artist, music executive, producer or lawyer know about selling, marketing, and/or collecting royalties on digital music?

Michael Brae:

It's all about convenience—the ability to buy now at a click of a button. This is a 'spontaneous buy' courtesy of the Internet. The music industry has adapted to the Internet world and learned how to meet the needs of consumers and monetize it in the digital marketplace. Digital music consumption is now the mainstream. Download stores continue to see steadily growing sales and are spreading globally. They represent around 70 percent of global digital revenues. In addition, music video streaming services are also seeing strong growth. YouTube, the most popular digital video service, has more than 800 million active users globally. Vevo and Warner Music Sound, are two of the top three channels on YouTube. Internet radio is also soaring in popularity, with leading service Pandora already accounting for eight percent of all radio listening in the U.S. With all this in place, my advice is to simply move away from the traditional platform of selling music and to position your music in all these new platforms. Strategically build a strong fan base to support your brand. At the end of the day, it's all about brand loyalty.

Where do you think the future of the music industry will take us?

Michael Brae:
I believe artist development is back, along with the rise of the Indie label. I believe that this is the future. History always repeats itself. Capitol Records, Interscope, A&M Records and Geffen Records (which was founded by David Geffen in 1980 and home to Donna Summer, John Lennon and Yoko Ono) were at one point all independent labels in which they positioned themselves alongside major companies. The label retaliation against poor industry numbers has historically been to invest less and less into developing artists in order to sustain long-term careers. The result is you see quick famed one-hit wonders and lots of crap on the radio. Labels will seize the opportunity by increasing their budgets and investing in apps, online radio, and social media. Labels will once again focus on developing sustainable careers, not one-hit wonders. Likewise, A&R will also become relevant again, which will lead to an increase in music industry jobs.

What advice would you give anyone who wanted to be successful in the music business?

Michael Brae:
Know your market and know who your fans are. After you have identified your value/brand, you must know 'who' you are going to communicate and sell to. For example, if you are about to release your single or album, who are the fans/customers that you expect will buy it? Can you easily reach them? If not, what are you doing to grow your database of fans? How will you place your music to thousands of potential fans? Most musicians don't think this strategically through, and as a result, end up as average musicians. Always be in the process of building your brand. YOU are ultimately responsible for your own career, regardless of whether you have somebody else promoting your music for you. Lastly, establish shows, tours, live interviews, radio, and

Internet promotions in supporting your music. This is a must. It's all about consistency. It's all about being in control.

What does it mean to be your own Ultimate Music Aggregator?

Michael Brae:
There are hundreds of digital retail stores worldwide. Who do you pick as your 'ultimate music aggregator' in positioning, promoting and selling your music to gain the most ground in supporting your overall digital sales efforts? I recently spoke to Steve Norris, one of the partners of MondoTunes, who commented, "While most independent distributors reach only 45-50 retailers, despite charging needless monthly and yearly fees, MondoTunes reaches over 750 retailers and mobile partners in over a hundred world regions without any monthly or yearly fees." He stated that they are the only global distributors that assists in marketing and promotions in supporting artists in getting music heard by the masses. They have a veteran team with familiarity and hands-on experience that covers songwriting, production, A&R, booking, tour management, marketing, distribution, media and licensing. MondoTunes boasts the largest music distribution in the world, and provides upstream services for many major labels in search of breakout artists. What makes MondoTunes unique is their ability to provide the largest global digital distribution in conjunction with a comprehensive worldwide online marketing campaign to maximize artists' hype and exposure. Artists retain 100 percent ownership of their own master recordings, publishing, and songwriting credits. My recommendation is very simple, 750 retailers in over 100 countries for under $38 an album. Check out http://mondotunes.com.

Contact:
info@hitmanrecords.com
www.hitmanrecords.com

Dr. Westbrooks:
Michael Brae strongly suggests that those who make a living from the music industry recognize changes in the industry and change with them or be left behind. He feels that some aspects of the old model will return such as artist development and strong Indie labels. He speaks about paradigm shifts and changing your way of thinking as necessary steps to successful careers. Just as the printing press was a game changer for the book industry, so has the new digital technology changed the game in the music industry.

CHAPTER THIRTY

DAVID WASSERMAN

CEO of Latin Cool Records and Latin Cool Now

"That product that I just sold for a 99¢ download automatically reinvents itself. It doesn't have to be stored, shipped, refrigerated or packaged. It's the greatest invention, even better than bottled water."

David Wasserman launched Latin Cool Records in September of 2002. Prior to that he spent 40 years on Wall Street as a senior stock market trader in the NASDAQ marketplace. Upon retirement, Wasserman's company was acquired, and he decided to pursue his passion for music. He started a traditional record company—Latin Cool Records—before transitioning into the digital arena. David describes the origin of the Latin Cool enterprise.

David Wasserman:
I launched a traditional record label called Latin Cool Records. We were primarily in the Latin Jazz world, because realistically, I knew I couldn't compete with Pop music and the five big labels. I hired a very experienced music veteran of the Latin world who had produced music for everybody from Tito Puente to the late Grammy Award-winning Ray Barretto. He was my A&R man. We did six CDs, three of which were Grammy nominated. Unfortunately, we did nothing but lose money because it was at the time when the music business was in its first throws of changing to an Internet based kind of industry.

We had to deal with all those issues traditional record companies went through, which was distribution, shipping, and not getting paid. It was unpleasant because it was unlike Wall Street where we got paid within five days or three days. In the music business, you didn't get paid. The only time you got paid was if you had a big hit and when they wanted more CDs. That's when you say, well you pay me for what you have first before I ship out more.

Fortunately, I had the vision where I saw where it was going. What I found was that one morning I came into the office, and without exaggerating, I had between 300 and 500 CDs that were self-produced

194

by artists that I would categorize as secondary or tertiary level artists. People who were gifted in the sense of their profession, but, basically, they had been shut out by all the major labels. They said, "Here, take my product and do what you can do with it. Do whatever you want with it." We began to realize that the music business was morphing into the Internet business, so we established one of the first downloading stores called Latin Cool Now.

We had a lot of effort and a lot of money. The idea was to take these albums, digitize them and have the artists be very genre specific. We had mostly Latin, and for each song, believe it or not, we went through and gave a special genre designation within the genre. For example Mambo, Cha-Cha, Bossa Nova, and other such genres were itemized. It was quite an undertaking. Again, all of my thoughts were how wonderful it was, but the reality was that iTunes opened at the same time and everybody went to iTunes.

After about six months of reluctance, I decided it made more sense to give my content to iTunes and the other stores. It was a pretty extensive catalog, and it covered most of the major independent Latin labels. It was great music and nobody really knew where it was. It was a successful choice because at my store where I made 100% of each download, on iTunes I made less but substantially much more in volume. I decided that was the route to go, and we signed a lot of labels. I became a licensor of their content. It turned out that's the greatest business ever invented.

How does licensing content affect the artists who had previously only just produced CDs?

David Wasserman:
I realized the great wonder of the Internet was that the person doesn't get the product until they pay first, unlike when we distributed and made CDs. The purchaser has to submit a credit card to these stores, and when it's approved, then they can own the music. The best part of it is that they download it, and guess what? That product that I just sold for a 99¢ download automatically reinvents itself. It doesn't have to be stored, shipped, refrigerated or packaged. It's the greatest invention, even better than bottled water. We are basically selling air that has to reappear as soon as you hit the button. And from that sense, it's there for perpetuity—forever. It's a very good situation. We get our revenue from the stores, and we, in turn, pay our artists. We pay them quarterly, we get reports and we also distribute, too.

Now we've grown from iTunes to approximately 240 stores throughout the world. We report quarterly to all of our artists and labels. We give them a complete Excel spreadsheet of every song that was sold everywhere in the world. They can review it and see that everything is in order. And similar to my Wall Street background where our motto was "My word is my bond," we take everybody at their word, that the report I'm getting from iTunes, Amazon and Google is exactly what happened. I never questioned them, and my artists never question me. So it's a very nice thing, but again it also has changed. The business is a very moving kind of industry. The business has changed not only for the companies, but for the artists themselves and I'm experiencing that right now.

In today's digital arena many times an artist or sometimes a manager believes that if your music is available at these digital sites, and if you post on Facebook and Twitter then you're going to be an overnight sensation. I'm sure there is a wide gap between your higher selling artists and those who aren't selling very much these days. What is the difference between the artists who have substantial sales and those who don't?

David Wasserman:
Yes, that's a fantastic question. I would say the majority of our labels and artists that give us the music to represent for them around the world think that that's enough to have their music sold. It's not, because there's millions of tracks out there right now. It's not like the old days, where you went into a Tower Records and you only had to choose from 50,000. Now you have to choose from 14,000,000. The actual game has changed in terms of the amount of music available. Number one (when you think about it), when you go in a store you see an album cover that's a thumbnail. The days of people wanting to have a physical CD in their hand is really past.

The premise of why CD sales were so effective at the beginning, was because of the actual convenience and quality of the music, although it was not as good as vinyl. You could play it, and it was so much easier to use and better quality than the cassette tape. First it was the vinyl. Then we had the 8-track tape, which was tedious, and you really couldn't control it, and it was a big bulky thing. Then came the cassette, which we loved. But the cassette really set off something in all people who love music. That was, I can take the cassette, once I figure out how to hook up my amplifier and my cassette player to my turntable, I can make my own greatest hits. I can take one from Rita Shelby's album, I can take one from Al Green, I can take one from Andrea Bocelli and I can make my own compilation that I like onto this cassette. So now, that's what people did. I could make "Dave's Greatest Disco Hits Volumes 1 through 12," and that was done by me.

Then they came out with something called the CD, which was so convenient to use. You didn't have to hold your finger down and fast-forward until you found where you wanted to go. You could just click and it would take you from track to track. It was easy to carry, and you could have a lot of them. What happened was, at the beginning people who had Al Green's Greatest Hits on either a cassette or an LP, bought the CD version of it. They were so pleased they could easily carry it, and it didn't scratch. The sales at the beginning of that whole generation were gigantic. A great part of the sales were people getting that same collection of what they had, but now they have it in a new format.

Then what happened was—like everything else in this world—the labels got greedy and they wanted $17.95 for that CD. The reality was if you heard a track on the radio that you liked, you'd have to spend $17.95 to buy the CD of which there were only two or three tracks that you really liked. That became costly and people didn't like it. Then the label said, "If we give them 50 to 60 minutes worth of play, they'll think it's worth it. It really started to show in the sales because people didn't want to pay that much. As prices kept coming down, then Steve Jobs (JOKINGLY: *and Dave Wasserman*) invented music download. This is where you could do exactly what you did with your cassette players. Except now you could go from music to music, and download what you wanted and make your own compilation for your car. I would say on that premise, out of the thousands of artists that we represent in songs, I would say less than one percent is for total album purchases.

So it's the singles that consumers wanted? The music industry saw this as a precursor to the CD entering the marketplace. In the 1970s and 1980s we had the 12-inch singles and the remixes.

David Wasserman:
You're right, of course. That was the disco era when that first came out. That had a very potent effect on the way music is thought of. You know, I have young artists to call me and say, "Mr. Wasserman, I've got the album. I've got 16 tracks ready for you." And I say, "What? Are you crazy? Take those 16 tracks and make it into two albums and put a different cover on them. Put a different face and have a little more visibility."

The premise of the artist today is totally changed. It used to be, if you had a great record and you would bring it to the radio industry—

without going into the ramifications of what that business was like—you got it played on the radio. People would listen to it and actually that whole radio concept is, if you got it played often enough, then listeners will start to think it is good. Your mind plays tricks with you. The more you hear it, you're almost convinced that this must be a really good song because I'm hearing it all the time. Believe it or not, that's not enough today. Today, you have to be involved in social media and you have to have connections. A lot of music is now sold by word of mouth, by Facebook, by Twitter and by Instagram. With that comes the need for young artists to have an awareness of what the Internet is, and how to maneuver and make your music show up frequently on the Internet.

As I have just learned, having done a new Hip Hop release in which I'm very proud of, I just got finished filming a music video. That's an important part of it. Although I'm not a believer in giving away anything for free (because it costs us money to produce these things) the reality is that's the way music is getting sold today. It helps if you find someone gratuitous enough to find a DJ that can help and a promoter to send the songs out to the record pools. It's not enough to make a quality record anymore.

I used to joke about my Latin Cool download side of the business, I wanted to call it the best music you've never heard because most music goes unheard. That's unfortunate. For musicians, that's their life's blood. A lot of them that really almost do it for nothing. It's a career that is love based. It's not a monetary thing, and I wouldn't recommend it if you're looking to make a lot of money. It's very stressful, and there's a lot of ups and downs and a lot of questions. I've yet to find an artist who didn't think his album was the greatest. It might well be, but that's not enough anymore.

What does 'record pool' mean for today's artists who are just entering the business?

David Wasserman:
I'm talking about music where the demographics of purchasers of this new production is 14-30. Believe it or not, the listeners of Hip Hop might probably be beginning as early as ten years old. They listen to this music. That's why this particular single that I've released has no profanity in it, and the subject matter is kind of upbeat and exciting as opposed to demeaning or anything like that. But let's say 18-30. These are the ages of people that go to nightclubs. You see enough of it in a movie when they walk into a club and are given music to play at these clubs. When we do a recording, we do a radio version. We do a version

where the artist can perform live above the backup track. And we do a club version, which is specifically a longer version for dancing, and they do play a part, they really do. Of course, the other places where we have to place music, the Sirius satellite stations and the Pandora digital outlets. Although I take objection to them because they don't pay.

Streaming is the big threat to the music industry in my opinion. There are two sides to the story. There are those that think it's great and those that think it's terrible. Streaming is a new music model whereby you pay a fee every month which allows you to listen to your music. There are different levels of fees. For example, Spotify (a digital music service) first comes to mind. On that site for $4.95 a month you can listen to any song that you want—any song that you've ever loved. They have a vast library where you just go on there and you look up the best of B.B. King or Carla Thomas or Rita Shelby, anybody you want. You click on it and it plays, and you didn't pay anything. It doesn't give you just a sound bite, it gives you the entire song. You can save it to a play list, and you can make a play list so that when you're sitting at your computer working or whatever it is you're doing, you can hear the music of your choice.

Unfortunately, the person who did that is having a wonderful time, but the artist and Latin Cool Records that paid $25,000 for that track is getting a payment based on the decimal that goes so far low from a penny down, that you could have 47,000 lines on an Excel spreadsheet that shows the song and its amount of streaming, and the royalty amount comes to $114. The premise with sites that stream was that while you're listening, we're going to show you advertising. That's going to be part of the mix as to what you pay. I frankly haven't seen it, and I think that's the threat. It's better than people not paying for music at all like on Napster, but I still think the artists and the labels don't benefit from the streaming world. But, we'll see.

Regarding legal matters, I just got through making sure I had all the proper clearances before I released anything. I'm telling young artists to make sure to get the right clearances before you put music out. If it's not a success, don't worry about it. But if it is, they're going to come and take everything that you made. So it's very, very important that you be aware of legal issues.

Contact:
Facebook.com/LatinCoolRecords

Dr. Westbrooks:
David Wasserman loves the new distribution platform of downloading music. Downloading does eliminate the manufacturing

aspect of the product. He feels the best part is getting paid immediately, even before the customer gets the music. This is completely different from how it once worked when you got paid for product at the mercy of others. That's the positive side. The flip side to that is streaming. I agree with him completely about streaming. It pays the content owner much too little if it pays anything at all. Hopefully in time, things will adjust so that the content creators can receive better compensation.

THE MUSIC DIRECTORS

INFORMED SOURCES

Ray Chew
Shannon Sanders

CHAPTER THIRTY-ONE

RAY CHEW

Musical Director, Composer, Producer—
Saturday Night Live, American Idol, and Dancing With the Stars

"Keep the craft at the heart of all that you do. Be the best musician that you can. Study music theory, study music history, study it all."

Ray Chew has conducted full orchestras for some of television's most stellar events such as Fox TV's *American Idol*, ABC's *Dancing with the Stars*, The *BET Awards* and BET's *Celebration of Gospel*. Chew's talents have taken him to Carnegie Hall and around the globe as a musical director for artists such as Aretha Franklin, Justin Bieber, Prince, Rihanna, Carrie Underwood, James Taylor, Anita Baker, Queen Latifah, Ne-Yo, Barry Manilow, T.I., Smokey Robinson, Pastor Shirley Caesar, Jennifer Hudson, and Quincy Jones. Chew is also the Music Director for Donald Trump's *Miss USA* and *Miss Universe* pageants. Chew has been featured on over a hundred Gold and platinum albums and has designs on scoring for major motion pictures. He is a diverse musician, composer, arranger and producer. He generously recalls some of his career highlights and promotes tenacity, training and versatility among emerging artists.

Ray Chew:
One of my career highlights was being musical director during the start of the inauguration celebrations for President Obama, our first African American president. The historical context cannot be overstated, especially if you go back over the past 50 years. We were denied the right to vote freely, and further than that when you consider slavery. So, it was a huge moment in history. As for the show that I worked on, there was a huge line-up that I was responsible for, including Beyoncé, Sting, Stevie Wonder, Alicia Keys, Mary J. Blige, Maroon 5, Mariah Carey, Shakira, Jay Z, and Will.i.am. The undertaking was supreme in putting all of this stuff together because we're absolutely talking about some of

the world's greatest artists, and everything had to be great because it was on live TV. It was definitely a career highlight.

Is it correct that you have structured events once or twice in Carnegie Hall?

Ray Chew:
That is correct. Actually, there have been a few others. I'll go back to the beginning of my relationship with Carnegie Hall. It started when they brought me in to work with the legendary opera star, Miss Jessye Norman. I produced several events as part of her festival that was called *Honor*. After that, they liked the work that I did and they asked me to come in and curate some of my own events. They gave me pretty much artistic freedom. They believed in me and the product that I did. So my first one was called the *Night of Inspiration*. We had a great night of inspirational and secular music. So I married on the great stage of Carnegie Hall a great line up of artists including Michael McDonald, Bebe and Cece Winans, Shirley Caesar, Patty Griffin, Phylicia Rashad and many more. We had a 50-piece orchestra and a 130-voice mass choir. It was one of the greatest nights in their history, and that was by their own account.

After that they asked me to do a video. Then they asked me to do another event, and we came up with the concept of presenting the great music of Motown. I always insist on bringing in a full orchestra for my productions. This is a great institution. Carnegie Hall is iconic, not just the music, but in terms of the building itself. It's a landmark and a great place to perform. It's just a great institution, and they sought me to bring in my own program, which is something I am very proud of.

Can you speak to the professional music director, conductor or composer? What kind of strategies would they need to employ to even touch upon your success?

Ray Chew:
First thing is that you need to arm yourself with as many great musical studies and skills as possible. These are acquired skills. A lot of people look at the pinnacle of some of the accomplishments, and it seems unattainable. They ask how do you do this? It's like building a house. A house does not go up all in one shot. You have to do it brick by brick. You don't look at a house and get to the 21st floor without having to go through floors 9, 10, 15, and 18. You have to build upon a great founda-

tion, and the first foundation is to arm yourself with acquired musical studies. I speak to young people. I want to see the next phase of talented musicians on their way up. I want to see the next crop of musicians learn everything there is to know about the craft, uplifting the craft. Keep the craft at the heart of all that you do. Be the best musician that you can. Study music theory, study music history, study it all. People underestimate the capacity of their own brain. I studied many instruments starting with piano at age six, and I got a scholarship to play. I also studied drums, percussions, violin, cello, bass and trumpet. I had the desire and the aptitude to be able to pick up any instrument and figure it out in an hour. Give me an instrument and I'll be able to play something within an hour. I'd say to the next crop, "Study up, study well." Knowing that the path to any kind of success is to dream a wonderful dream and divide it into goals and sub-goals, and then divide that into tasks. Something seems far out of reach, but you have to build a road to it. It starts with a wheel and then the steps to get things rolling.

In any industry it is about reputations. You have been able to build great relationships and establish a reputation with Donald Trump, the producer of the Miss USA and Miss Universe Pageants. How did you approach working with Mr. Trump?

Ray Chew:
The *Miss Universe* and *Miss USA* pageants are the brands of Donald Trump, and are very special endeavors. The focus is on knowing that music is to underscore and to drive the energy of the show. This is not the type of show where there's a lot of out front musical performance, although there are a few during the course of the show. The main focus is on the girls. So I take the approach as if I was scoring for a movie. I want to underscore the moment and give each moment the right kind of energy. I compose the music for *Miss USA* and *Miss Universe* which includes the themes and the many different pieces of music that you hear throughout the show. There are also special performances and special pieces of music that I put together that will make the swimsuit segment have the right kind of rhythmic walk. Those are the types of considerations that I use when doing that show. I am excited about being with a brand that is synonymous with excellence. When you think of the Trump brand, there is nothing that isn't excellent about the things that he does. Putting politics aside, there is absolutely nothing that you would not love about excellence and maintaining that.

Let's talk about the politics of aligning yourself with a network such as BET. How does one build a relationship with a network, and how did you prepare creatively to mount those productions?

Ray Chew:
The relationships are cultivated and developed over the years. My first BET show, which was about ten years ago, was the *Celebration of Gospel*. It all comes from somebody wanting to give you a break and giving you a chance. You can have agents, you can have managers, and you can have lawyers. They are all important, and if they can get you an opportunity, then great. But the first big thing you need is access. You have to have access to get to the right person so that you can perhaps get an opportunity to display the wonderful things that you have prepared. So I have been fortunate in being able to come across somebody when they need you.

My first television job was *Saturday Night Live,* and I got that job because I was sitting in a Sushi bar in a Japanese restaurant. Sitting next to me was the producer of *Saturday Night Live.* The musical director at that time was trombonist and multi-instrumentalist Tom Malone, who is now with the *Late Show*, and we started chatting. He knew of my work and he said, "There's a slot open on *Saturday Night Live*, are you interested?" And I said, "Yeah!" That came about because I first had access to him as a person, and secondly I had some kind of a previous relationship with him. The opportunity presented itself and then with me being totally armed and prepared for that opportunity.

The worst thing that you can do is go and engage an opportunity and not be prepared. Some people's equation for success is preparation meets opportunity equals success. I take it a step further. I say preparation plus opportunity, plus God's good grace and luck, and every other thing that you can imagine is what gives you an opportunity perhaps for success. That doesn't create success in and of itself, but you are certainly on the right path.

My BET relationships have developed over the years with meeting Stephen Hill (President of Music Programming and Specials for BET) and Marilyn Gill (producer of BET's *Celebration of Gospel*). Marilyn was the executive producer, and she called me and said we'd love for you to do *Celebration of Gospel.* She had knowledge of me doing shows for many years for *Showtime at the Apollo*, so she knew me from that show. That didn't necessarily sell me in itself as far as making me the right choice for the *Celebration of Gospel.* Still, she decided to give me a shot doing that. So I thank Marilyn Gill because that was the first special that I did for them. From there my relationship continued to grow based upon me doing that. For me it's about delivering excellence and going above and beyond, and making sure that our artists and producers are happy. I'm always that main link to bring them together.

From there my relationship grew to the *BET Awards*. The late John Cossette was the executive producer of *BET Awards* and formerly the *Grammy Awards*, he was familiar with my work. I was at the front door step when they were putting together the *BET Honors*, and I have also worked on the first three seasons of *Sunday Best*. It's about cultivating great relationships based upon a brand of excellence.

You have been in the Music Director's spot on American Idol and now Dancing with the Stars. On the music tip, what advice do you have for those whose careers take longer to manifest?

Ray Chew:
I would say there's a lot of many wonderful jobs out there. It's a lot to look for. There are many things that I haven't done yet. I aspire to write Academy Award-winning scores for major motion pictures. I have trained for it, I've studied it and I've worked on the craft. I have aspired to do that, and I have people who are going to be opening some doors for me for those opportunities knowing that I deliver excellence. Sometimes it's the Catch-22 that they do find themselves in.

If you don't have any experience in being a music director for a big time show, then how do you get one? So I get it. I've run into that with my initial push into major motion films. I did some shorts and small budget films. I did the music for them and that was great, but I want to do *Star Wars*. I want to do the next big movie like that. I certainly have the capability and the chops. It's just a matter of someone giving me an opportunity and giving me a shot.

That is pretty much the way it works for the next crop of musicians. A lot of times it's a matter of placing yourself in the vicinity of an opportunity. I think it's a lot to do with timing and placing yourself in the right vicinity, so young musicians keep going for it. Don't stop if you haven't reached your goals thus far because that's a goal along the way. You have to see yourself a lot further, you have to dream a lot bigger than that anyway. I expect to go a lot further than where I am. I expect that, and I am constantly looking for goals to reach that are just beyond my grasp. Why go for something that is easily there? You have to reach beyond that.

What would you say to all of the artists and musicians who compete in big talent shows, banking it all on a big break, but they don't win?

Ray Chew:
I would say don't block your whole capabilities and don't limit yourself. You may start down one corridor, and there may be an opportunity for you down another. I look at everything that has music in it and consider myself as being someone capable of doing that. I used to do a lot of music for commercials. At the same time I was doing *Saturday Night Live*. I was doing jingles and music for radio and TV commercials. I did that for many years as a first call musician and arranger and producer. There is a great market for that.

For young talented producers with a lot of imagination, there is music for video games and there is music for all types of things. The life blood of our industry, the entertainment industry, is always the emerging new artists. There's going to always be that. We're going to always want to see that there is never going to be a shortage of appetite for seeing who's going to be the next Alicia Keys, or the next Justin Bieber or the next Beyoncé. Never limit yourself. Always keep aspiring and never stop.

Do you have any advice for musicians across all genres?

Ray Chew:
I think the opportunity has shifted. People who are looking at the traditional roles of how music is being presented, communicated and acquired are looking in the wrong place. You have to shift and look differently. There is a lot of chatter about the record industry not doing well because CD sales are down. Yes, CD sales are down, but many other streams are up. We've got people making record amounts of money that they have never made before. Justin Bieber made $80 million. There are DJs making $20 million. DJs! For some people that's surprising. He's up there spinning records and these guys are making ten and twenty million. They are making a lot of money.

If you're looking at CD sales, then you're looking in the wrong place. If you are into the CD sales business, then your business is down and you're in the wrong business. If you're a CD manufacturer, yes and you need to get out of the CD manufacturing business and go on to these other things. I say to these musicians and other artists, make sure that you are looking forward—looking at where the new advents are and the new types of revenue streams and things that are going on.

There is certainly no shortage of appetites for entertainment. People want to be entertained. They will pay for it; they just won't pay for it like they used to. The kids have found a way to download for free. They're not buying CDs, but they are buying other things. You still have people making tons of money. Justin Bieber, Jay Z, and DJs making millions of dollars. You can't point to another period like this. If you look back 30 or 40 years ago, who was making even the equivalent of that? Jay Z is on pace to be a billionaire. So yes, there is an appetite for entertainment and the preservation of it is in that next crop of artists who have to really push down and go for it.

Contact:
www.RayChew.com

Dr. Westbrooks:
Ray Chew urges artists to always work on their skills and be in a constant state of practice as much as possible to be the best that you can be at your craft. He describes the success of his career as having come through not just hard work, but through relationships he's built through the years. It wasn't just because he knew someone or someone knew him, it was because he was also very qualified and professional. He encourages positive thinking and envisions himself going further in his career. It's best to always be prepared because you never know who is watching you and what opportunity you might be presented with.

CHAPTER THIRTY-TWO

SHANNON SANDERS

**Grammy Award-winning Singer/Songwriter, Musician,
Producer and Music Director for India.Arie**

*"Never invest more into someone's project than they're willing
to do for themselves, whether it be time, money or energy."*

Shannon Sanders is an artist, songwriter, musician and producer who has worked with John Legend, Eric Benet, Johnny Lang, Anthony David, Marc Broussard, Heather Headley, India.Arie, and more. He has also partnered with Drew Ramsey, in addition to producing solo projects such as *Outta Nowhere*, *It Ain't Easy* and *Man Up*. Shannon has won two Grammys, two Emmys and a Dove Award. He gives an overview of what it takes to win, what happens afterwards and what it takes to maintain in the music industry.

Shannon Sanders:
I have got to say that the first thing is that you just have to do the work. It's funny because to win an award is to have what you consider to be one of your 'older' works celebrated. By the time you win a Grammy, you are awarded for something that came out last year, which means it's something that you recorded the year before that. So you're way past where the award process is if you're doing what you're supposed to do, which is to continue to be creative and not get caught up in it. It's funny because it's nothing you can try to do. When it happens, it happens.
As for winning the awards, it was definitely nothing that I was trying to do. It was nothing that was even in my radar or that was even on my mind. In the moment I was really just thinking about doing great work, and then hoping that it would reach people. The beautiful part about the Grammys in particular is that it's a peer award. It's nothing that's voted on by the public. It's nothing that fans can decide. It has nothing to do with that. It's not a popularity contest, it's a peer award that's voted upon by people in the music industry that see you as having the best work of the year. That's what gives the Grammys the prestige that it has, it being a peer award.

As far as changing your life, it does. But the thing is, it doesn't come with the check. They don't send you a Grammy and send you a check. But from then on, you can always say you are Grammy nominated or Grammy Award-winning. What that does is validate you to a degree, and it lets it be known that you do know what you're talking about and you do know what you are doing. Does it change your life per say? Not necessarily. It doesn't change anything else about you, but what it does is put more pressure on you because people expect that everything you do has the potential to do that. At the same time, not all of that is you. A lot of the exposure is because of record companies and publishers and people that make your works available for people to hear, and be exposed to. It has a lot to do with a lot of factors, not just the music you create. In that way your life changes, but it really does put you right back on the grind. If anything, it made me want to work that much harder, because after the second time I knew it really wasn't a fluke. I knew it wasn't a fluke the first time, but I think everybody else was like, "Okay, it really isn't a fluke. He really does know what he's talking about. He really does know what he is doing. He is somebody that we really do need to pay attention to and respect the opinion of."

Exactly what pieces of your work were awarded the Grammys, the Emmys, and the Dove Award?

Shannon Sanders:
The first Grammy was in 2002 for India.Arie's *Voyage to India* album. I produced more than 50 percent of that record, so I won for Best R&B Album that year. The next one was with Johnny Lang who won for Best Rock Gospel Album of the Year in 2007. That's what the second one was for. The two Emmys both came for work we did with Robert Randolph & the Family Band. There was a song called "Get There" that was used by the Madison Square Garden Network to promote New York Knicks games. They used that song two years straight, and they won two years straight. That's what that was for. The Dove Award is for Nicole C. Mullen's album that I worked on called *Everyday People*.

You have made commentary about a calling that a producer has to have on his or her life. You have mentioned that you just can't wake up and say, "Okay, I'm a producer," because being one entails certain skill sets and gifts. Would you describe them please?

Shannon Sanders:

I feel like to produce is to facilitate. Even beyond the musical gifts, I just think that you have to have the spirit of a facilitator and of somebody that makes things happen. You've got to be a self-starter and you've got to be a motivator, otherwise things don't happen. To produce is to bring forth. So my job is to bring forth the greatest performances from everybody—from writers to musicians to engineers, everybody. For anybody involved in the production or the bringing forth of the final product, it is my job to get the best out of everybody and anybody that will touch the project. That's the thing. It's not all musical for you to be a producer, and you have to have gifts that are outside of music. You have to be somebody that can bring people together.

Talk about some of the names that you have worked with who are now possibly household names such as India.Arie, John Legend and Eric Benet. Let's go down memory lane with some of the most precious moments of working with them and developing them as artists.

Shannon Sanders:

A lot of them were developed already. I worked with India the most in that way because I'm a musical director as well. I spent the most time with her over the years. For the most part, John Legend's career was already well on the way when we got together and wrote a song. It wound up being a great song that was on his *Evolver* album called "Good Morning." We also toured with John and that was great. Usually, I tell folks that being a producer is like being a contractor. You kind of come in and do what you're hired to do. If it's to fix drywall, or if it's to frame a house—whatever it is—that's what you do. And then you're gone a lot of the time.

Long-term relationships or just kind of being around is usually not the case because people work with lots of writers and producers. My situation with India is different because I'm her musical director. I'm around her not only in the studio but live. Because we spend so much time together, we end up writing a lot of songs in the down time. That's why I'm so heavily involved in her career. On top of that, we're just really good friends. But anybody else, we definitely have great times in the studio. I can say with everybody that my approach is to get to know folks before we start writing. Even if it's as simple as having lunch or having dinner. It's good to do that just because you get to know folks. I believe that great songs come from great conversations.

It's always good to be able to sit around and connect. Before you attempt to connect with the artist, you should first connect with the person and then the artistry comes from there. With all of them I could tell you something, especially with Johnny Lang. Recording his album was a transcending experience just because of who the guys were in the room. We had Michael Bland on drums, and we know Michael Bland from Prince—the early Prince days. We know Jim Anton. He's just a regular bass player, but he's a monster. My production partner on a lot of this stuff was Drew Ramsey, who played rhythm guitar and he's a monster. I played keys and Johnny played lead and it was just a magical experience to be in a room with those guys. To be able to play songs that were so strong at the same time. It was just crazy. That experience I would say was a game changer for me because I had never done that. I had never been in a room and been able to play with guys of that caliber and just run a record down. A lot of it was just because the sessions were so well organized that we could just run the songs down. There was nothing for them to think about, they just had to come in and play and be who they were and contribute as players. So that experience was crazy.

In many cases you have situations where a producer is a multitalented, multidimensional entity who can sing, write, produce, play, and all of that. So for other people who are just like you, what would you say are three things a multidimensional artist must do?

Shannon Sanders:
　　The first thing I would consider is having all of those things like a toolbox. I don't need everything for every job and that's just it. For some things I don't have to be a singer, for some things I don't have to be a writer, and for some things I don't have to be a musician. It just depends on what the artist brings to the table or what they have available for them. Sometimes people have their bands and have people that they're close to that they want to be a part of their thing. So I think the thing is, just because you can doesn't always mean you should. You should definitely be able and willing to remove your ego from a situation. At the same time just be conscious and know that it's not your record at the end of the day, so you don't force what it is that you do on people. Just use your gifts to enhance other people's gifts. I would say you don't have to do everything for every project. Every project doesn't require you to bring all of those things. It's good to be able to do those things, but just on an as-needed basis. I would say to be able to get your ego out of the way, but at the same time always continue to develop.
　　I know for me, it bothered me if I could do one thing better than another. I always wanted to write, sing, produce, and play everything at the same level. Whatever it is, continue to develop, and research is the

key before starting any project. Don't go into something thinking that you know it all, or thinking that you know somebody. Do the research to see what it is they are listening to or what they are feeling right now. Everybody wants to be brought something new and/or something fresh. Just to see where they are at the time, it's important to know where an artist is, or where a creative person is or whoever you're working with. It's important to know where they are in the moment. Like, what are you feeling at the moment, what songs move you in the moment, and what production styles move you? That's what you want to be able to tap into.

Sometimes producers are great at enhancing other people's projects, but many times their own projects get pushed further and further back as a result. What advice or assurance would you give to multifaceted producers and writers whose own music gets put on the sidelines?

Shannon Sanders:
You just have to know that it's all about timing. For whatever reason, I know that I can make my own records, but should I? I do things or I create my own records when my heart is moved to do so. I record songs when my heart is moved to do so. A lot of it is just making sure that you're doing it for the right reason and not necessarily for commercial gain. If you're at it for making a living, then you're making a living. A lot of times it's for that. It's like saying, *"Okay, why do I really want to do this? Is it because I have something to say?"* If you have something to say, then just say it. It shouldn't be determined by somebody paying you to do it. A lot of times that's the hard part. You're so busy making records on everybody else.

It's funny because I'll see cosmetologists that do hair and style people's hair all day long and make people beautiful. A lot of times they have their hair pulled back into a ponytail just to stay out of the way or just so they don't worry about their own while they're on the job. Just because their job is making people beautiful, it's not like they necessarily have the time to do it for themselves. It's the same thing with writers and producers. It's kind of like when that is your job, then it's really a very selfless place. They say, "Let me get mine out of the way just so I'm not conscious of it, so I can help you be or get the most beautiful presentation on you that I possibly can."

What happens is a lot of the time we wind up doing our own thing in our spare time, but how many other things do we have to do in our spare time or in our down time? It's almost like the last thing you'd want to be doing. Sometimes you want to just go to a movie and not be working on your own thing. Yeah, but I probably don't have the emotional wherewithal or the emotional energy that it takes right now because I just put it into this other project that I'm working on. A lot of times you're just emotionally exhausted or creatively exhausted by the time it comes around to doing your thing. Honestly, it's your baby, so it does take a lot of energy. A lot of time that's why these things get pushed to the side, because of the energy that it requires. People just don't have the muster to do it for themselves.

What is the biggest lesson that you've learned, and what is the greatest source of encouragement that you can share with someone regarding the music industry?

Shannon Sanders:
I think the biggest lesson would be putting too many eggs in one basket. You never know what's going to go or what's going to take off. There have been projects where I almost thought that I could predict that they would do well, but the one thing that you can't gauge is the hustle until the project comes out. You can gauge how talented someone is or how musical they are, but you can't tell how hard somebody is going to go. I would say more than anything, never invest more into someone's project than they're willing to do for themselves, whether it be time, money or energy. Be able to read or see those signs early on. If they're not willing to do what you're willing to do, then you don't need to be doing it. I've worked with some very talented people, but if they're not willing to match your hustle or match your grind, then it's not going to go, especially when their picture is on the front of it.

There will be certain situations where you just can't have more resources or financial resources than they do. At the same time, you see something in them where you'll say I know I can't predict what the sales are going to be, or I can predict what it's going to do. I know that it's good, and so I'm willing to invest that way. But when they're willing to give everything they have and they're willing to sow it and spend every working moment so that it's successful, then, yes, you've got something. This is not just a reference to success from a commercial perspective, but success from a creative perspective as well. It's making sure that people know about the project, and the artist is doing everything they can to make themselves available to contribute to the success of whatever the project is. You've got to have somebody who is tirelessly promoting the project or tirelessly promoting their career and your own career. You've also got to watch out for selfish people. When you're helping people and when you're developing situations, like when you're working with people and they're quick to keep all the credit, or not to share credit, or not to tell people how much you've contributed to help, then that's something you've got to watch out for. Because if you're stingy with credit, then you're going to be stingy with money.

Now that you have acquired all this wisdom, what is the greatest encouragement that you can offer?

Shannon Sanders:
I tell folks to be real. Be real with yourself, look at your situation, and figure out where you can get in. I've been reading a book about stress. It talks about how we spend so much time and energy attempting to develop a weakness. By the time I take something that is an area of weakness to the point where it is even average, somebody is already good at that. They're closer to being greater at that than I am. Just because I've spent all of this time and all of this money doing this, doesn't always mean that I'm going to be great at it. That's a great realization. Look at something that you're already good at, and with that same amount of effort you can be great at it. That's the main thing about being real with ourselves.

I might want to be this kind of player. I might want to be this kind of singer, but what am I good at? If I'm not good at that now, then what's it going to take? Do I really have the time, energy and resources to become that when it's really not in me naturally? What am I good at naturally that I can become great at with some effort? If I throw my whole self at it, what is it I can be great at? You might not need to be a musician. You might not need to be an artist. You might be a much greater natural organizer. You might need to be in management. It's not to say that you don't need to be in the business, but you may need to look at where in the business your gifts are and enhance those. Throw yourself where your real gifts are and that's where you're going to be great, and that's where they're going to flourish.

I really think that things don't happen for people because they're really not in alignment. For me, I can't do anything else. This is what I do and it's been like this since I was a child. The writing was on the wall for me since I was nine years old. There was no wondering if I could, the question was just if I would. Am I willing to do what it takes to go from being good to great? That's the question. Could I? That was never the question. Would I, was the question. It's the same thing that I think we all have to look at and ask ourselves if I really need to be doing what I'm doing.

If I've been at it this long and nothing has happened, then I need to look at my situation differently and have some real conversations with people and ask them how they really see me. And I really need to listen. When I hear the same thing over and over and they are resounding themes, you need to pay attention to that. When I keep hearing the same themes, you're good at this or you're better at this, or this is where you're strong, then you need to pay attention to where people are saying you're strong, because that is how people see you, regardless of how you see yourself. This is how people see you, and this is where people have placed value on you. If you become great where people already see that you have value, you can't help but win.

I like to tell people that you have got to keep your mind open because the game is forever changing. Somebody told me one time that in the music business, you've got to do as much in a day as most people in other industries do in a week, because it changes that fast. You have to be that busy in order to stay relevant. You have to be consistent in your output in everything that you do knowing that one particular opportunity leads into the next. You need answers as soon as possible because the answers from today will help figure out what I'm doing tomorrow.

Based on what I find out today and based on work that happens today is what dictates my tomorrow. So the thing is, you've got to keep your feet moving and just understand that the game is changing. There's a lot of people who are drowning. They're failing because they don't really get how the game moves now. It moves so quickly and it keeps changing. It's ever changing, it's like water. It's like being in a boat on water, you can't make it and it doesn't stop. Even when it's calm, it's not still, and you can't make it stop, you can't make waves go in another direction, you've just got to be prepared to go with them. If anything, build your ship sturdy to be able to handle wherever the game takes you—wherever the waves take you—because you can't predict it, you can't stop it, and there's nothing you can do about it. That being said, build your ship strong and make your ship sturdy so it can be able to withstand whatever the game throws at you.

Contact:
www.shannonsanders.com

Dr. Westbrooks:
Shannon Sanders speaks on reality and being realistic about what your strongest talents and capabilities are and finding your place in the industry. Just because you want to sing doesn't mean that you should.

Maybe you'd be a better producer or manager. Try to see your strengths and see yourself the way others see you and not how you see yourself. Shannon thinks that you should never put all your eggs in one basket because this industry is in a constant state of unpredictable change. Some signs you can see coming and some you can't, so keep your eyes, ears, and mind open and always be prepared. His perspective might be viewed as philosophical to some, but it is very honest and could be very helpful if utilized.

THE GOSPEL/CHRISTIAN ARTISTS

INFORMED SOURCES

Bishop Donald Hilliard, Jr.
Vicki Mack Lataillade
Prophet X

CHAPTER THIRTY-THREE

BISHOP DONALD HILLIARD, JR.

Pastor of Cathedral International

"Gospel music is not about sex, it's not about seduction or sensationalism. It's about God."

Bishop Donald Hilliard, Jr., is celebrating more than thirty years as lead pastor of Cathedral International. It is a church that has grown from 125 members to 5,000 with three locations in Asbury Park, Perth Amboy, and Plainfield, New Jersey. In 2006 Bishop Hilliard launched "From the Pulpit to the Palate," a premiere collection of over 70 pieces of original art. Hilliard is a member of the Joint College of African-American Pentecostal Bishops, and he's a lifetime member of the NAACP. He has earned numerous awards and distinctions including a Doctor of Ministry degree from United Theological Seminary in Dayton, Ohio, as a Samuel D. Proctor Fellow. Bishop Hilliard is the author of several books. Among them are *Pentecost: Real Power for Real Times*; *Midlife, Manhood, and Ministry*; and *Stop the Funeral*. The bishop is married to Reverend Phyllis Thompson-Hilliard, who is his partner in life and in ministry. Under their leadership, their church has also birthed a prolific music ministry that has added greatly to the Gospel industry. Bishop Hilliard speaks on today's Gospel industry, the evolution of it, and how we got to where we are today in the Gospel industry.

Bishop Hilliard:

The Anatomy of the Music Industry from the Gospel perspective is a very interesting and much needed topic. You can't think of how we got to where we are today without calling to memory the great Mahalia Jackson, Clara Ward, Aretha Franklin or Roberta Martin. Those people paved the way in Gospel music. I'm 56, but I remember in the late '60s, the Hawkins Singers came out with "Oh Happy Day." Many of our churches wouldn't let the choirs sing that, because they thought it was too racy, and it was a recorded song. (Edwin Hawkins and his family were the pioneers of contemporary Gospel). We've come a long way from "Old Happy Day," because they thought it was worldly. So many

219

of our churches, especially the Methodist church that I grew up in, thought that this kind of music was worldly.

I think the great evolution in Gospel music overall is a good thing because it reaches different demographics and a different genre of people. I'm one that can enjoy James Cleveland's "Peace Be Still." I can enjoy hearing "What a Friend We Have in Jesus," and I can also enjoy Kirk Franklin, Israel Haughton, Karen Clark-Sheard and these new contemporary artists. I think the bottom line is that the message is pure.

Now on the other hand, I think that the message should not be polluted by worldliness. This is a message of light, a message of life, a message of empowerment, and a message of hope. I think that as long as the music is offering light; if it's going to be Gospel music and not just inspirational, there is a difference. I appreciate all music, I appreciate Jazz, I appreciate Luther Vandross and all of that, but, if it's going to be Gospel music, it's the good news of Jesus Christ. You just can't call anything Gospel. If it's not pointing people to Christ, that's not Gospel music. It may have a nice sound, it might even have a Gospel sound, but it's got to have the message to be classified as Gospel music. I think as long as we stay within those parameters, whichever genre as long as it's clean and pointing people to God, I think it's good.

We have come quite a long way because some Gospel music now is so hip and funky that it's unrecognizable, not only from the beat but also from the lyrics. There used to be a time when you started grooving, and then you would kind of catch yourself with shame because the dance you were doing wasn't your 'holy' dance. So do you see this happening a lot when the music itself draws no distinction?

Bishop Hilliard:
You see, you're right. I remember when the Clark sisters came out with "You Brought the Sunshine." They started playing it in some of the clubs and I remember friends of mine saying, "I can't dance on that because my mother would kill me if I were out in the club dancing to 'You Brought the Sunshine'." The message was great. I still love that song and that great beat, but I think that's the danger that we're facing now. It's when you're not sure.

Sometimes you've got to throw something out there that's really edgy and different, and then bring the people along. What I'm saying is you can start out sounding like it's going to be one way just to get the people to open up their ears, and then you bring on the Gospel. But I agree, and I think that with some of the beats and things of that nature, there really should be a difference. If it's going to be Gospel music—

music is wonderful—but if it's going to be classified as Gospel music, I do think there should be some kind of difference in Gospel music.

Gospel music is not about sex, it's not about seduction or sensationalism, it's about God. And I think that's clear. It's clearly important, but I don't think we all are on that same page. That is what's dangerous, and we don't have monitors to monitor what's what. We have to help people monitor, and we have to ask God for discernment so we can now see where we're going in this arena.

Many people believe that they are inspired by God and because of that pure inspiration, they will be granted supernatural instructions to guide them and pave the way for every aspect of their success. What would you say to someone who has a passion for Gospel music who is now ready to take it beyond a worship experience in a religious arena and into a product which they hope to be profitable in the music business arena? What is your pastoral and business advice for them?

Bishop Hilliard:
My pastoral advice would be to make sure they have a word from God to do it. My business advice would be, "Don't quit your day job." Very few artists can make it in the industry to the point where they can live off of this industry. It's a very, very difficult industry. It has its own jungle mentality. You're number one today, and there's another one coming out tonight, and another number one coming out the next day. I think it is wonderful to be inspired, but if you're going to place your entire livelihood on that alone, you'll have to be extraordinary or willing to be on the road most of your life. It's going to be very challenging to have a family and do that. Many Gospel artists who have been inspired and who have 'made it' in the business still work. They're ministers of music at churches, they're song leaders and they are on salary.

You've got to think about things like: Where are you going to get your benefits, your insurance, and your 401k retirement plan? You certainly just can't get that being on radio shows or singing here and there. You can't be guaranteed, particularly in this economy, because pastors are not inviting Gospel artists in for paid performances like they used to. It's not because we have a problem with Gospel artists, but the economy has dictated that some things we'd have to cut and adjust.

So I think that you've got to have a real word from the Lord, that's my pastoral advice. But my business advice is to stay on your day job. You really need to know where your basic bread and butter—your mortgage money, your insurance money, and your health care is coming from. It's very challenging for you to move into that arena because every day a star is born. And very, very few people make it to the place where they can live totally off of the industry alone.

I am even advising young ministers now. When I do webinars, one of the things that I tell them and the pastors that I cover as bishop, is to diversify. Maybe you need to be a schoolteacher and a pastor. Every church in this environment may not be able to support a full-time pastor. I think we've become so enamored with the pastors who've been able to build these wonderful expansive ministries that have given us a comfortable lifestyle. I am very grateful for how good God has been to me. I came from 125 people, and we have exploded, but that's not the norm. The average church in America has 84 people. So the same advice I would give to them, I give to pastors—diversify. What are your other gifts? You should never just have one stream of income. You should always have three different streams of income.

Contact:
www.donaldhilliardjr.org
bishop@thecathedral.org
Twitter.com@Bishop_Hilliard

Dr. Westbrooks:
Bishop Donald Hilliard is a proponent of the purity of Gospel music and that it should be distinctive from what is considered worldly music, and he feels there should be no confusion about it. He listens to traditional Gospel as well as contemporary Gospel but the message must be clear. He also speaks on the reality of today's economy and how it affects Gospel music's bottom line. Because of the uncertainty of the economy, he encourages Gospel artists to diversify and seek additional revenue streams.

CHAPTER THIRTY-FOUR

VICKI MACK LATAILLADE

Founder of GospoCentric Records
CEO of Lataillade Entertainment

"You've got to be determined, get a good education, learn your law and learn your economics."

Vicki Mack Lataillade is one of few Gospel music executives who has mounted the extraordinary task of establishing a new brand of contemporary Gospel. She and her husband Claude formed a label called GospoCentric Records in 1993 in Inglewood, California. The label gave rise to such artists as Kirk Franklin, Curt Karr, Trin-i-tee 5:7, and more. She has been instrumental in promoting the Winans, Tremaine Hawkins, Andrae Crouch, Byron Cage, Dorinda Clark-Cole, David and Tamela Mann, the Clark Sisters, J. Moss and Kelly Price. She is considered the most powerful woman in Gospel music. Currently she presides over Lataillade Entertainment, and is now in partnership with Central South Distribution, the number one distributer of faith-based music in the world. Vicki shares her inspired history in the business and why she decided to tackle the Gospel music industry against all odds.

Vicki Mack Lataillade:
It's really interesting because Logan Westbrooks was around when I started my career in the mid-1970s. The reason that my husband and I decided to do this was for our children, who were really little at the time. They are now in their early 30s, but we didn't want them to listen to a lot of the music that was out there at the time. We saw that it was very degrading to women, and we used to have conversations with them about the music. I didn't ban them from the music completely, but there were songs out like "Poison" by Bell Biv DeVoe (The lyrics state that a certain girl is poison.) and "Nasty Girl" by Vanity Six (the hook of the song says "Do you think I'm a nasty girl?"), and other songs like that. We'd have long discussions with our children at about seven or eight years of age.

One day my daughter was dancing in our living room to "Do You Think I'm a Nasty Girl?" She had very little clothing on and I said, "Whoa, wait a minute. I really don't want you to listen to this, that's not what we listen to." She was only eight years old. She was so frustrated with me that she declared, "Mom, you're in the music industry, do something about it!" I thought, *"Oh wow,"* and I really began to pray, and I thought, *"Can one person really make a difference?"*

I asked that question in my prayer. Then my husband (who has really been an inspiration) was such a strategic planner. He said that I need to go back to the company that I was with at the time and had promised me a production deal, but they hadn't done it. He told me to go back and talk to them, and we need to do something because this music is really needed. Our kids are coming up and this music that they listen to is awful.

So I went to the company that I was with and asked them to do a deal. A production deal is what I wanted and they said, "No, you're going to have to do it like this and we'll give you a label deal, but you're going to have to spend all of the money on it." I signed two artists. My first artist was Donald Lawrence and the Tri City Singers, and another artist was Betty Griffin Keller. My third artist was another brand new artist who had never had a record out named Kirk Franklin. I didn't have money to get any established artists to sign, so I went with new artists. I told them that if they signed with me, I would work very hard for them, and the rest is history.

I started in the industry with RCA Records, and I then went to Sparrow Records, and then Sparrow was bought by Capitol. As I was working through all of that transition in the Sparrow/Capitol Records deal, I got a label deal. There were two people who were instrumental in making that happen. There was a guy named Jimmy Bowen. Jimmy didn't make any kind of differential between any kind of music. If it was selling, he was willing to get behind it. He had Liberty Records. That's what started it, then Sparrow/Christian, which is now EMI Christian, and it might be Capitol Christian or something like that now. It helped with my distribution, but the great part about it was that I did all my own marketing and all of my own promotion. I had all of these years before with RCA Records where I had learned how to work Country music. When I came into RCA records in the 1970s, I counted Elvis inventory before we had computers. Somebody had to do all of that counting, and that's what I did. In the long run, I ended up selling my company to the company that I started with RCA/BMG twenty plus years later.

How did being backed by a larger company assist you in garnering mainstream airplay for your artists back then?

Vicki Mack Lataillade:
In the beginning they really didn't do mainstream. I got that from Black independent radio. The mainstream companies that I was with didn't help me with any of that. There was a group of Black women in the music industry that would bring their extra paper, extra envelopes and whatever they had, and they did independent work for me. There was a person in particular, the late legendary record promoter Alan Lott and his wife Lygia that helped me. The major companies were not willing to put the kind of dollars into it that we put into it at that time or you would have seen Gospel artists rank much earlier on a more consistent basis. I had the support of not just Black women, but a lot of Black people in the industry that worked for other companies and helped me on the side. They didn't have the vision for it like that.

At the time you formed your company in 1993, the body of worshippers were becoming more contemporary. Do you remember how this music was evolving?

Vicki Mack Lataillade:
Yes, I remember. First of all, I did it for my daughters because the young kids didn't have anything to listen to. Number two, the reason you heard that more is because for the first time Black people were in charge of Gospel music. I didn't have to ask someone else's opinion. I was going to church and my kids were there, and for the first time I could do (market and manufacture) what I knew was being played in the church and what my kids wanted. Before that the big companies that were mainly doing things were not Black owned. You had to do what they wanted and their sensibilities, which was different from what I wanted for my kids and what I knew was happening in the church. You had a lot of people who were making decisions who had never been in predominately Black churches, and they were dominating what was happening and what they thought Gospel music should be. What made what my husband and I did so significant was that we started to get unprecedented support.

This was the time megachurches were starting to experience growth spurts. I'd go to Faithful Central Church in Los Angeles, which was a huge church. We were being backed by a lot of the megachurch pastors. They wanted to support what my husband and I were doing, and they did. It wasn't much anybody else could do to dominate. These gentlemen and women were saying, "Baby, just come to my church, talk to our people, we'll support you," and they did. A lot of what we did wasn't because of the major companies at all. What the major distribution companies did was back us with the dollars for the pressing of the product. We got to the point where we were shipping platinum and there was no way I could have done that on my own without the distribution company helping me. There was no way for me to pay that kind of bill on my own.

When it came to the creative, when it came to the power of radio and all of that, at first that was not a major factor. That did not become a major factor for me until I went to Interscope Records and worked with Jimmy Iovine. Everybody was beating up on me because I was going to the company with Suge Knight, Tupac and Dr. Dre. My husband and I had prayed on it, and it was one of the best things I ever did. When we got there, we were able to do things with radio that I could not do on my own because he'd pick up the phone and he'd introduce us to a lot of people. He just wasn't insecure. Some of the other people we worked with didn't care about Gospel, but the way Jimmy thought about it was totally different. It was one of the best experiences I have ever had in a lot of ways. He introduced me to all kinds of people, and that's how I had my biggest seller, which was "Stomp" by Kirk Franklin. It did over three million. That was when the power came in. We were already selling platinum on our own. When we got to Interscope, the power was there to support what we were doing. It was amazing.

We appreciate all the specifics because we are putting this book together not only to chronicle stories of those who have been legendary, but to serve as a guidepost for new people who are constantly entering the industry and the older people who are reinventing themselves in the industry. So now with today's world, there is the idea that artists and smaller labels can do it all by themselves. There are only a handful of independent radio outlets, the rest are run by corporations. With all of that as a backdrop, what advice do you have for today's artists?

Vicki Mack Lataillade:
I am now one of the owners of Central South Distribution, which is a 40-year old distribution company. I know that everyone thinks that they can do it themselves, but really I've found that most people cannot. You still need that power behind you like I had before, because there are a lot of things that you don't know. We get independent labels every day that come to us and they really don't understand the music business. They

don't understand basics like intellectual property and that you can't just use somebody's product.

If someone sits in and writes with you, and you say, "That's my friend, we got a good understanding." There is no understanding. This is still about law and economics. It's a business. It's about legal entities and economics, and you can't make up new economics. It is what it is. One plus one still equals two, and most people still can't do those basic things. You cannot have someone in the studio with you that adds a sentence or a big producer that helps you produce a song, and you can't think that you are not going to have to share some of that intellectual property. A lot of people think that it's all theirs or that they can do things because 'That's my boy or that's my girl.' There is no such thing as all of that. That is the first thing I have learned that people do not understand. The creative process is a small part of it.

The other thing with the technology is that people think that they can produce. I've heard some of the most horrific sounding music because a lot of these people don't know anything about playing an instrument. They don't even know how to work a computer that well, so a lot of the parts that come in, they don't know how to get it finished properly. There's a lot of rudimentary things that are missing now because people think that they can just pull something together.

Still, when you look at the majors or with anybody that's selling anything, first of all the sales are a lot different. A project that we used to do a half a million on, might sell 80 to 100,000 units. The average Gospel project that used to do 40,000, now might sell 8 to15,000 because all of the independents are gone. Interestingly enough, in our business as of 2014, believe it or not, some of our biggest projects like Tamela Mann right now that is about to go Gold, 70 percent of those sales are in physical products, not in digital sales as people might think. So faith-based music and Country music are behind the curve in terms of what's selling on the Internet.

Also (as of 2014) we find that digital sales are down for the first time this year. Physical sales have been down, and the new area of growth is in subscription Internet. For example, look at Pandora and Spotify and companies like that, the money you make from subscriptions are very low. The interesting thing in today's market is surveying how many people will be able to thrive doing music when we are operating from laws that were made in 1950. And now we are in 2014. Nothing applies, and you're getting paid pennies for what used to be payment in dollars.

It is a very interesting time that we live in. I'm not sure where it is all going, but it's not the same now. In two or three years it is all going to be different. Right now it's the growth of subscription based. This is the first year that Internet sales have been down. So it's very scary and then we've also got YouTube. Some of my friends believe that they don't have to buy products. If they're looking for an artist, they'll just look them up on YouTube. I hate to say it but some of the church mothers now have their phones, and they don't think it's illegal to record or share music. One person will buy the product and they'll share the product with 20 people, or they'll buy one CD and share it with the whole church choir. We've got some really interesting things to look at.

I was in Washington, D.C., where they were meeting with Congress to talk about these intellectual property challenges that we are having. It looks like in the future people are going to be looking more at festivals. Also there's reality shows, which are very interesting. A lot of people who are doing reality TV shows aren't selling as much product as they were, but they don't care because they are making money from the reality shows. That's something different. You've also got tours and concerts. We used to have the church that was supporting us with the big ticket items, but we see less of those as well. It's an interesting time. I'd like to think of it as a definite time for reinvention and an exciting pioneering time for those of us that were used to making money in certain ways, but it's not going to be there.

For the young people, they think they know something that they don't, and I think we all should come together a lot more. For example, in faith-based right now Hip Hop is very big. We have an artist named LeCrae with us in our distribution label, and they are selling 200 to 300,000 without any airplay. They have a very strong social media base. I also have an artist named Canton Jones who is coming out. These young guys are able to sell real products through their social networking.

With faith-based Hip Hop there are still some real odd kind of things that artists don't know, and some of them are still learning. Even in the case of LeCrae (I'm sure it will change), but a lot of our sales are still physical products. So if Walmart or Target decide to get rid of music, faith-based in particular is going to be in a lot of trouble. Also, if we don't have CD players any longer in cars (which we won't in a minute), that's going to cause problems, too. We've got to get innovative really quickly because music is not going to be sold the way it was before. Someone told me, "Well, it used to be 45s and then the albums." So (referring to the changing of the times) we've got to work with all that to keep laws in place that allow people to make a living from the music that they are making.

With Gospel, Christian or Spiritual music comes the challenge of keeping a delicate balance that a Rock star, Pop star or R&B star does not have. *There is an expectation that the motive for the music stays in its proper spiritual perspective, but at some point the popularity of the music makes the artist in demand. You have done quite well embellishing the brand of Gospel music, but there are some who covet stardom as much as they do the desire to spread the Gospel. Do you have any advice on how these inspired artists can get specifics about the business from a spiritual and business perspective?*

Vicki Mack Lataillade:

There are a lot of really good churches and conferences. You've got the Full Gospel Conference. T.D. Jakes has an incredible conference every other year; it's amazing. But I think that what poisons the well, so to speak, is reality TV. What happens is that now you can have a contest where someone sings well, and he or she could actually be an atheist and not care about anything that is faith-based at all. They could win and have a platform and be the devil himself, and there is nothing you can do about it because that platform can be so large. We are starting to see that now. We are starting to see all kinds of wild stuff that we really didn't have before. Of course, some of it might have been hidden, but now I think a lot of people don't care because there is not necessarily a standard. So you're going to get some of both of it, unfortunately. There's a new television show with a group of ladies who aren't even necessarily successful in music, but they are successful in drama. Now their platform is going to be elevated, and it's going to be interesting.

The amazing thing about being in faith-based is that God always has the remnant. You can say all these things will happen, but God will lift up someone at any moment. Just like God lifted up me and my husband. That's why I'm really encouraged, even with reality TV or some other kind of platform that we may not totally agree with completely. And for the record, not all reality TV is bad. There have been some that are very good but, there is always going to be a remnant. God is always going to use the foolish to confound the wise. That's exciting.

You and your husband defied the odds years ago with the start of GospoCentric. Please reflect on the biggest and most joyous moments of the journey.

Vicki Mack Lataillade:

In terms of my career, one of the things that I remember was the first time I hit 100,000. I had borrowed $6,000 from my dad, and that seemed like so much money back then. I promised him that I'd pay him back. When I hit $100,000 that was amazing to me. We had this thing. It was Kirk Franklin's first record, and I said that if this record goes Gold, I'm going to get on the street corner of Florence and Centinela (in Inglewood, California) and testify about how good God is. We did that. I remember that very well. The next time when my company went platinum, we got out there and we just praised God on that street. People were honking their horns at us, and we were praising God and saying how good God was. I remember that, and I remember the first song we got on Kurt. I remember with Kurt Carr, the first time we hit a half a million (the record went Gold) without any kind of crossover. That was significant to me.

We kept doing it over and over again. We would ship records, I remember the stuff with Interscope then and now going full circle really. I'm working again with David and Tamela Mann, who were with Kirk Franklin and the Family. Now Tamela's record went Gold with a half a million in sales in this day and time. That's so amazing to me. Working with LeCrae and having a Hip Hop record hit. It's just God allowing me to be on the cutting edge of this genre. I'm not a genius or anything, so it's got to be God, because it doesn't even make sense how many times I've had hits and been on the cutting edge of something. And I'm still doing it today. I know it's the grace of God. There are so many people I've worked with who have since passed or are older, so it's pretty amazing to the point where I know I can't take any credit for it.

Any final words for those who might aspire to be a Gospel artist, manager or publisher?

Vicki Mack Lataillade:
You have got to think out of the box right now. It's a whole new frontier. For example, my old partner Jimmy Iovine got with Dr. Dre and sold his Beats headphones for $3 billion. Look at Oprah Winfrey. Look at people like David and Tamela Mann, who took the television route in a very positive way with Tyler Perry and reinvented themselves. They will have two wonderful, beautiful reality shows that will be very positive. Just keep thinking outside the box and really get educated about the business. With regard to Hip Hop, who would have ever thought that rappers would be as strong as they are? You have got to be determined, get a good education—learn your law and learn your economics.

We see more and more Gospel musicals that are on the road. What should playwrights and producers do who want to pursue this and use previously recorded Gospel music?

Vicki Mack Lataillade:

They need to contact us as a publisher (because I also publish music) to get permission to use our songs. If it's some new songs that you want to use, what you'll find out is a lot of times we'll work with you gratis. In that regard let me say this, one wonderful playwright named David Talbert took Kirk Franklin and put all of his music from the first record in one of his plays. I gave him that music gratis because I wanted him to help me make the record go platinum, and that's exactly what happened. We went on the road with it, and we let him use that music for no charge because we knew he was hitting a platform and a group of people that were very faithful and would buy the product. He helped that record go platinum. Being a playwright is more important than ever because you look at a lot of these people now—Tyler Perry or Shonda Rhimes's successful TV shows—and a lot of these people who start with plays could end up with huge movies. We should also consider the potential of working with videographers. And I remember a guy who did some of our first videos, like the Trin-i-tee 5:7 video. He ended up doing a big Sci-Fi movie. A lot of people who worked with us in the beginning—who worked with us for almost nothing—are now major movie directors or playwrights. Just look at Tyler Perry, my goodness! He's a playwright and very successful movie producer. There are just so many ways to do this now.

Contact:
Facebook.com/VickiLataillade
VLataillade@MackRecords.com
www.MackRecords.com
(NO UNSOLICITED SUBMISSIONS ACCEPTED)

Dr. Westbrooks:

Vicki Mack Lataillade was inspired to start her Gospel label to create a viable music option for her children and others who thought that secular music had become too racy. It can be said that the GospoCentric label is purposed driven with the intent of counteracting the pervasive sexual and violent lyrics that were dominating the airways. Her goal was to offer messages that were spiritually uplifting, positive, and backed by powerful voices and quality music.

Using a combination of opportunity-driven, business-savvy, and strategic decisions, she signed unknown artists who are now household names, such as Kirk Franklin. She got help with distribution, but controlled her own marketing. This worked out great for her because she understood her audience much better than the distributor did. That enabled her to tailor promotions for her demographic. Those efforts, in addition to receiving unprecedented support from the faith-based community, resulted in a phenomenally successful Gospel label.

Lataillade stays abreast of trends and changes in the industry and understands that she must change and adapt to maintain her success.

PROPHET X

Pastor of Freedom Fellowship Church

"I would say in the now world, make music that is intelligent because the music that is coming out now is artificially intelligent."

Prophet X is the name that describes a young man who earned the nickname from his family and friends because his wisdom exceeded his years. Prophet is now the Owner and CEO of Prophecy Records, Inc. and Prophecy Productions, a Christian Rap label and music production company that specializes in Hip Hop and film scores. Prophet gives a synopsis of his past several years in the music industry.

Prophet:
I have produced music for literally a Who's Who of people in the Gospel industry, mostly in Hip Hop Gospel, such as Sevin, Tha Gim, Priesthood, and Remnant. I do all the production on my own albums, of course, and then there are the artists that are signed to our record label such as Khanchuz, Prodigal Son, and Fewfaze. I also produce music for a lot of secular artists. They purchase from me through my websites. They are artists such as Raskass or Canbus.

Let's move more specifically into some of the dynamics of how you do what you do. First of all, where are you from?

Prophet:
Originally I am from a very small town called Lima, Ohio, but I've have lived in Los Angeles for thirty years, so I feel like I am from California.

How did you go about forming a Gospel Hip Hop Christian, or a label that mainly deals with Christian artists?

Prophet:
The record label, Prophecy Records, is exclusively for Christian Hip Hop artists. That's the way that it was started 14 years ago, and the way we still operate. Over the past years we have released 14 albums and some mixtapes. I think we're one of the only Gospel Rap or Christian Rap labels that is still going. Over the last few years many companies that started have since closed their doors.

So there is the music label side and also the production side. How do you acquire your artists, and explain whether you offer standard record deals? What is unique about your legal agreements with your artists?

Prophet:
With Prophecy Productions, we've been doing acts for about three years. All our clients are acquired through the Internet. We have a website, and we kind of pioneered the idea of providing exclusive music, which means that it's not licensed. So when you purchase the track from us, you get the exclusive rights to use it, no one else is using that music. So what that does is this. It gives the artist the ability to copyright the music, which is not very popular lately in the music industry. There are so many music production companies that are selling multiple artists the exact same track. And if multiple artists have the exact same song or music bed, there is no way that they can copyright their finished song, because they are using music from someone else's copyrighted song.

So what you're saying is that basically a track that is sold to your artists grants them ownership and all subsequent rights free and clear?

Prophet:
Yes, when they purchase it, they get all the rights. We don't sell it to anybody else, they own it. We don't even play it for anybody else.

On the record side, explain the interconnectivity of all of this?

Prophet:
The Internet makes it possible to network with artists that are in other states and other time zones half way around the world. Several albums on our label have been produced entirely over the Internet where

234

we did not actually meet person to person. I would find them on the Internet and say, "Hey, check out my music."

I have an artist named Lyrix who lives in Fresno, California. His entire album was produced by sending tracks back and forth across the Internet. He does the recording there, he sends it back to me. I do some recording here and send it back to him, and then I do some mixing and mastering. So the Internet has opened up an infinite amount of doors for expanding your reach in the music industry.

You are well versed as an artist, a multi-instrumentalist, a businessman and a producer. You've created a business model that benefits you by getting your revenue off the top by selling your tracks free and clear, and the artist benefits because they can retain all royalties they generate. With your deal, the artist bears the responsibility of marketing and promoting their own music, much in the way that a standard label used to do. Is that correct?

Prophet:
Yes, that's correct. That's kind of a new model, it wasn't always like that. Usually, a producer gets points (or royalties) on the back end. Now we're in a market where everyone and their mother produces music because you can buy a program for $50, take it home without any knowledge of music theory, and start producing tracks. So producers had to figure out a way to get our money up front. There's no back end money, because a lot of artists are making their own music. So we came up with a way where we create the tracks in advance, and sell exclusive rights to one person. We get our money up front, but there is no back end income or back end cost to the artist.

What is most rewarding about this as a businessman and as a versatile producer and artist?

Prophet:
The most rewarding thing for me is working with new artists who have raw talent. As a producer, I'm always looking for someone who has talent that they have not fully honed or some ability that just needs to be developed. I then work with that person to bring out more than what they know is in there. That for me is the most rewarding thing because it's creating art, and at the same time it's advancing someone's ability to create art.

Now let's talk about the flip side of it. Creatively, you have found a way to merge the lyrical, the musical, and the production end, but what are the rewards and challenges of producing music in this niche genre of Christian Hip Hop music?

Prophet:
That's a very good question. In this genre, it is still a fledgling genre. It is still the equivalent of what Hip Hop was 20 years ago where most of the artists that do Gospel Rap or Christian Hip Hop have never sold 500,000 albums. There is one Gold Gospel Rap album. It's still new. It's still brand new, and because of that it's still like we're trying to make enough waves for the world to realize what we're doing. It was only in 2013 that the first Grammy for a Gospel artist went to a Christian Hip Hop artist named Lecrae. So that makes it a little bit difficult, because we're fighting just to be noticed.

There are different thoughts on the importance of radio airplay. What is your perspective on that?

Prophet:
For my genre, there is like one percent coverage throughout the United States who will actually play Gospel Rap. One percent of stations who are only Christian stations are playing Gospel Rap music. I think that is part of the reason that the genre is not more popular. Pop music is still dominating. When you turn on most popular radio stations, you're going to hear the most popular songs. Because Gospel Rap is not able to break through that wall to get on any of the popular radio stations, it's almost like a genre of music that you have to dig and look for under a rock to find out what's going on with it. Radio still dominates the popularity of music. Radio can still complement the exposure that music gets online.

Explain the steps that you have taken to be this committed to the Gospel in your soul and in your craft.

Prophet:
For me, everything that I do or have the ability to do came out of necessity. I was at a place in my life where I needed to make a change. It was either going to be everything dedicated to God or keeping everything dedicated to the streets, and I knew that wasn't going to last. I formed my record company out of necessity because I needed to take

my music to the next level, but I did not have the resources. I had to spend the hours and the time and the dedication to learn what I was going to be talking about, and then learn the music and build the company and find some people to support it. All of it came out of necessity and a lot of years of dedication. I have been doing it for 14 years, going on 15 years, and I don't foresee stopping. I'm sure I won't be rapping over the next few years, but I will be creating opportunities for other artists to have their music produced and released by the label.

What encouraging words would you have for any inspirational artist anywhere in the world? They have no previous reference, they live in the now world.

Prophet:
I would say in the now world, make music that is intelligent, because the music that is coming out now is artificially intelligent. It is regurgitated music from the last 10 or 20 years. Artists are no longer coming out and saying that they're going to make intelligent music and establish themselves as artists. They are more focused on establishing a hot song, getting radio play, or being the flavor of the month. That's one reason the music industry overall is on a rapid decline. There are no more Marvin Gayes, there are no more Princes coming out, and there are no more Bob Marleys. Those people were artists first, and popular second.

Contact:
www.theprophetx.com
www.prophecyproduction.net

Dr. Westbrooks:
As a producer and label owner, Prophet has totally embraced the Internet as his sole method of finding artists and them finding him to get music produced, create albums, and for all other business related to his label Prophecy Records. He encourages artists to create intelligent music and not just throw anything together that might be a hot song. Prophet explains that his genre of Christian Hip Hop is very small, but one of his goals is to create opportunities for more Christian Hip Hop artists that will help expand the genre.

THE LEGAL ANALYSIS

INFORMED SOURCE

Gary A. Watson, Esq.

CHAPTER THIRTY-SIX

GARY A. WATSON, ESQ.

Entertainment Attorney
Owner of Gary A. Watson & Associates

"First and foremost it is best to educate oneself when it comes to digital media."

Gary A. Watson, Esq. has provided legal expertise for clients such as Michael Jackson, Yahoo!, Motown Records, Def Jam Records, Tommy Boy Records, Jimmy Jam and Terry Lewis's Flyte Tyme Records, and Dr. Dre. He has been in business for thirty years and offers a full range of legal services for the music, television and motion picture industries, as well as new media and ancillary industries. Watson also served as lead attorney for Universal Pictures on *The Guardian*, a film by William Friedkin, who was also the director of *The Exorcist* and *The French Connection*.

First of all Atty. Watson, please give us information on your background in the music industry as it relates to entertainment law specifically.

Gary Watson:
I am a Stanford University Undergraduate with an Economics Major. I got my law degree from U.C. Berkeley's Boalt Hall Law School in 1984. Primarily, I started my practice doing some music in 1984 at a large law firm that had a vibrant music department. In that law firm I participated not only in an entertainment practice but also in a corporate practice.

My involvement on the entertainment side at that juncture was with respect to doing personal management agreements, recording contracts, and other small deals that related to the music industry. I then went to work for a film and television law firm, and later I went to work for a motion picture studio. At the film and television law firm I didn't do much music, if any at all. At the studio I was involved with music on a very limited basis with music that went into the films produced by the studio. I was a production lawyer and responsible for garnering all of the rights that were necessary for the production of films. Every now and then we'd have a music issue that the music department didn't handle.

My next foray was after I was recruited into a firm that represented clients primarily in film, but our largest client was Michael Jackson at the time. I'm talking about the period from about 1991 until 1993. In that period we were quite involved with Michael Jackson's *Dangerous* tour. Specifically, my involvement was a lot of the work on the production of the *Dangerous* tour and, therefore, contracts that were entered into on behalf of Michael Jackson concerning all of the elements that went into production.

For example, one deal was very unique because, of course, Michael had a wonderful stage show. His show involved him flying off the stage at the end of his show and ending with him exiting the stadium in the air. One of the deals that I did was for a company that actually helped with producing the backpack that he would strap on his back and the jet propulsion fuel that would be used to fuel the machine that actually lifted him from the stadium stage out of the arena. I also did work with his nephews The 3 Ts who had a recording that was done for the mini-series about the Jacksons. We worked on sponsorship arrangements that were done with the Heal the World Foundation that Michael Jackson had established.

Another one that comes to mind was a music video that Naomi Campbell starred in that was for the track off the *Dangerous* album called "In the Closet." Herbert Ritts was the photographer and the director for that video. He was a very well-known photographer, and the visual style dictated that they wanted someone special that could render a special look, so they hired him to do the music video that model/actress Naomi Campbell appeared in.

After that juncture at that law firm, I decided to start my own entertainment practice, and that was from around 1983-94. At that point I had the opportunity to represent clients that were active in the music industry as a large portion of my practice. I was involved in representing companies such as Motown Records, Def Jam Records, and Tommy Boy Records and really helping them on special projects and working with them to supplement their in-house staff with doing recording agreements.

When Johnny Gill came out with a new album and Motown had him perform at the Regal Theater in Chicago, I did agreements involving the rental of the theatre and the joint venture between Black Entertainment Television and Motown, whereby that performance for the new album was then televised on BET. We did a lot of overflow work for the record companies. For Motown we did some recording agreements, publishing deals and everything else that was needed.

For Def Jam, we did multiple agreements for a soundtrack album for a docudrama called *The Show*, as well as multiple recording agreements for various artists that were assigned to the record company. I represented individuals that signed recording agreements and artists such as producer Dr. Dre, who was doing work in recording and producing. There was a myriad of other deals like personal management agreements, publishing agreements, and songwriting agreements. I continue to work with artists overall. A lot of their needs center on personal management agreements, production agreements, demo production agreements, recording agreements, producing agreements, publishing agreements, and songwriting agreements.

What would you say would be the basics that any person encountering today's music industry should expect from a legal perspective?

Gary Watson:
First I would go back and retrace from the point in which I started my own law firm, and therefore, I was doing a lot of work in the music industry. What you saw was that record companies were selling units of CDs, which could be millions for successful artists. The artist was in need of and primarily desired to obtain a recording contract with a major company. The artist would often start pursuing that goal by perhaps getting a personal manager. That was a basic agreement that was entered into. It is important for an artist to understand and appreciate the terms and conditions of a personal management agreement. They want to become aware of how a personal manager helps them along in the process. Typically, you have an industry standard commission that is paid to the artist. You want to look at what the terms and conditions are that focus on the range of representation, and the duration and terms that the artist is going to sign with a personal manager.

It used to be that you had the production agreement that the artist entered into, and those production agreements were very important. Those were agreements where the artists would have someone produce tracks with them or for them, and then try to pitch those tracks to a record company and get a deal signed. You still have a similar thing in a sense now. What artists are seeing now is that they can do one of two things. They can still pursue that recording agreement and, therefore, look to sign with a major record company, but often times now they are looking to sell their own music in the market. They have to be careful then as they do now regarding any deals they enter into with people that are helping them produce music.

A producer agreement centers on how much the producer will make from producing the track, whether it be solely an upfront payment or an upfront payment as well as a percentage or royalty provision. That's really very important because now you don't see many units that are being sold because of downloading as opposed to the sale of physical units. More importantly, now there is streaming of music, so you have to look at what type of structure you're going to have when it comes to paying and what type of deal you're going to have when it comes to paying a producer royalties.

If you do go with the recording agreement, it used to be much more simplistic. It simply covered the recording services that the artist rendered. Usually the artist was signed fully and exclusively for recording services. Therefore, they could seek out other opportunities for other services they might bring to market like acting in television or feature films or performing live and touring, therefore, with live performances of their music in front of audiences. Nowadays you see more situations where if the artist is interested in signing a recording agreement, the artist has to be concerned with what is known as the 360 deals. That's where the artist is being signed to exclusively render services to the record company for recording, but the artist is also looking to render services that the record company is going to commission for their touring and for film and television appearances.

Producing agreements are still important just like they were in the past. The producer is going to be actively involved with the artist in helping along with producing work that the artist is going to record. Again, the complexity of those deals is enhanced by the fact that streaming is going on.

Publishing has always been important, but I think that artists have to be very careful about protecting themselves with respect to their publishing. It used to be that a recording artist was signed to a recording agreement. As a result of recording for a major record company if they were a writer or songwriter, they might often be signed to a publishing deal. If they were successful in selling records, then there was a lot of money to be made on the publishing side. That still continues. If an artist mounts their own project, they have to be very careful in protecting the music they have created that they are going to record. For example, maybe copyrighting that music and looking at how they are going to monetize the public performance of that music and all other aspects of that music being utilized in the industry.

Overall, the basics that an artist has to look at now centers more towards downloading and streaming. Therefore, artists have to look at how they really protect their interests when it comes to music being downloaded and streamed.

If you had one or two cautions to put out to today's new artist who is just entering the playing field and has no concept of how the industry used to be, what would you say to them about protecting their intellectual properties as it relates to digital media?

Gary Watson:
First and foremost, it is best to educate oneself when it comes to digital media. Clearly things are evolving quite rapidly. For example, I have an article in front of me that was written in May of 2014, and it states that digital downloads fell for the first time ever last year. People have turned to streaming services like Spotify, Google, YouTube and Pandora to listen to music according to Nielsen SoundScan. Artists need to be aware of what is happening as far as how consumers are consuming music so that they are really abreast of what they need to look at given the hope and desire that they will be able to generate money and revenue from their music. That's changing year to year oftentimes.

So where they may have thought that downloading was the most important, maybe now streaming is most important. They have to concern themselves about when their music is streamed and how they are going to make money on that. When they find that consumers sign up for streaming subscriptions, how is the artist going to make money? Therefore, is a streaming service a case where an artist is getting money for each unit that is listened to in that streaming, or is it some other way the artist is being compensated?

Artists have to be very careful about how they keep abreast of what is going on when they look at what they are going to reap as far as benefits. Self-education is important in order to get proper representation to help the artist with cutting deals. Even though artists may have become somewhat knowledgeable, they are going to need expertise from a lawyer's standpoint such as someone who has worked in the industry long enough to have entered into deals on behalf of artists or negotiated deals on behalf of artists. Beyond that, they should have at least five years of experience in how those deals pan out, and they should have worked on those deals to perfect their knowledge. In other words, they want to make sure that they have someone that really knows what they are doing.

You want that lawyer to be able to work with you in helping you understand the deals and any shortcomings you have despite bolstering your understanding. You want that lawyer to help you with getting that understanding. Of course, you want to have a lawyer that is going to be able to provide you services at a rate that is going to be manageable for you and for your budget and your needs. I would say it's really about educating and then finding representation that is really going to be astute about servicing the needs given the ever-changing marketplace.

For songwriters and publishers what is the very first thing that they should do as far as protecting their intellectual properties?

Gary Watson:
First, if the song is written with someone else, then be very clear as a songwriter on what the splits are that exist between you and whoever you write a song with. In fact, you should document what portion of the song you, as the songwriter, are going to own and what portion of the song is going to be owned by the other person that you write the song with so that it is absolutely clear what you actually are entitled to with respect to the song and what the other person is entitled to. Between you and the artists and any other persons, be very clear in terms of who can actually license that song or make that song available. If you write with someone else, you have to be very careful about the fact that the other person might be able to make that song available to a third party and have that third party either record the song or have that song exploited. It can happen if you don't have an arrangement with them that dictates the terms under which they can do that or that says they cannot do that.

Next, copyright the song and make sure that you take advantage of the copyright laws that we have in the United States that protect that creation, song, or composition. If there is ever a question of ownership and there is ever a need to address a problem with ownership such as someone using your song without having rights to use your song, then you have the proper protection from copyright law. These are real basic and important things to consider when writing.

Third is to really look at the ways in which a song could be utilized and how revenue could be generated from the song. Make sure you understand what happens in terms of the public performance of the song and the revenues that are thrown off from the public performance of the song. Be sure you understand what happens when units of a recording are sold, such as with CDs and what revenue you are entitled to and can achieve in terms of all the ways that you can get revenue.

Make sure you protect yourself so that you get revenue in all of the ways you can from the exploitation of a song.

What about the poor man's copyright? Yes or no?

Gary Watson:

The poor man's copyright? By that I think you mean the process of putting the music in a sealed envelope and mailing it yourself and, therefore, designating that you have had the music in existence from the time that the postmark is found and affixed to the envelope. The reality is that under copyright law the creator of the song does own the song from the very inception of their creation, so you are protected by general copyright. However, the level of protection is heightened much more by actually filing with the copyright office.

The process is not that expensive. It's a matter of filling out some basic forms, and you can do it online. All things considered, you're better off actually filing with the United States Copyright Office. Filing procedures can be found at www.copyright.gov.

In addition to this book, of course, what is your most suggested book for general information on the music business?

Gary Watson:

What I've found useful in the past is Donald Passman's book *All You Need to Know about the Music Business* (Free Press 8th Edition Dec. 2012)

Contact:
Attorney Gary Watson
1800 Century Park East, Suite 600
Century City, CA 90067
(310) 229-5725
www.GaryWatsonLaw.com
gwatson@garywatsonlaw.com

Dr. Westbrooks:

There are countless stories of artists signing bad contracts that cost them untold amounts of money and sometimes even careers. In the early days of the music industry, many artists were taken advantage of because they didn't know how to read or didn't read or understand the contracts they were signing. Even though we've all heard these stories, there are artists today that still sign terrible contracts. There is unlimited amounts of information—even free information—available that creates awareness about the pitfalls in this industry.

Every artist has the responsibility to protect themselves by becoming educated about the business and by obtaining legal advice. Having a good attorney to assist you in navigating your way through this legal maze is an absolute necessity. Contracts can be complicated, and entertainment contracts are especially so. It is best to shop around for an attorney with a good reputation, but who will still be assessable to you. It will cost you, but it will also save you in the end. Before you sign your name to anything, consult an attorney. Look at it this way, as an entertainer you specialize in creating art. An attorney specializes in the law. Let attorneys do what they do, so you can relax and do what you do.

PRESENT STATE OF AFFAIRS

CHAPTER THIRTY-SEVEN

THE ARTIST THAT MUST DO IT ALL

The New Indie Artists

The notion and definition of just what makes an artist Indie or a DIY artist has become blurred. In a general sense, an Indie artist is someone who produces music independently without the support of major labels. It is creating your own opportunities to make things happen using your own resources. Historically, Indie artists operated outside the mainstream and directed their music to their target audience. But, in the new model, even that is changing.

In today's music industry, all artists have a shot at getting their music heard. The one thing that will separate one artist from the others is creating music that truly connects with listeners. This is the real challenge that all artists must face—both Indie and major labor artists. Listeners are in control and don't have to rely on record labels and stores to get to the music. Everyone (with Internet access) has access to unlimited amounts of music and can decide what they want to stream or download. With so much competition for the attention of listeners, artists will be forced to create better and better product.

In the old model, money was invested in artists and they had the support and muscle of a huge money machine to guide their career. The power of money and marketing expertise often resulted in handsome profits as a result of creating a superstar. Today's artists, without the benefit of a machine to back them, are left to their own devices to figure it out. Today's infrastructure provides the means to create music and the avenue for it to be heard, but it doesn't allow for a support system to lift Indie artists over the competition. In essence, they are left to flounder among the other millions of music creators, with few of them attaining legendary status. In spite of that, there are many Indie artists now making the charts and selling a large number of units of music. It's truly amazing how easy it is to express yourself musically and be heard, particularly if the product is worthy.

The power of funding and marketing was the hallmark of the old model. Because the new model does not provide these resources, doesn't mean that we should return to the old model. Indie labels operate on a different business model than a major label. There is little upfront money, but they often have a 50/50 split between artist and label. Under this model, an artist that sells 100,000 units would be considered a big success. With a major label, the reverse would be true—100,000 units sold would be considered a failure.

Currently, there are a string of Indie artists that have obtained mainstream success that continue to blur the lines because of partnerships with major labels for distribution and promotion. Grammy-winning artist Adele was discovered on Myspace by XL Recordings. Her album *21* was promoted and distributed by Columbia (Sony) and sold 26 million albums. Macklemore & Ryan Lewis, an unsigned act, had *The Heist* album distributed by ADA, Alternative Distribution Alliance, and promoted by Warner Music Group, resulting in the number one spot on Billboard's Hot 100 and won numerous awards.

So the question is whether they are actually Indie artists or is this the new normal for Indies in the new model? The reality of the new model seems to have benefitted Indie artists because they are still able to create music without the confines of the majors' templates while also receiving the funding for mainstream success that can only come with the influence and resources from a major label.

This kind of success, however, catches the attention of the majors who then begin to buy up the really successful Indie labels. This demonstrates why the majors are majors—because they have the money to push artists to superstardom that still eludes Indie labels. At first glance, the success of Macklemore's song "Thrift Shop" appeared to have been generated by a grassroots marketing strategy because it was an Indie. In reality, the power of a major label is actually what propelled "Thrift Shop" through the stratosphere. The song was labeled Pop rather than Urban even though he is a Hip Hop artist. He got commercial radio airplay, which is still controlled by the major labels. Even with the decline of FM, commercial radio is still a powerful force.

The major labels benefit from this arrangement as well because everyone is trying to carve out their positions in the new model and seek out alternative revenue streams. The partnership between Indies and the majors seems to be a win-win situation for both parties. Indies can create independently then reap the benefits of major label resources, and the majors don't have to bet on an artist's success because they only support Indies with a completed project that is a sure thing. But, the question to be answered is if an Indie partners with a major, are they still an Indie? Or can artistic approach keep one an Indie even if they partner with a major?

One downside to this arrangement is that the opportunity is still only given to a chosen few, which mirrors the opportunity at majors—only a chosen few are signed. One thing is certain—the new model and technology promises to produce more Indie artists who will seek support from major labels, who in turn will be eager to partner with self-produced artists with already completed products and proven track records. For the majors, it's still a bet, but they would be considered safe bets.

Today's Indie or DIY artists have their work cut out for them. The new model, powered by easily accessible technology, has opened the floodgates for everyone with talent and even some who are not so talented, but are ambitious and able to produce music. There is a lot more competition and the expectations are now higher. Indie artists who have become superstars have certainly raised the bar for all artists, not just Indies.

Distribution

The problem of distribution has been adjusted and eliminated by downloading. In addition, Indie artists can have a free or inexpensive marketing presence online through artist sites like ReverbNation, CD Baby, TuneCore, Bandzoogle, BandCamp, and many others. BandCamp presently seems to be the standout among these sites because there are no setup fees. It also allows artists to customize their sites, and more significantly, it allows for direct digital downloads to customers, which eliminates the need for a middleman.

Physical distribution still presents a problem for Indies in big box stores because space is limited with the lion share of shelf space going to major label artists. In addition, Indie record stores and mom and pop shops still exist, but continue dwindling in number.

The New A&R

Entry into the music industry was once heavily influenced by A&R, which is now ostensibly dead. Artist development was once under the purview of A&R, which has been all but eliminated, especially for Indies. Without artist development, artist do not have long-term career potential. Say what you want about the old model, but it was the aspect of artist development and quality control that helped create longevity and staying power for artists in a very competitive industry.

Even though most of the gatekeepers are gone, they have been substituted for new ones. A&R has been replaced by a variety of options, such as artist websites, music supervisors, LiveNation, crowdfunding, and music blogs. The power and influence of music blogs should not be underestimated. A positive review can help make an artist by shining a light on them. It can get an artist worldwide attention depending on the reputation of the blog.

It can also be argued that A&R has been replaced by the new model itself. So many aspects of the new model are now being done independently, such as production, marketing, and distribution. Even artist development is now being done independently. This means the artists have to set their own level of quality control. Quality is a relative concept, so there won't be an 'Indie industry standard'. One artist's quality is another artist's garbage.

The Offline World

There are also other options out there for artists. Everything I've discussed so far has been based on an online perspective. However, there is still an offline music world out there with millions of people going about their business listening to commercial radio in their cars, at work, while doing housework, and just regular life. And there are plenty people who still buy physical CDs from stores.

People still attend concerts—small and large—and still support artists by purchasing their merchandise. The revenue stream from this depends on their fan base and how hard they hustle.

Future Possibilities

The ideal situation would be for the listener to purchase directly from the music creator, totally eliminating all gatekeepers. But, what is the likelihood of that? Most artists don't have an infrastructure in place that would take them directly to the fans. Also, this concept is lost on most listeners. They just want the music, so they go directly to the most well-known source, which is currently iTunes, Amazon, or CD Baby. Any support for the artist is good, but a middleman lowers the profit margin for the artists. Artists can't fully capitalize on the popularity of their work without a successful direct-to-fan infrastructure. Creating awareness in fans and listeners on how to better support music creators is the next step to freedom for artists.

My Assessment

We are where we are, and we can see that the new model is also not perfect. Even though it isn't perfect, it's still more beneficial to artists than the old model, if only because it opens the door for anyone to enter rather than just the chosen few. However, artists need to understand that just because the doors are now open, there still is no automatic guarantee of success. I think the solution lies somewhere in between the old and the new models.

There are some artists who will be able to make a living at this, and some who might even make an okay living from their craft. But, under the old model less than ten percent of the artists were able to attain superstardom. Under the new model, the percentage will be the same and probably even less. Left to fend for themselves, artists under the new model should be realistic about their career capabilities regardless of the degree of their talent.

Artists should not operate with 'stars' in their eyes. Rather, they should get a clear understanding of the nature of this business. Artists must now become business savvy themselves because the business of the music industry still has to be handled. Under the old model, all an artist had to do was create and perform. Under the new model, they must do everything themselves. Under the old model, the label was like a bank loaning money to the artists and expecting a return on their investment. That's simply how that business model worked. For many under the new model, you are now the bank, but you should still strive for a return on your investment.

What was once known as the big time is no longer that big. We could be looking at the last of superstar artists like Michael Jackson, Whitney Houston, the Rolling Stones, Prince, and Beyoncé. Still, there are more winners among music creators than ever before. This means the public wins as well. With more artists maintaining control of their own careers and creating music, the listeners have more choices. This is a good thing for all music lovers who can look forward to the arrival of good music to be presented to the world.

However, opening the door to everyone can be a doubled-edged sword. There is a lot of superb music available that once might have slipped through the cracks because of gatekeepers. The other side of that is now there is also an abundance of music that I'll generously refer to as 'low quality' for lack of a better word. One of the good things about gatekeepers was that they were able to separate good songs from bad ones. They were like filters. Now, completely eliminating the concept of artistic quality control, any and everything can be put out there. That's still not so bad a deal if you don't mind sifting through garbage to find music that is glorious, and, at least the artists can keep their copyrights. A few years ago that opportunity would not have existed, but it's possible now that barriers have been lifted for both artists and listeners.

There is an exciting new Indie artist that arrived on the scene in 2013 named George Tandy, Jr. His debut single "March" garnered quite a radio buzz. It was ranked #7 by BDS, #5 on Mediabase Urban AC Radio Charts, and #7 on Billboard's Adult R&B Chart. It was in rotation in the top ten of 45 radio stations in major markets across the country. He signed with the Indie label RedStar Entertainment. This is one of many examples of what an artist can and must do.

Singer Melonie Fiona—who won several awards, including two Grammy Awards for "Fool for You" recorded with CeeLo Green—is now an Indie artist. She's excited about creating new music under her own terms and said that there are no rules in the industry today, and that she can now be as free and experimental as she wants to be.

Singer Tyrese (Gibson) is also now an Indie artist. Upon releasing—what is being promoted as his final album—*Black Rose*, he became his own PR/Marketing man for the album. Tyrese put together a very successful grass-roots campaign. He promoted everywhere from stores to radio to television and even on a bus where we first saw him singing on the Coke Cola commercial. He hustled and made a personal appeal to all his fans and lovers of good music to pre-order and buy Black Rose. The result? According to Nielsen Music, Black Rose opened at No. 1 on the Billboard charts, selling 83,000 copies of the traditional album and more in downloads and track streams. Tyrese also has a very successful acting career starring in the *Furious 7* movie franchise and the popular movie *Baby Boy*.

CHAPTER THIRTY-EIGHT

THE PROGNOSIS

The Expansion of Streaming

I, and other contributors, have spoken a lot about the impact of streaming on the music industry. It has become a common part of the discussion. But, exactly what is streaming? Simply put, streaming is listening to music without having to own a physical copy. Streaming is the latest format in the new music industry model and is still morphing into its final shape. It can be a bit confusing, but you need to understand it. Also, anyone interested in earning a living in the music industry must understand the money flow in streaming. It is very complicated, but I'd like to describe the basics.

The first important thing to understand is that not all streaming services are the same. Some of the major players are Spotify, Pandora, Tidal, Apple Music, Google Play Music, iHeartRadio, Slacker, Rdio, Rhapsody, Deezer, Songza, and YouTube Music Key. There are several specialty streaming services such as This is My Jam, TheSixtyOne, Hype Machine, SHOUTcast, Jamendo, 8tracks, and many, many more. Some of these services are free to listeners and some are supported by ads and/or subscribers.

The major free services are Pandora, Songza, Spotify and Deezer. They are free but they have ads. Ad-free service requires a paid subscription. Terrestrial radio can also be considered a free streaming service because you can hear music free, but with ads. YouTube is still free with ads for now.

Paid streaming services include services like the iTunes/Apple Music hybrid, the YouTube Music Key/Google Play Music hybrid, Rdio, and Rhapsody. They do not offer a free tier. YouTube Music Key is requiring content creators to sign a new agreement, and a lot of them are displeased with some of the terms.

Another difference is that some services are interactive and some are non-interactive. Streaming services such as Spotify, Rhapsody, Google Play, and Rdio are considered interactive because listeners choose the songs they want to hear when they want to hear them. This is considered on-demand streaming and they pay performance royalties as well as mechanical royalties that are monitored through Performing Rights Organizations.

Non-interactive streaming services would be like Internet radio stations Pandora, Sirius XM, NPR or IHeartRadio. Here the listeners tells the service the type of music they like by genre or by artist name, and an algorithm creates a playlist with that type of music. Non-interactive streaming services are like terrestrial radio and requires licenses. They pay only performance royalties that are monitored by SoundExchange and Performing Rights Organizations.

Like it or not, streaming is the current model of delivering and receiving music. It's very efficient, convenient, and inexpensive for the consumer. It's a great mode of exposure for new and Indie artists to get their music heard. However, it also pays very little to content creators, which is the crux of the pushback from some well-established artists. Artists Thom Yorke, Will.i.am, Pink Floyd and others were very vocal opponents of Spotify.

Taylor Swift became somewhat of the poster child against on-demand streaming, and Spotify in particular. She said to Yahoo, "I'm not willing to contribute my life's work to an experiment that I don't feel fairly compensates the writers, producers, artists, and creators of this music." [Willman, C., 2014, November 6, *Taylor Swift on Being Pop's Instantly Platinum Wonder...And Why She's Paddling Against the Streams* http://yahoo.com/music].

Even though streaming services are operating smoothly for the most part, things are still being figured out. Pandora lobbied to lower its royalty payouts. Spotify determined that seven tenths of a penny is what a stream is worth. Some people rationalize that it beats piracy, where the content creators got absolutely nothing. I have to agree with that, but it's also like offering a starving person a crumb. New and Indie artists will not be able to make a livable wage on fractions of a penny no matter how many spins a song gets.

Piracy has contributed to the extreme devaluation of music, but it is not alone. Labels overcharging for CDs with one or two good songs and the rest just fillers fueled discontent among consumers. In 1999 P2P file sharing and Napster changed the game of access to music, but it was illegal because of copyright infringement. When iTunes introduced single downloads in 2003, it changed the game further. Consumers could now legally buy only the singles they wanted at a reasonable price.

When on-demand streaming came about, the major labels quickly bought into the new delivery model after negotiating and receiving millions of dollars in lump-sum payments for use of their catalogs. In addition, Spotify had to negotiate with each label separately for their rates. Also Spotify doesn't pay the artists directly. Content creators are paid by the labels because Spotify already gave the money to the labels. Spotify pays out 70 percent of its revenue.

Some of the anger directed at Spotify should be aimed toward the labels who keep the lion share of the profits and give the content creators a small portion. In the old model, major labels justified this by saying they were recouping production costs, marketing and everything associated with bringing the music to the world. Now that production costs have gone way down in the digital era and delivery is a matter of clicking a key to upload, it's hard for them to justify keeping such a large portion of the payout.

It's not just some of the artists who are after Spotify to cough up more money. Now the major labels—Universal Music Group, Warner Music Group, and Sony Music are pushing for more from Spotify. They argue that Spotify should cut back on its offerings in the free tier hoping that will encourage more paid subscriptions.

Now that Apple has entered the streaming world after purchasing Beats Music from Jimmy Iovine and Dr. Dre and relaunching it as Apple Music, you can expect competition for paid subscribers to heat up even more. Spotify is the streaming service that people either love or hate and has not yet turned a profit, but its value is said to be in the billions.

Podcasts

Podcasts are another popular medium. A podcast is a program or series in digital audio format that is available by downloading over the Internet. The programs can be either a music show or a talk show. Very similar to a radio program, the main difference is that you can listen to a podcast at your convenience and not necessarily at the time it is broadcast.

Through the ingenuity of podcasts, anyone can be a DJ or have a talk show. Leading hosting services in this industry are BlogTalkRadio, SoundCloud, Amazon S3, Rackspace CloudFiles, Spreaker, Podomatic, PodBean, Buzzsprout, Blubrry, LibSyn, Archive.org, and many more. Like music streaming services, podcast hosting services also have a free tier and paid tiers.

Conclusion

It seems that almost every day there is a new development in the music industry. Artists and labels—both major and Indie—are coming up with creative ways to become or remain relevant and earn income from their music. Major labels are working to re-secure their tightly-held position as gatekeepers in the new music industry model, even though now there is competition from streaming services.

Download numbers are down and streaming is up. Streaming is replacing downloads that replaced CDs that replaced tapes that replaced vinyl. Indie artists have seen their potential music revenue dwindle to fractions of a penny per spin. When people know that the music they want can be found for free on the Internet, the perception is that it has no or little value.

On the other hand, the amount of revenue earned is relative to how you look at it. An artist can receive between 70 cents to 90 cents per download. But, if you count up how many times a song can be streamed over the course of 10, 20, 30 years, that revenue amount will be much larger from streaming, even at fractions of a penny, than on a single one-time sale because quantity in streaming makes the difference. But, who wants to wait 10, 20, 30 years to see a profit?

Since streaming is still relatively new, it probably caught content creators off guard when they realized what was happening to that income stream. I think that in time, revenue that content creators earn from streaming will balance out because there will be a reckoning comparable to the civil rights struggle for fair and equal pay.

In fact, music executive Irving Azoff has formed an organization called Global Music Rights. In an article by *The Hollywood Reporter* Azoff said, "GMR is going to give songwriters and publishers an opportunity to engage in meaningful licensing for their intellectual property. The trampling of writers' rights in the digital marketplace without any regard to their contribution to the creative process will no longer be tolerated." [Gardner, E., 2014, Nov. 12]

I understand technological advances, expansion, and the new distribution platform of downloading. But, I don't understand how someone can decide to pay fractions of a penny to use someone else's music. One song in particular "Wake Me Up" by Avicii was streamed 168,000,000 times in the United States, and they received just $12,359. [MusicTimes.com 11/08/14].

Streaming services are making money for the major labels, the advertisers are happy, and the listeners are elated. Everyone seems happy except the people who created the music that everyone loves to listen to for practically free. It should be noted that not all artists are displeased with streaming. And many opponents of streaming have now accepted the inevitable, even though some artists have chosen specific services to be associated with.

Today music is being consumed more than at any other point in history. Many people get it free and those who pay, are paying very little for it. As far as streaming goes for the content creators, they are told to be patient and that minute payouts are better than nothing.

Physical media is on life support. According to the Recording Industry Association of America (RIAA), in 2014 revenue from stream-ing surpassed CDs for the first time. Streaming has changed listeners' habits with the ease and availability of enjoying music. That genie can't be put back in the bottle. The only thing that will turn people away from streaming is the next big thing that will come down the pike, which possibly will be even more convenient and pay content creators even less.

As more and more content creators become disgruntled, they will start a movement and demand their music stop being de-valued. This should be done using a multi-pronged approach. It could be done by changing outdated federal laws which make the current de-valuing of music possible. It could be done by more and more content creators protesting and demanding their content be removed from the streaming services unless they receive better payouts. It could be done by creating awareness for the consumers to know how streaming effects the content owners. I'm sure it will be an uphill battle.

Yet, I have developed a more philosophical perspective about streaming. Now that music has moved beyond the physical, it makes me wonder if this is how it should be anyway. In the pre-broadcast era before the invention of the radio and records, people would listen to music being played live by real musicians. People could listen to music without having it in a physical form; they enjoyed it ephemerally. They had it for that moment and filed it in their hearts and minds.

After a century of having physical forms of music, the digital era is returning us to an era without physical copies once again. This time, however, the music is retained and digitally preserved into infinity. The music is not always produced by live musicians. Today music can be produced by people who aren't musicians, but who know how to use a computer program. It's not for me to say if it's right or wrong, but that is the way it is.

Some people say that artists are wrong to think that the world owes them a living. I don't agree with that attitude. I think that anyone who creates something that is desired by someone else should be fairly compensated for it.

If you open a clothing store, should people be able to go in and take what they want? If you open a restaurant, would you want everyone to come in and eat free or lower your prices? Why does no one question why an attorney or a doctor charges for their services? Better yet, why do record labels think they should get paid? These are honest questions, and the answer is because they all offer something that someone else desires. It should be the same for content creators to expect to be paid for their services, especially when they incur costs to create them.

My experience and viewpoint is from that of a record executive, but I have expanded my perspective to see the new music industry model through different vantage points. I now have a granddaughter who is an aspiring musical artist. This is her world. Where I see streaming as not paying enough to labels and artists, she might see streaming as a blessing that will help introduce her music to the world. Having never experienced making lots of money that once flowed for successful artists, her expectations are different.

This tsunami of change in the music industry for me has been like a whirlwind 50 years in the making. I've experienced several aspects of it: as a pioneer African American record executive; as a witness to the systemic racism in the industry that I fought against and helped to change; as a witness to the emergence of the new music industry model; as a teacher who shared what I learned; and as a student of life who marvels at the extreme changes I've seen over the decades and who is giddy with excitement about future possibilities. In the end, it's all about the music…and the business of it.

SPEECH TRANSCRIPTS

CHAPTER THIRTY-NINE

"BLACK LEADERSHIP IN THE MUSIC INDUSTRY"

Logan H. Westbrooks
February 2013

Hello everyone. It's a pleasure to be here with you today. I want to thank you for letting me share my thoughts with you about leadership in the music industry. Let me start by saying that MY music business is not YOUR music business! My God, so many things have changed! An avalanche of technological advancements have turned the music industry upside down since I've moved on.

In spite of that, strong leadership is still a necessary prerequisite in order to garner any form of success in this business. In fact, good leadership is required to run any successful endeavor. That is something that has not and will not change.

The first thing a smart leader must do is to surround him or herself with a good team. You need a solid team of music professionals to produce a successful project—meaning the business, the music and the artist. When I organized my team, I sought out people that I knew were ideally suited to perform specific tasks.

For promotions I brought in Armand Mckissick, Bill Craig, Gerry Griffin, Chuck Offutt, Glen Wright, Speedy Curtis, Leroy Smith, Ralph Bates, Granville White, Harold Costner, George Chavous, and Fred Ware. A promotion person requires a certain type of personality. They must be observant and adaptable. They have to be extroverts and highly sociable. Promotion people—promoters—live life in the moment and are able to quickly adapt to situations as they pop up.

They keep themselves in the thick of things to be in a position to efficiently handle their network of people. Basically, they have to be skilled people-persons. So, I put those people in place to handle that aspect of the business, and they did their jobs very well.

My team was empowered as my representatives, all working together toward the same goal. You see, it's important to do more than create a product, and you must never be satisfied with the status quo. This means always reaching farther and farther to create a product that creates not just an impact, but a POWERFUL impact. That was our goal, and that is what we always strove to achieve.

As a leader, you are responsible for creating the vision and directing the path for the fulfillment of that vision. It means sometimes having to work in an unfamiliar and unpredictable atmosphere, where perceived advantages can disappear in the blink of an eye. But, also where a surprise streak of luck can change misfortune into great fortune.

An effective leader has to envision every possible outcome in the face of uncertainty. You have to be five or six steps ahead of the moment. That's what you call changing a mistake into an opportunity. That's when you take the risks, when it's either "try it or it's over."

Keep in mind, however, that you, the leader, are ultimately responsible whether your vision succeeds or fails. Your team must be free to move forward unhindered by the fear of punishment for the uncertain outcome of a project. Fear prevents experimentation and exploration and risks, which translates to no innovation.

Everybody's looking for the next big thing. Innovation is what drives the music industry. It's what drives any industry. You need to have a team that understands you and understands your vision. It is the magical combination of the right people engaged in a common cause that fuels the engine of success. That's the kind of leadership you should aspire to.

In the music industry, the singers and musicians are the stars. But, the engine behind the stars that opens doors and guides and directs their path to stardom starts with the business aspect. It starts with the executives, the decision-makers. Music is art, but it is also a business—a business that needs effective leadership to be successful.

There are a number of African American music executives and music industry leaders that have had very successful careers, even though we had to work harder, run faster, and jump higher than our peers just to prove we were as capable as they were. Some of them are: Larkin Arnold, Clarence Avant, Berry Gordy, Don Cornelius, Al Bell, Sylvia Rhone, Suzanne De Passe, Quincy Jones, Buzzy Willis, Oscar Fields, Dick Griffey, Ron Mosley, Dr. George Butler, Brenda Andrews, Ray Harris, Tom Draper, Sidney Miller, Henry Allen, Cecil Holmes, Jack Gipson, Otis Smith, Kenny Gamble and Leon Huff.

Of course, there are many, many others, but time doesn't permit me to mention everyone. They all worked very hard and left a powerful legacy in the industry. We've come a long way since the days of 'race music'. African American music executives are no longer a rarity, and African American singers, musicians, and entertainers have made music and had careers that are the stuff of legends.

We experienced racism and resistance from some, but we saw ourselves as trailblazers and we were on a mission. We understood the role we played in the cultural landscape of the country, and we also remembered from whence we came. We could not walk away from our responsibility to the African American community, and we were proud to support organizations and causes that uplifted our community. Some of the organizations were The Mufandi Institute, PUSH Expo, Project 75, MLK Center, the Black Caucus, Mt. Morris Park, and Wattstax.

Music and business are both global forces that transcend the boundaries of language, ethnicity, nationality, and class. And music provides many examples of leadership and of people working together to create great achievements.

Music executives, singers, and musicians face common issues in dealing with teamwork, change, achieving performance value, and competing to succeed. I hope future generations of African American music executives and singers understand the significance of their roles in society and grasp their opportunity to take the music higher.

It's also necessary for me to share an example of leadership that was once dynamic, focused, and extremely successful. In the last couple decades, however, they have dropped the ball and fallen from their perch of leadership at an astonishing rate. There was a vacuum in leadership because they rested on their laurels as if their leadership status would be eternal. That leadership vacuum appeared in none other than the music industry itself.

It was 1981 when I wrote *The Anatomy of a Record Company: How to Survive in the Record Business.* It's been almost 30 years, and I have witnessed a transformation of the music industry that is comparable in scope to the Industrial Revolution when there was widespread replacement of manual labor by machinery.

Some of the driving forces at that time were the steam engine, steel, electricity, and the automobile. The major driving forces today are the Internet, digitized music, and the mobilization of music. The major labels no longer hold autonomy as to who enters the 'gates'. Even though their influence is still powerful, they are no longer seen as the only avenue for artists to break into the music industry.

Political, sociological, and psychological factors have also contributed to a major shift in the paradigm of the entire notion of music –how it is delivered and how it is received by today's music consumers.

Radio has been consolidated by corporations, which are virtually monopolies such as Clear Channel. So now, corporate entities rather than program directors decide what music does and does not get played. This shift has diluted the sense of familiarity and the 'flavor' of radio's appeal to local communities.

The major labels have gobbled each other up and now there are only three remaining: Sony/BMG, Universal Music Group, and Warner Music Group.

Nowadays, many artists prefer independence and choose Indie labels. Artists opt for the freedom of creativity provided by an indie label rather than the conformity of commercialized music.

The creation of peer-to-peer (P2P) file sharing, where you can get the music free if you choose to, has presented a huge dilemma as well as a tremendous loss of revenue for the major labels. Many people don't care about owning the music, they prefer access to it. They can stream it whenever they want to hear it through their computer, their phone, their pad, and other devices. They could care less about the physical CD.

Technology and the internet has made it possible for everyone to enter the gates on their own terms, create the music they want, target the audience of their choice, and worry about pleasing no one but their niche market and themselves. They might not make as much money as they would have under the major labels, but at least their voices can be heard. And the public is exposed to a more abundant assortment of music rather than the cookie cutter allotment permitted by the majors. This doesn't necessarily mean that the Indie path is better than the major label path. I'm saying that now there is at least a viable option.

I'm not trying to bash my industry, I'm just speaking the facts. But, the question remains...how did the major labels allow themselves to be pushed aside by technology that was as available to them as it was to the independent artists and consumers that have embraced it and utilized it to their advantage.

The fact is that the tables have turned and the business of music is wide open because the gates have come crashing down. I'm sure I'm not the only one to ask this question.

I have one more thing to discuss that has been weighing on my mind for several years. Who, among the younger generation, is going to step up to accept the challenge of the messengers? Yes, the messengers are still watching us. And, just as they came to me and explained my responsibility to the music, that responsibility is now yours.

I know that times change; what's acceptable and what's not acceptable has changed; styles change, and genres morph from one to the other. But, as an elder, it is also my responsibility to give guidance to the youth when it's necessary. My age and experience have earned me that right.

The lyrics, the images, and the messages of some of today's music is disheartening. I never thought I'd live to see women referred to as the "B" word. I never thought I'd see women refer to themselves in that way.

And after all the struggles from the Civil Rights era, all the battles we fought for equal rights, all the sacrifices we made for your generation to be able to advance...after all that...some of our youth prefer to degrade themselves with the "N" word. It's like you're turning your back on those who fought for our freedom—on Malcolm X, on Martin Luther King, Jr., on Harriet Tubman, on Fannie Lou Hamer.

Glorifying drinking, and drugs, and guns, and sexing multiple partners in the music and videos can be detrimental and turn back the clock on advancing ourselves as a people. The music of the '70s helped to inspire us and motivate us to overcome all obstacles. Those words sunk in and influenced us in a positive way. So, if you sing songs about hope, pride, redemption, and power, that's what you reach for. It's something psychological about it.

By the same token, if you sing songs about drinking, guns, killing, and going to jail as a rite of passage...that's what you'll reach for. It's something psychological about that, too.

I've heard that the major labels wouldn't give rappers a deal unless they sang 'gangsta' rap. I hope that's not true. But even if it is, now you can do something about it. Now, you have the freedom to make whatever kind of songs you want. What will you do with that freedom of creativity? Will you step up and take responsibility for the music? Will you listen to the message from the messengers?

Just as we're discussing history today, one day your generation will be history. What will your legacy be? What will be said about the music you create? What do you want to leave to the generation after you? The gatekeepers can no longer keep you out. The labels can no longer tell you what to sing in order to get a contract. The choice is now yours. What are you going to do with that kind of power?

It's up to you to decide...but remember, it's not just your future. It's all of our future, so use your power wisely. Thank you very much for having me.

CHAPTER FORTY

"THE GOLDEN AGE OF BLACK MUSIC"

Logan H. Westbrooks
June 2014

I could not begin to write about music without qualifying my message with a confession about my love of Black music. It is as much a part of my life and as natural for me as eating or sleeping. I, therefore, consider it a blessing to have had the opportunity to be a part of bringing a very special period of Black music to the forefront. That time is affectionately known as 'the '60s and 'the '70s. I call that time the 'Golden Age of Black Music.'

I am proud to have represented an era in music that focused on talent—raw talent, finessed talent, and everything in between. Music that elicited real emotional responses; from the angst of the Vietnam War ("War" by Edwin Starr and "Bring the Boys Home" by Freda Payne); the anger of political turmoil ("You Haven't Done Nothin" by Stevie Wonder); the sense of freedom of disco music ("Le Freak" by Chic); the power of the funk phenomenon ("One Nation Under a Groove" by Funkadelic), the energy of women's empowerment ("I'm Every Woman" by Chaka Khan), and the passion of love, sweet love ("Turn Out the Lights" by Teddy Pendergrass).

Black music is distinct unto itself, and is the bedrock of American music, with Gospel, Blues and Jazz at the root of it all. Black music in the '60s and '70s was robust and dynamic with the pre-imminence of horns and the powerful and pulsating rhythms. Black music of that era had an undeniable and irrefutable impact on the tapestry of American culture, and delivered almost an embarrassment of riches through classic hit after hit after hit.

My area of expertise in this Golden Age of Black Music was behind the scenes. My job was to open doors for development and exposure of Black music to the mass market. Just as the American pioneers opened up new areas to land development, my role was similar in the sense of developing new musical concepts, ideas, and inroads for Black music.

Clive Davis, one of the top honchos in the music business during that time, had an affinity for and deep appreciation of Black music. Because of his influence, he played a crucial role in creating the landscape for its acceptance and its crossover appeal. Clive Davis made it possible for me and my peers to introduce Black music to the mass market on a broader level than ever before. He respected the audience and knew they would accept good music if it was presented to them in just the right way.

After forming my own record label—Source Records—I signed a relatively unknown Chuck Brown & the Soul Searchers where he got his first hit record "Bustin' Loose" in 1978. It was a powerful song with an undeniable '70s sound and appeal that transcended time and space when it was covered in 2002 by rapper Nelly with the #1 smash hit "Hot in Herre," which is still popular today. In March 2014, San Francisco radio station FM 105.7 put the song on endless loop replaying it nonstop for more than two days while the station re-launched with a new format. Radio Insight described the song by saying *"There is a strangely hypnotic quality to listening to Nelly's 2002 smash hit endlessly on a loop. You feel like it's Friday night no matter what you're doing."* [Radio Insight 3-17-2014]. The same thing was done at an Austin, Texas, radio station in 2003.

It was music from this era that became the backbone of Rap and Hip Hop, with rappers sampling music from James Brown, George Clinton, the Barkays, Leon Haywood, the Isley Brothers, Kool & the Gang, Lynn Collins, Sly & the Family Stone, and many, many, many other artists from this period.

There was something about music from the '60s and '70s that will resound eternally. It raised the standard of what was musically capable. And, culturally, it came to represent a time of change that, ironically, to this day no one wants to leave behind—the clothes, the hairstyles, the attitudes, the dances, and most important, the music. Today, on a regular basis, there are '70s themed concerts and parties held all over the country celebrating the musical culture of that decade. The '70s even had its own television show—*Soul Train*.

Soul Train was created, produced, and hosted by Don Cornelius in 1971 and lasted 35 years. It was a music, dance, and variety show that showcased the hottest Black musical acts and fantastic dancers, some who became celebrities themselves. All the Black artists wanted to be on *Soul Train*, and Don Cornelius presented the best of the best—James Brown, the Jacksons, the Temptations, Gladys Knight & the Pips, Smoky Robinson, and too many others to mention.

Soul Train also had a huge and lasting impact on America and the world with the Soul Train line that has become a part of all parties and family reunions. Don Cornelius had a deep, classy voice and made popular such sayings as "Love, peace, and soul," "The hippest trip in America" and "You can bet your last money, it's gonna be a stone gas honey." The ebullient *Soul Train* was created and existed all for the love of Black music.

There were a variety of elements that helped to create this phenomenon of the '70s. The front aspect was the music, the production, and the artists. But, long before the public was served this delicious music, a lot of background preparation had to take place. Credit must be given to the talent scouts who found and discovered new talent; the A&R personnel who groomed the talent; the marketing team that promoted the music; and yes, the record executives who orchestrated each project through strong leadership, decision-making, and vision. All of these integral parts happened behind the scenes by the unheralded participants, the unsung heroes and sheroes whose roles were as significant as the front people—the stars. If not for those behind the scenes, the stars would not have become the successful artists that the world came to know and love.

This era can also be considered the Golden Age of Black Music because it was the last decade of totally live musicianship. In the '70s, most bands averaged eight to ten members. But in the 1980s synthesized music began to dominate the industry, virtually putting live musicians out of work. It can be argued that it also changed the feel of the music. Today, one person alone in a studio can create a fully orchestrated song. It's good music—some of it great—but, it will never be as impactful as the feel of '60s and '70s music. To hear it and to see it performed live demonstrates that the human element is irreplaceable.

That could explain why the world clings to the music of the '70s. The children of children who were born in the 1970s now embrace and claim that era of music as their own. And it's not unusual to see an 80-year-old person singing along with people in their teens...because they're all singing songs from the '60s and '70s.

Music from that Golden Age ushered in an unprecedented number of songs that became classics; songs filled with innovative grooves, polished productions, and unparalleled vocalizations. Another crucial component to the music was the emotive effect the songs had on people individually as well as on the larger society. All these different elements were integrated into the music—some intentionally and some by happenstance.

A marketing plan can be well crafted, 'feelers' can be sent out, and strategies put in place, but until the song is actually released, there is no guarantee of a measurement of success. There have been many surprises, and many hits and misses. There are also many songs that should be revisited because when they were originally released, the time might not have been right. Maybe the world wasn't ready for it. And, there are some hits that just happen. Then there are songs that have a message that is right on time; songs whose relevance is the same 30, 40, 50 years later. Those songs are called classics.

One song in particular that resonated strongly in my soul was "Wake up Everybody" by Harold Melvin & the Blue Notes with Teddy Pendergrass on lead vocals. That song exemplified the Golden Age of Black Music. More than just a song, it was a charge—a call to action. "Wake up Everybody" delivered the best of everything—writing, music, production, strong vocals, a danceable beat, and social consciousness on a global scale. It used the universal language of music to raise awareness that we are all responsible for each other, and that we are, indeed, our brothers and sisters keepers.

Written by Gene McFadden, John Whitehead, and Victor Carstarphen, and produced by Kenneth Gamble and Leon Huff in 1975, "Wake up Everybody" is a musical triumph of message music. It deserved and received critical acclaim. It was produced in 1975, right in the middle of the decade—symbolic of a master scale of balance—grabbing the best of the first five years of the decade and influencing the second half. The song was breathtaking in its scope of covering the landscape of societal ills that effected the poor, the elderly, children, as well as the apathetic.

Black singers sang of both love and social issues because they could not escape the reality of some of society's deficiencies. For Black artists, it was as natural to sing of one as it was the other because both were a part of our lives. Marvin Gaye sang about inner-city blues as easily, as effortlessly, and as sincerely as he sang about getting it on. Teddy Pendergrass told everybody to wake up as genuinely as he told his woman to close the door. It was all a part of who we are. To sing of one and not sing of the other is like living in denial.

"Wake up Everybody" was covered by several artists, most recently in 2010 by the collaboration of John Legend, the Roots, Melanie Fiona, and Common. It has introduced the song to a new generation of listeners worldwide.

What better way to express our joy and our pain than through music...beautiful and timeless music. Thanks to classics like that, the Golden Age of Black Music will always be with us.

Thank you for letting me share my thoughts.

CHAPTER FORTY-ONE

"BUSTIN' LOOSE: BREAKING RACIAL BARRIERS IN HE MUSIC INDUSTRY"

Logan H. Westbrooks
February 2013

Good evening. Is everyone doing okay? It's a genuine pleasure for me to be here with you...to have the privilege to share my thoughts with you. When I look around the room, it makes me smile inside. I see myself in so many of you.

It was 42 years ago that I opened the door to my office at CBS Records. I stopped just inside the door and I inhaled. I breathed in the air that smelled of possibilities...Possibilities that were moving more toward probabilities...Probabilities that would become actualities.

Yes, that office was more than a room. The room was more akin to opportunity. I say that because I was now in the position to affect real change. I had been around the industry for a while, but this was different. I was now in the big league.

Inside the room, I slowly approached my desk, looking around at the bare walls. I envisioned the greatness that would soon decorate the beautiful but generic wallpaper. I sat down at my desk in a high-back, black leather swivel chair, and I continued to survey my surroundings. I delicately ran my hands across the desk, then I sat back in my chair and closed my eyes. Only then did I exhale.

The room was totally silent and there was a stillness in the air, but I heard the feint sound of music, and I surrendered to the moment. It was the song of all those who had come before me delivering the message that I had an obligation to open doors. To open doors not by knocking on them. Not by asking someone to let me come in. Not by pushing, trying to force my way in.

The message was that I was to facilitate the removal of barriers and to usher in great music that would make the doors open by themselves as if being assisted by a gust of wind. The message was that I was to help bring forth powerful music that could not be denied. The

270

message was that I was to deliver compelling music that would stand the test of time.

My answer to the message was, "YES! I will abide by my obligation to those in the past who paved the way for me to sit behind the desk of this powerful organization." And my answer was, "YES! I understand my duty and responsibility to those who will carry our music forward to the future."

You must understand that the message was not spoken out loud. There was no one physically in the room with me…I was alone. But, I felt it and I understood it clearly, and my mind went back to those in the world of music in this country who had come before me.

It is imperative to know your history, because without what was, nothing is. With that in mind, it's important to share a brief historical overview of Black music.

The history of Black music started in the 19th Century during slavery. The music started out as rhythmic work songs, field hollers, and hymns that were sung to get the enslaved workers through endless days of hard labor. The songs were also used to convey coded messages of healing and escape.

Wade in the Water – a Negro Spiritual, is a song that is still very popular today. Its message was to stay in the water so the bloodhounds could not follow your scent. Negro Spirituals were also songs of faith, hope, and survival.

Blues evolved from the work songs and hymns in the latter part of the 19th Century. Blues was music of heartache, pain, and adversity. Blues is also considered one of the first American music forms, and is the root of all other American music. Also around this time, Black music was given a classification called 'race music.'

Jazz was created in the early 20th Century in the melting pot of New Orleans. Jazz was a fusion of Blues, Spirituals, and African and European music. Scott Joplin, the Father of Ragtime music, was the first African American to become a famous celebrity, performing at the 1893 World's Fair in Chicago. There was a movie made about his life called *Ragtime*.

Rhythm & Blues entered the scene around the early 1940s when bandleader Louis Jordan became the best-selling artist of his time. He sang a duet with Ella Fitzgerald called *Choo Choo Ch'Boogie* in 1946 that was a multi-million seller and changed the history of Black music.

This thirst for 'race music' produced the formation of several White-owned record labels specializing in Black music and artists. The labels started during this era were Savoy, King, Atlantic, and Aristocrat.

Doo Wop emerged on the West Coast in the 1950s. Groups like the Penguins, the Platters, the Ink Spots, the Jewels, the Coasters, the

Flamingos, the Cadillacs, and the Chords were all a part of the Doo Wop explosion.

In 1954 the Chords had a hit song called "Sh-Boom" that was covered by a White group called the Crew Cuts. Even though the song was bland and watered down, it made the charts and started the trend of White groups covering Black songs.

Rock & Roll also developed in the mid-1950s. Some of the early stars of Rock & Roll were Little Richard and Chuck Berry. The person set atop the pedestal of Rock & Roll, however, was Elvis Presley. Although talented, Presley was actually interpreting Black music. Most of his hits were covers of R&B songs.

On the other hand, Chuck Berry wrote his own songs and created his own dance—the duck walk. And Little Richard gave the best description of it when he said, "Rhythm & Blues had a baby and some-body named it Rock & Roll."

Soul music originated in the late 1950s, early 1960s. It was a blend of Gospel and Rhythm & Blues. Soul music was like returning to the roots of Black music. Soul music was sung with intense vocals. Ray Charles is credited with one of the first Soul songs in 1954 called "I Got a Woman."

Singers like Aretha Franklin, Otis Redding, Johnny Taylor, Al Green, and James Brown embody the epitome of Soul music. Most Black music lost its popularity during the British invasion with acts like the Beatles and the Rolling Stones who were heavily influenced by artists such as Little Richard, Chuck Berry and Muddy Waters.

Aretha Franklin and James Brown are credited with saving Black music around this time because their sound was not easy to duplicate. James Brown's music would later become the most sampled music in the world.

Hip Hop/Rap is stylized rhythmic music accompanied with a rhyming chant called rapping. DJ Kool Herc is considered the first Hip Hop artist, and is credited as the Father of Hip Hop. Rapping began in the Bronx, New York, in the mid-1970s, and was performed live at house parties and block parties.

In 1979 the first Rap recording was made by the Sugarhill Gang titled "Rappers Delight." Gil Scott-Heron and the Last Poets were the forerunners to this genre. When it was first introduced, it was thought to be a fad. However, Hip Hop has become one of the most influential music genres in the history of American music. Hip Hop artists sampled a lot of its music from Soul artists from the 1960s and '70s, which also revitalized the careers and bank accounts of those artists.

Go-Go artists Chuck Brown & the Soul Searchers had a hit song in 1979 titled "Bustin' Loose." In fact, I signed Chuck Brown to his first record deal, and "Bustin' Loose" was his first hit song and the first hit for my newly formed label, Source Records. "Bustin' Loose" remained on the Billboard charts for a number of weeks.

In 2002, Hip Hop artist Nelly used "Bustin' Loose" for his song "Hot in Herre." It was #1 on the Billboard charts and was four times Platinum. "Hot in Herre" also earned Nelly a Grammy for Best Male Rap Solo Performance.

That's what can happen when you create great music. Music that transcends genres. Music that is unhindered by the demographics of age, race, and geographic location. Music that sounded good then…that sounds good now…and that will sound good in the future.

So, that was my message from the messengers. That was my charge. I didn't necessarily have the guarantee of a solid blueprint to follow, so I had to follow the spirit of the message that I would be guided by the music. Needless to say, I felt the pressure. But, I shrugged it off, lifted my shoulders and went to work. I was on a mission.

The first act selected was the O'Jays* and their song was titled "Backstabbers." "Backstabbers" was #1 on Billboard's R&B Chart and #3 on Billboard's Pop Chart. The next act was Harold Melvin and the Blue Notes, and their song was "If You Don't Know Me By Now." That song also went to #1 on Billboard's R&B Chart and #3 on Billboard's Pop Chart. After that, it was Billy Paul. His song was "Me and Mrs. Jones." Another hit! "Me and Mrs. Jones" went platinum, selling over two million copies and Billy received a Grammy Award.

I now had a definite guideline to follow. But, having three back to back successes also set the bar rather high. With each project, I gained more confidence. We found new and innovative ways to deliver successful and unique projects. We had to.

Awards and accolades started pouring in for the artists I had brought in. I beamed with pride with each success. I was proud of my accomplishments. I was elated for the artists. And I was pleased that I was able to fulfill the commitment of the message given to me when I first entered my office.

I was sometimes disappointed when a song that I felt was a sure winner wasn't as well received as I thought it would be. Johnny Mathis was a very successful singer of standards and popular music, but he always wanted to reach the R&B market. We paired him with hit producer Thom Bell and lyricist Linda Creed, and he recorded the song "I'm Coming Home."

We all felt that song would be a big hit, but it went nowhere. Thom blamed CBS for not promoting it. We gave the same song to the Spinners and it was a big hit for them, with Phillippe Wynn singing the lead. So, we were not successful with Johnny Mathis, and that was a big disappointment.

There was another group called the Ebonys out of Philadelphia. Of all the vocal groups out during this time, they were among the best singers. But, they just didn't make it. They had a couple songs to chart, but no real hits. It was unfortunate and a big disappointment.

But, I didn't give up. I looked at each setback as merely a temporary obstacle and kept it moving. I stayed positive. I had to. There were people looking up to me...depending on me. I chose to embrace constructive thinking that could propel us onto a better direction. I got back up, brushed myself off, and tried again.

I was armed with determination and persistence, a duty to my mission, and my belief in the music. I kept an enthusiastic attitude and refused to be distracted from my purpose. I had long-term goals that were bigger than me and my position at CBS Records. My innermost goal was to take our music higher; to make it everlasting. So I had to keep my eyes on the prize.

There's a big difference in where we were, and where we are today. Race relations in the music industry paralleled race relations in the country at that time. Where there was discrimination and racism in the larger society, so it was within the music industry.

Things were separated along racial lines, including the songs and where they were played, live performances and where people were seated, where the artists stayed while on tour, and what kind of contract artists signed. Black music—Jazz, Blues, Gospel, R&B, and any other music that was considered Black was played solely on Black radio stations.

I wanted to create a new way of listening to the music of Black America. In order for this to happen, the world had to learn to appreciate its profound contribution to the entirety of American music. I wanted to demonstrate the enduring vitality of Black music. Simply put, I wanted the same thing for our music that was provided for White music. I advocated for adequate budgets for my projects, and I fought for more Black authenticity in the promotion of that music.

We were trying something that had never been done before, and we knew that the old way wouldn't work. They wanted us to give them songs that would crossover to the Pop market. They told me if I could give them a Top 5 song on the R&B chart, they would cross it over. The importance of crossing over was because you would be exposed to a much larger audience.

We got the hit songs, but they would not help us. In fact, they blocked everything we tried to do. Black staff worked Black radio stations and White staff worked White stations, and the White program directors would not cooperate with Black staff. Not to be deterred, we knew that we had to be innovative in our approach.

A member of my team named Bill Craig was friendly with a man in Canada who could get music played at a Top 40 radio station there. We crossed the border and got our music played in Canada. Once our songs got airplay there, we were able to get their affiliate station in Chicago to play them. And that's how some of our songs moved across the country. Believe it or not, things really didn't begin to change much until MTV began playing Michael Jackson's videos.

At first, some people at CBS were not happy with the changes, and they resented me coming in as part of that change. Some of the sales staff were 'rednecks' that came up through the ranks, and quite frankly, they were resistant to the focus on Black music. They felt too much attention was being paid to the African American artists. But, they quickly came around when they saw the numbers. And they also bene-fitted financially from the rise in those numbers.

When I arrived at CBS, there were no African American publicists. I advocated for an African American publicist to help promote our music. Keep in mind that everything was totally separated. There was a White music division and a Black music division. The White publicists were not effective for our music. This led to the hiring of Ed Wright & Associates as publicists for the African American acts. Having promotion specially designed for our market made all the difference in the world. We knew how to talk the language…we knew what we liked. They didn't.

I probably could have taken the easy route by not making waves and by following the rules as they were already being played. But, that's exactly why it's important not to simply accept the "way things are" as some unchangeable reality. It's a fact of life that things change, that innovation happens. However, change only happens because of gentle nudging or aggressive pushback. Whatever it takes. However, when all was said and done, the power of the music spoke for itself.

When I retired, the bare walls of the office I entered when I started at CBS were now decorated with Gold Records…a testament to the music. That's what I envisioned happening and it became manifest. I started with the end in mind, and we got there. But, I had to follow the path of the message that was given to me in order to get me there.

I must say that I was given strength and inspiration by the socially conscious music of the time. Similar to the old Negro Spirituals with the hidden messages, there have always been messages in our music during periods of social change. The O'Jays acknowledged that in 1976 with their song "Message in Our Music." It had an infectious no holds barred groove that captured the mood of '70s music—both lyrically and rhythmically.

There was also a particular feel that was created by the legends of Black music. These sounds moved from Blues, R&B, Psychedelic, Funk, Pop, and more. However, what was significant about the '70s is that it was a period of change. Change from Jim Crow racism to the Civil Rights Era and anti-war era—a period of protest.

This protest emerged in the aftermath of Martin Luther King's assassination and the urban rebellions across the country. This was a period of a rising "Black Consciousness" and "Black Identity."

One artist—the High Priestess of Soul, Nina Simone—had a regal appearance that added more dimension to an already powerful voice. She was unapologetic in her socially conscious songs of freedom. She shined a spotlight on racism in the South with her song "Mississippi Goddamn!" in 1964, which focused on the assassination of Medgar Evers and the bombing of the church that killed the four little girls. In 1966 she made "Four Women" about four distinctive personas of African American women. In 1970, she gave us the anthem "Young, Gifted and Black."

There were artists whose music became the soundtrack for the Civil Rights Era. Curtis Mayfield wrote soul stirring anthem-like songs starting with "Keep on Pushing," "People Get Ready," "Choice of Colors," "Check Out Your Mind," and "If There's a Hell Below." He wrote songs of empowerment like "We're a Winner" and "Move On Up." Curtis Mayfield, was very effective at using music to exemplify the political ideology of the Black Power Movement.

James Brown went through a period of transition during this time. After the assassination of Martin Luther King, there were riots all across the country. The mayor of Boston pleaded with Brown to come and perform and ask the people to be calm. He was also summoned to Washington by President Lyndon Johnson to do a concert benefitting non-violence. After that, Brown became a social activist and released songs like "I'm Black and I'm Proud," "Santa Clause Go Straight to the Ghetto," "I Don't Want Nobody Giving Me Nothing," "The Big Payback," and "Funky President."

Stevie Wonder became one of the most popular R&B artists during the 1970s who also used music as a vehicle to enlighten and raise public awareness to society's ills. Even as a child star, he delivered a message with Bob Dylan's "Blowing in the Wind." He gave us a song so beautiful it was almost a prayer with "Heaven Help Us All." Then came the acclaimed 1973 album *Innervisions*, which gave us "Higher Ground," and "Living for the City."

Stevie told us to rise up, reminding us of ghetto traps. And he challenged government claims of aiding Black and poor people with "You Haven't Done Nothing." Stevie ended the decade of the '70s playing a major role in getting a holiday in honor of Martin Luther King, Jr., and blessed us with "Happy Birthday to You"—a song that is now commonly sung at birthday celebrations.

Some other significant socially conscious songs were:
- The Temptations "Ball of Confusion" 1970
- Gil Scott-Heron "The Revolution Will Not be Televised" 1970
- Edwin Starr "War! What is it Good For?" 1970 (protesting the Vietnam War)
- Marvin Gaye "What's Going On?" 1971
- Tower of Power "Urban Renewal" 1974
- Harold Melvin & the Blue Notes "Wake Up Everybody" 1975
- The Isley Brothers "Fight the Power" 1975
- McFadden & Whitehead "Ain't No Stopping Us Now" 1976
- Grand Master Flash & the Furious Five "The Message" 1979

These were just a few of the hit tunes we heard over the airwaves. Some of these songs were banned in the South. Black-controlled but White-owned radio stations refused to play anything which raised the consciousness of Black people. They feared it would incite resistance to the established order of things. They didn't want us demanding equal and equitable rights. They didn't want us to speak for ourselves and be proud of ourselves. These songs encouraged us to be proud.

Moreover, these songs fed our souls by giving us hope and faith for a better tomorrow, just like the Negro Spirituals from centuries before. They allowed us to weep and to laugh. They allowed us...gave us permission not just to sing, but to shout and scream!

We were telling our own story in our own way. We created a culture that gave us legitimacy. We validated ourselves by wearing African clothes and natural hair. In the late 1960s and early 1970s we created Black national organizations, separating ourselves from racist organizations in areas of medicine, social work, law, psychology, etc.

Music of the '70s gave voice to the earlier messages of Malcolm X, Fannie Lou Hamer, Ella Baker, and other voices of protest and resistance. We rioted, and we saw so-called ghettos crumble, but the people rose up and responded to oppression with passion.

I need to mention a significant event of the 1970s involving Black music and social consciousness. You cannot speak about music of the '70s and not mention one specific event. This event was Wattstax, a 1972 music festival in the African American community of Watts in Los Angeles.

It was held at the Los Angeles Memorial Coliseum. It was organized by Al Bell and Stax Records to commemorate the seventh anniversary of the Watts Riot, a rebellion that lasted six days in August 1965, where over a thousand people were injured and 34 people were killed. It was the most severe rebellion up until the riot stemming from the Rodney King case.

Bell said the purpose of the festival was, "To create, motivate, and instill a sense of pride in the citizens of the Watts community."

Tickets for Wattstax were sold for $1, and was attended by 112,000 people. The festival was totally peaceful. Rev. Jesse Jackson gave the invocation, which included the poem *I Am Somebody*. The first song of the festival was the "Star Spangled Banner," followed by "Lift Ev'ry Voice and Sing"—the Black National Anthem, sung by Kim Weston.

People stood with their fists raised in the air. Needless to say, everything about the concert reflected the African American experience. Musical performers included Isaac Hayes, the Staple Singers, Rufus Thomas, Kim Weston, Johnny Taylor, the BarKays, and Albert King. After the concert, Bell said, "It caused us to see ourselves differently."

The concert was filmed by Mel Stuart. Footage also included interviews with Richard Pryor and others that discussed the African American experience. The film was screened at the 1973 Cannes Film Festival and was nominated for a "Golden Globe" award for Best Documentary Film; a film that was fueled by the power of Black music.

In 2005 the President of the United States, George W. Bush, honored African American musicians. During the ceremony he said, *"Throughout our history, African American artists have created music with the power to change hearts and reshape our national conscience. The songs of Black musicians heralded social change. Music like Jazz and Blues communicated across racial barriers. That music began in America's country churches, and urban clubs of Chicago, New Orleans, and Harlem. Today it is cherished here at home and around the world."*

I think that says it all.

I'd like to close with this thought. Music changes lives, affects politics, fuels economies and shapes cultures. The American Dream is personified through its music, its influences, and its bold and original qualities. It is a fascinating and transforming force—a force with the power to enrich cultures the world over. When it comes to music, everyone on the planet speaks the same language. Music is that universal language. Music is a powerful thing.

I want to thank you for sharing this time with me. And I've enjoyed sharing my experiences with you. I hope you understand that there is still a lot that we have to overcome. And I urge you to consider your responsibility to those who came before you, and to fight for the integrity of the music. We owe it to the children. Remember...they are the future. Thank you again.

* This is a correction from the first printing of this book, which stated that I signed the O'Jays.

PHOTO GALLERY

NANCY WILSON

P2

Norbert Simmons
Pres MCA New Ventures

Lew Wasserman
Pres MCA/Universal

Sid Sheinberg
VP MCA/Universal

P3

P4

P5

P6

P7

P8

SHARON PAIGE

P10

Opus 7

Direction Exclusively:
Ed Smith Management Enterprises
170 Shaddowmoore Court
Martinez, Georgia 30907
(404) 796-1177

P11

ANDRAE CROUCH
VOICES OF JOY
BOYS CHOIR

LOGAN H. WESTBROOKS
280 S BEVERLY DR SUITE 206
BEVERLY HILLS, CA 90212
(310) 868-4868

P12

John Buchanan — Richardo Wellman — Jerry Wilder — Chuck Brown (sitting) — LeRoy Fleming — Gregory Gerran — Curtis Johnson — Donald Tillery

Chuck Brown and The Soul Searchers

Exclusively On

SOURCE

.MCA RECORDS

P13

P14

P15

P16

P18

P19

P20

P21

P22

KEY TO PHOTOGRAPHS

P1   Nancy Wilson

P2   In Lagos, Nigeria: Local Radio Personality L-R Ginger Baker, Paul & Linda McCartney

P3   Westbrooks presenting Gold Record to Norbert Simmons. Norbert Simmons, President MCA New Ventures; Westbrooks; Lew Wasserman, President MCA/Universal; Sid Sheinberg, Vice President MCA/Universal

P4   Presenting an award to the President of Senegal, President Diouf and his wife (Interpreter is in the center)

P5   NATRA Convention, L-R Chuck Scruggs, Westbrooks, Stanley Scott (Whitehouse, President Nixon)

P6   Tom Nix (Stax), Al Jackson (Stax), Revae Gipson, Logan & Geri Westbrooks, Jo Bridges, Mrs. Al Jackson, Dr. Benjamin Hooks

P7   Source Record Logo

P8   Event on Capitol Hill, L-R Chuck Brown, Congressman Clay (MO), Sidney Miller, Max Kidd

P9   Sharon Paige

P10   Mable John signing to Source Records

P11   Opus 7

P12   Andrae Crouch Boys Choir

P13   Chuck Brown & the Soul Searchers

P14   Nelly sampled "Bustin' Loose"

P15   Indiana University Display, Black History Month – Source Records, Logan Westbrooks

P16   Indiana University, February 13 Lecture

P17   Vanguard Award recipient

P18   Westbrooks receiving Honorary Doctorate of Humane Letters 2014,
L-R Dr. Cheryl Golden; Robert Lipscomb, Board of Trustees;
Dr. Johnnie Watson, President of LeMoyne-Owen College; Jeff
Johnson, Commencement Speaker; Logan Westbrooks

P19   HEROS Lincoln University Alumni Award 2014

P20   Dr. Westbrooks received Key to the City of Memphis 2014

P21   Dr. Westbrooks & Wife Geri at Jus Blues Awards where Westbrooks
was honored 2014

P22   The Westbrooks Family, Logan & Geri in front, L-R son-in-law Jeremy
Moxey; grandchildren Jordan Moxey, Amelia Hart Moxey, Elliot
Moxey, Brienne Moxey, and daughter Babette Moxey

INDEX

X

Y

Logan H. Westbrooks

Dr. Logan H. Westbrooks is one of the first African Americans to work as a major label Music Executive. Dr. Westbrook's impact in the music industry is undeniable. He is recognized as a pioneer who paved the way for African American Music Executives of today.

Made in the USA
San Bernardino, CA
10 October 2016